# African Governance Report III
## 2013

Economic Commission for Africa

OXFORD
UNIVERSITY PRESS

# OXFORD
## UNIVERSITY PRESS

Great Clarendon Street, Oxford, OX2 6DP,
United Kingdom

Oxford University Press is a department of the University of Oxford.
It furthers the University's objective of excellence in research, scholarship,
and education by publishing worldwide. Oxford is a registered trade mark of
Oxford University Press in the UK and in certain other countries

First Edition published in 2013

Impression: 1

Published in the United States of America by Oxford University Press
198 Madison Avenue, New York, NY 10016, United States of America

British Library Cataloguing in Publication Data

Data available

ISBN UNECA 978–92–1–125120–3
ISBN Oxford University Press 978–0–19–964505–3

Typeset by Communications Development Incorporated, Washington, D.C.

Printed in Great Britain by Bell and Bain, Glasgow

Cover photos: United Nations Photo Library; Staton Winter (top),
Eskinder Debebe (middle) and Martine Perret (bottom)

**Foreword**      ix

**Acknowledgements**      xi

**Abbreviations**      xiv

**Executive Summary**      **1**
Monitoring governance trends: Marginal progress      1
Elections and diversity management      1
Note      15

**1   Political Architecture: State-building and Diversity**      **17**
Diversity in Africa      18
Pre-colonial and colonial political systems      22
The post-colonial state      25
The reform period: Renegotiated architecture and recurrent issues      32
Conclusions      42
Notes      43
References      44

**2   Democratic Transition, Elections and Diversity Management**      **47**
Background to democratic transition      48
Patterns of democratic transition      49
Democratizing trends      51
Leadership      59
Diversity issues in the democratic transition      60
Conclusions and recommendations      70
Annex 2.1  Alternation of presidential power in Africa, 2007–2012      73
Notes      76
References      76

**3   Diversity and the Electoral Process**      **79**
Managing diversity      80
Elections      81
Electoral systems' strengths and weaknesses      84
Tackling diversity issues in the electoral process      88
Representation of women and minorities      96
Religion and diversity management      102
Challenges for managing diversity      103
Conclusions and recommendations      104
Annex 3.1  Prevalence of electoral systems      107
Annex 3.2  Women holding cabinet appointments in African countries,
            January 2010      109
Notes      110
References      110

**4   Electoral Management Boards**      **113**
Evolution      113

Powers and functions        116
Autonomy       120
Performance       126
Promoting electoral integrity        126
Oversight of political parties        132
Conclusions and recommendations        134
Annex 4.1  Structure and composition of EMBs: Southern Africa,
             July 2010       137
Notes        139
References        139

5  **Competitive Elections and Conflict        143**
Electoral competition        143
Electoral systems and violent conflict        145
Election-related conflicts        146
Party democracy and conflict        150
Role of media in election conflicts        156
Managing electoral conflict—state mechanisms        157
Managing electoral conflict—other approaches        163
Conclusions and recommendations        167
Annex 5.1  Inter-party violence in six African countries        171
Notes        173
References        173

6  **The Economics of Elections        179**
Election resources and political competition        179
Election spending and effect on GDP        181
Funding electoral institutions and parties        183
Campaign finance and corruption        191
Regulating political finance        193
External funding and assistance        194
Conclusions and recommendations        198
Notes        201
References        201

7  **Electoral, Constitutional and Political Reforms        205**
Dynamic links among electoral, constitutional and political reforms        205
Electoral reforms        206
Constitutional and political reform issues        215
Conclusions and recommendations        222
References        225

8  **Policy Recommendations        227**
The political system        227
Electoral institutions, processes and finance        230
Managing electoral conflicts and disputes        233

Regional and international organizations and promotion of electoral integrity    236

Policy dialogue, training and research    237

**Appendix**
**UNECA Project on Good Governance: Background, Methodology and Calculating the Indices    239**

Rationale and objectives    240

Methodology    241

Project implementation    243

Note    244

**Boxes**

1      Africa's elections, 1996–2012    3

1.1    Examples of identity and politics    19

1.2    Diversity and conflict in Africa    21

1.3    A difficult graft    26

1.4    The tyranny of the majority    29

1.5    Ethnicity and party support    31

1.6    The African Charter on Human and People's Rights    34

1.7    Devolution in practice, Ghana    35

1.8    Failure and success in extending term limits    40

1.9    National Cohesion and Integration Commission, Kenya    40

2.1    Four transition trends    50

2.2    Social media promoting democratic change in Nigeria    51

2.3    Guaranteeing Nigeria's federal character    61

2.4    Ethnic overlays on political parties    64

2.5    Ethnic diversity as an asset rather than a liability    65

2.6    Shifting citizenships    69

2.7    Culture and constitution favour men in Botswana    70

3.1    Managing diversity in Africa    81

3.2    Grievance lay just below the surface in Côte d'Ivoire    82

3.3    Mali's recent conflict    84

3.4    Constitutional provisions on diversity    89

3.5    Diversity in electoral management boards    90

3.6    Gender balance on Malawi's Electoral Commission    90

3.7    Educating voters on diversity    94

3.8    African Governance Forum workshop, Accra    102

3.9    Some disabilities overcome in Sierra Leone    103

4.1    Origins of electoral management boards in Africa    114

4.2    Interlocking electoral management board responsibilities, Sierra Leone    119

4.3    Two approaches to appointing and removing electoral commissioners    122

4.4    Heavy staff demand around elections    126

4.5    Factors in the independence and effectiveness of Africa's electoral commissions    128

4.6   Good and bad practices in election administration and management in
      Africa     132
4.7   Electoral integrity     133
4.8   Party liaison committees in Lesotho and South Africa     134
5.1   The African Union and the 2011 Elections Year: Challenges and
      successes     148
5.2   Freedom marred by violence, South Africa 1994     149
5.3   Electoral violence and the indigenous–settler divide in Nigeria     149
5.4   From electoral violence to civil war in the Congo     150
5.5   Commendable practices in Cape Verde, Namibia and Senegal     156
5.6   Youth and political violence in Sierra Leone     157
5.7   Potential areas of electoral conflict     158
5.8   Managing electoral appeals in Tunisia     158
5.9   Malawi's reform of adjudication     161
5.10  Party liaison committees in South Africa     163
5.11  KwaZulu-Natal Democracy and Elections Forum, South Africa     164
5.12  The Continental Early Warning System     165
5.13  Key lessons from past election crises in Africa     168
6.1   Reaching out to voters     180
6.2   Electoral outcomes     181
6.3   Per voter election costs     185
6.4   Challenges of election funding in Africa     186
6.5   Grass-roots view on incumbent advantage in Uganda     189
6.6   Candidate funding in Nigeria     190
6.7   Banho in São Tomé and Príncipe     193
6.8   Kickbacks and donations to campaigns funds     193
6.9   Four gains from regulating political finance     194
6.10  Foreign funding and campaign spending in Tunisia     196
6.11  Are all governments convinced by democracy?     197
6.12  Donor-dependence concerns     198
7.1   Pressures from below     206
7.2   Three strategies of electoral reform     207
7.3   Constitutional bans on ethnic-based political parties: Ghana and
      Kenya     214

## Figures

1     Governance indicators, AGR I, II and III     2
2.1   Mass media—completely free or only infrequently violated by the
      government or ruling party     52
2.2   Legislative control of the executive branch—usually or always effective     54
2.3   Respect for human rights     55
2.4   Government respect for due process and the rule of law—mostly or
      fully     56
2.5   Role of civil society organizations in promoting transparency and
      accountability     57
2.6   Tripartite breakdown of governance in Sub-Saharan Africa, 1988–2011     60

2.7 The government and leadership represent all segments and diverse interests 62

2.8 Sectarian groups have a heavy influence on a country's political process 66

2.9 The constitution promotes diversity and minority interests 67

3.1 Voter registration is credible and accepted 92

3.2 Women play a major role in the electoral process—mostly or always 101

4.1 Adequacy of the electoral law for managing diversity at elections—mostly or fully 121

4.2 The procedure for appointing and removing the electoral commission is open, transparent and credible—mostly or always 123

4.3 The electoral commission is independent and fairly or fully competent 127

4.4 Performance of electoral commissions 129

4.5 National elections are free, fair and generally transparent—mostly or always 130

4.6 Local elections are free, fair and generally transparent—mostly or always 131

5.1 Electoral violence is a recurring phenomenon at general elections—agree or strongly agree 147

5.2 Violence is a major feature of political campaigns—agree or strongly agree 151

5.3 Security forces are fair and non-partisan in their role in the electoral process 155

5.4 Election disputes are usually well managed to the satisfaction of the political parties 162

6.1 Political parties have equal access to electoral resources—mostly or always 182

7.1 Proportional representation promotes electoral stability and diversity management—agree or strongly agree 208

7.2 Appointing and removing electoral commissioners should be handled by an independent non-partisan body—agree or strongly agree 210

7.3 Positions of electoral commissioners should be advertised for national competition 211

7.4 Electoral management boards should have relative autonomy in political, administrative and financial independence—agree or strongly agree 212

7.5 Political parties practise internal democracy in electing party officials and party candidates for national elections 216

7.6 A quota system should be adopted for appointing women to executive positions and parliament—agree or strongly agree 217

7.7 Significant or full constitutional checks and balances among the different branches of government exist in most countries 218

7.8 Judicial corruption remains daunting 220

7.9 Formation of coalition or national unity government is a viable option—agree or strongly agree 221

7.10 Access to public services remains a major challenge 223

7.11  States have weak capacity for managing intra-state conflicts in most
      countries     224

## Tables

1     Overall index of governance trends in Africa, AGR III      3
1.1   Diversity-related factors for conflicts and tensions in countries that have
      completed the African Peer Review Mechanism      20
1.2   Party systems in Africa, 2004–2006      37
1.3   Presidential term limits in Africa      39
1.4   Horizontal democracy-promoting institutions, selected African
      countries     41
2.1   Relationship among constitutional diversity guarantees, composition of
      government and sectarian identity      68
3.1   Women in African parliaments, lower or single house, October 2012      98
3.2   Women in African parliaments, upper house or senate, October 2012      100
3.3   Female presiding officers in African parliaments, January 2010      100
4.1   Models of African electoral management boards      117
5.1   Electoral systems and violent conflicts      146
6.1   State funding for parties, 2011      187
6.2   Countries that ban or allow foreign donations to political parties and
      campaigns     195
6.3   Examples of external sources of funding, 2007–2010      196
Appendix table
      AGR III collaborating research institutions      245

Improved governance remains central to Africa's peace and security and to its economic transformation. This is reflected in the strong interface between better governance and economic progress on the continent and in the increased demands by citizens for democracy, accountability, civil liberties and the rule of law. How these issues are resolved will shape public policies and influence economic performance.

A major message of this third edition of the African Governance Report (AGR III) is that there has been some progress on governance in Africa, with the political narratives shifting positively. Many African countries have more regular elections, more political parties and greater political space. But these trends do not mean that democracy is fully fledged. Indeed, electoral processes are still a concern because they may become instruments for exclusion rather than inclusion. This concern and the diversity of populations in many African countries made it essential to examine the dynamics surrounding *Elections and the Management of Diversity in Africa*.

The report's key question: How do Africa's electoral systems respond to plural African societies? Put differently, do African elections promote inclusiveness and participation and improve the quality of governance? To uncover some answers, we conducted extensive research, including surveys and focus group discussions in 40 African countries. Despite the expected differences among countries, some general policy conclusions can be drawn.

First is the need to avoid the "winner takes all" syndrome. The surveys revealed a broad preference for proportional representation.

Second is preserving the integrity of electoral processes by ensuring the administrative and financial autonomy of election management bodies from the executive branch.

Third, governments could consider constitutional and legislative reforms to ensure that minorities and hitherto excluded sections of society take part in political decisions—women, the disabled, youth and the poor should have voice beyond voting in elections.

A fourth conclusion relates to term limits. The power of incumbency can subvert fair electoral competition. Countries might seriously consider adopting term limits to increase the chances of changes in government and inject new ideas in leadership and governance.

Finally, elections by themselves will not promote democratic values and practices, nor will they guarantee political stability. The judiciary, anticorruption bodies, public accounts regulators, parliaments and political parties all have to be strengthened.

The United Nations Economic Commission for Africa and the United Nations Development Programme have worked closely in producing this report. We commend it to governments and other stakeholders committed to improving governance in Africa. We hope that its findings will contribute to consolidating the democratic project in Africa and to enhancing the quality of elections and governance.

**Carlos Lopes**

*United Nations Under-Secretary-General and Executive Secretary, United Nations Economic Commission for Africa*

*Addis Ababa*

**Tegegnework Gettu**

*United Nations Assistant Secretary-General and Director, United Nations Development Programme Regional Bureau for Africa*

*New York*

February 2013

# Acknowledgements

The preparation of this report was a long and painstaking process of roughly three years. The long process arose from the complexity and comprehensiveness of the project, in which national research institutions were engaged that conducted field-based research and desk studies in 40 African countries. Given the sensitivity of elections and diversity management in many African countries, against the backdrop of varying levels of democratization and political tolerance, the United Nations Economic Commission for Africa (UNECA), United Nations Development Programme (UNDP) and the national research institutions had to negotiate the process carefully in some countries to undertake the country studies. Overall, most African governments and political authorities lent their support to the project, without any attempt to unduly influence or control it, for which we are immensely grateful.

This report benefited from the institutional leadership and guidance of two UNECA Executive Secretaries—Mr. Abdoulie Janneh and Mr. Carlos Lopes. Also, the support of the Director of the UNDP Regional Bureau for Africa, Mr. Tegegnework Gettu, is most appreciated. The Deputy Executive Secretary of UNECA, Mr. Abdalla Hamdok, offered invaluable support in preparing the report.

This report was prepared under the direct intellectual and administrative leadership of the Director of the Governance and Public Administration Division (GPAD) of UNECA,

Mr. Said Adejumobi, who is also the coordinator of the African Governance Report (AGR) project. A team comprising Said Adejumobi, Lloyd Sachikonye, Adele Jinadu and Godfrey Assinwe prepared the chapters. Useful background papers were prepared by George Kieh, Godwin Murunga and Mohamed Salih. Francis Ikome provided useful background inputs, while Gedion Gamora, Christian Mahillet and Anita Wanki provided excellent research support. Legesse Ayane, GPAD statistician on the AGR III project, offered remarkable statistical services and prepared the methodology chapter.

Special appreciation goes to the 40 national research institutions that undertook the AGR III national country reports. The diligence and commitment with which they carried out the task is most commendable.

While preparing the report, several technical meetings and workshops were organized including three methodology workshops and two expert review meetings. The two expert meetings were held in Pretoria, South Africa, in May 2011, and Addis Ababa, Ethiopia, on 1–2 October 2012. UNECA and UNDP are grateful to the following people who served as reviewers, panellists and participants at those technical meetings and workshops: Ademola Abass, Musa Abutudu, Wale Adebanwi, Adigun Agbaje, Emmanuel Akwetey, Yusuf Bangura, Asmalash Beyene, Abdalla Bujra, Sheila Bunware, Louis Amedee Darga, Joseph Brian Diescho,

Mamadou Diouf, Kole Godana, Karuti Kayinga, Abdul Rahman Lamin, Pascal Mihyo, Winnie Mitullah, Ahmed Mohiddin, Patrick Molutsi, Mustaq Moraad, Rachel Mukamunana, Royson Mukwena, Florence Mutesi, Regina Mwatha, Janah Ncube, Ebenezer Obadare, Oka Obono, Adebayo Olukoshi, Shola Omotola, Selowani Onalenna, Okey Onyejekwe, Eghosa Osaghae, Liepollo Pheko, Severine Rugumamu, Simon Rutabajuuka, Mohamed Salih, Ebrima Sall, Getachew Demeke Shefarew, Wahab Shehu, Issaka Souare, Tegegne Teka, Christiana Thorpe, Ilona Tip, Ibrahim Wani and Charlotte Wonani.

The staff of UNECA and UNDP also provided invaluable support in undertaking the country reports and the AGR III continental report. The UNDP country offices provided administrative oversight of the national research institutions in some countries, while UNECA directly managed the project in others. Siphosami Malunga and Khabele Matlosa from UNDP were quite instrumental and supportive in producing the country reports and the continental AGR. Other colleagues from UNDP who supported the AGR III project include the UNDP Resident Representatives, Country Directors and Governance Advisers in some countries and also Evlynne Change, Brian Kagoro, Ken Lewis and Arthur Phiri of the UNDP Regional Bureau office in South Africa.

The GPAD-UNECA team provided substantive planning, technical and administrative support in preparing the country reports, which Valerio Bosco and Guy Ranaivomanana diligently managed as focal points. Other staff who provided technical review and administrative support to the process include Jalal Abdel-Latif, Kojo Busia, Sam Cho, Guillermo Mangue, Kaleb Demeksa, Hodane Yousuf, Gamal Ibrahim, Emebet Mesfin, Gonsalves Juliana, Constanze Westervoss, Grace Chisamya, Yeshimebet Araya, Misrak Worku, Loule Baltcha, Tsigereda Assayehegn, Abijah Yeshaneh, Bethlehem Teshager, Gebremedhin Tadesse, Lia Yeshitila, Meaza Molla, Genet Beyene, Bilisson Hassan, Monica Bonfanti, Saba Kassa and Kassahun Shiferaw.

The UNECA division of administration including Doreen Bongoy-Mawalla (the division's former director), Etienne Kabou, Charles Ndungu and others assisted in the administrative and technical processes of the report. Bruce Ross-Larson and Jack Harlow at Communications Development Incorporated deserve our special commendation for their commitment to excellence in the editing process. We also thank Oxford University Press for their support in publishing the report.

The development partners and sister African institutions that supported the AGR III project include Norway, Sweden, the African Governance Institute, the African Union Commission, the Council for the Development of Social Science Research in Africa, the U.K. Department for International Development, the International

Development Research Centre, International Institute for Democracy and Electoral Assistance, the Organization for Social Science Research in Eastern and Southern Africa, United Nations University Institute on Comparative Regional Integration Studies, and Trust Africa.

UNECA and UNDP are immensely grateful to the above people and institutions and to some others who may not have been mentioned but contributed to the report and the entire AGR III project. It is hoped that the report will contribute significantly to understanding and resolving the challenges of conducting free, fair and transparent elections in Africa and promoting inclusiveness, participation, respect for diversity and violence-free elections that are necessary for engineering democratic stability and consolidation on the continent.

# Abbreviations

| | |
|---|---|
| AGR | African Governance Report |
| AU | African Union |
| CEWS | Continental Early Warning System |
| CSO | Civil society organization |
| EAC | East African Community |
| ECOWAS | Economic Community of West African States |
| EISA | Electoral Institute for Sustainable Development in Africa |
| EMB | Electoral management board |
| FPTP | First past the post |
| GPAD | Governance and Public Administration Division of UNECA |
| INEC | Independent National Electoral Commission of Nigeria |
| SADC | Southern African Development Community |
| SAP | Structural adjustment programme |
| UN | United Nations |
| UNDP | United Nations Development Programme |
| UNECA | United Nations Economic Commission for Africa |

This summary is in two parts: the first is on trends in governance in Africa against the background of the first African Governance Report (AGR I) of 2005 and the second (AGR II) of 2009; the second is on the theme of elections and diversity management in Africa.

## Monitoring governance trends: Marginal progress

Africa's democratization remains fragile and contestable. Although the continent has recorded a 1 percentage point gain in its governance indicators overall since AGR II, that falls short of the 2 percentage point improvement made between AGR I and AGR II (figure 1).[1] Mali—a country previously regarded as a success story but that has succumbed to a military coup and conflict—attests to this fragility.

Still, the democratic transition in North Africa—starting with Tunisia in 2010 with effects on other countries in the region including Algeria, Egypt, Libya and (partly) Morocco—shows the complexity of the continent's democratic trajectory, as confirmed by the 2012 governance-tracking data.

The slight improvement in governance challenges African countries to intensify their efforts in deepening democratic culture and practices and in upscaling their governance performance. Steps include: enhancing the institutional capacity of democratic structures like parliament and the judiciary and of horizontal accountability bodies like the office of the auditor general, ombudsman, anti-corruption institutions and other public agencies; enacting freedom of information laws that grant to citizens and the media greater access to information; meeting demands for accountability from the political leadership; and providing better public services, social infrastructure and public security.

Although performances differ, the challenge for African countries is to raise governance outcomes so that the democratic project has tangible meaning in the lives of their citizens (table 1).

## Elections and diversity management

*While diversity may be a source of creativity and positive growth, when poorly managed, diversity often becomes a source of unhealthy competition, conflict and instability*

Ban Ki-moon, United Nations
Secretary-General, 2011

Since democratization begun in Africa in the 1990s, elections have become more regular on the continent (box 1), as a mechanism for popular expression, leadership selection (and change) and political accountability.

However, these elections have differed in form, content and quality, and greater regularity has not necessarily enhanced their value. Sectarian mobilization, intimidation and violence are major features of some African countries' elections, which have become conflict triggers rather than instruments for resolving differences, as in Côte

1

## Figure 1 Governance indicators, AGR I, II and III

Scores, average across project countries (%)

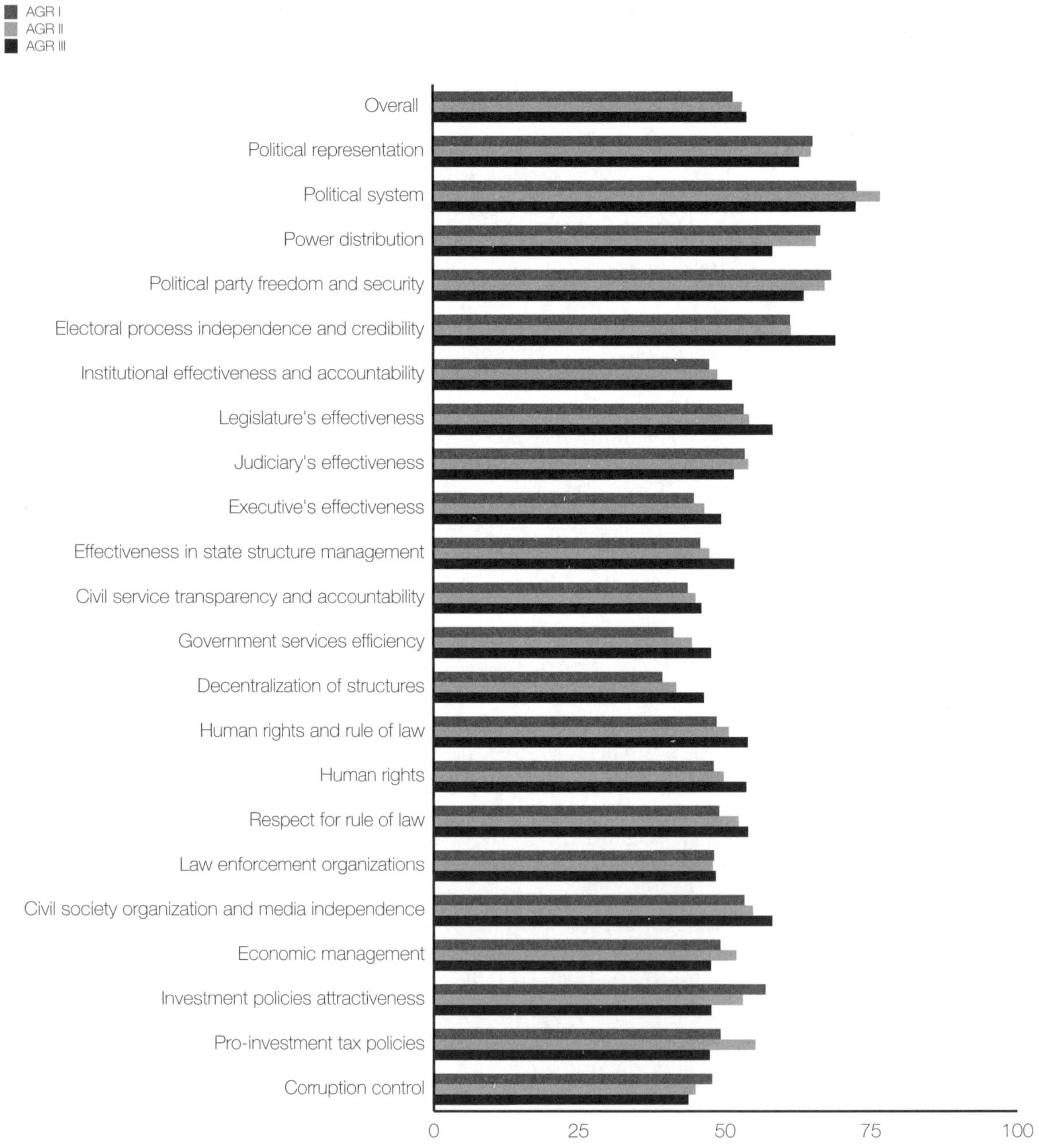

■ AGR I
■ AGR II
■ AGR III

|  | |
|---|---|
| Overall | |
| Political representation | |
| Political system | |
| Power distribution | |
| Political party freedom and security | |
| Electoral process independence and credibility | |
| Institutional effectiveness and accountability | |
| Legislature's effectiveness | |
| Judiciary's effectiveness | |
| Executive's effectiveness | |
| Effectiveness in state structure management | |
| Civil service transparency and accountability | |
| Government services efficiency | |
| Decentralization of structures | |
| Human rights and rule of law | |
| Human rights | |
| Respect for rule of law | |
| Law enforcement organizations | |
| Civil society organization and media independence | |
| Economic management | |
| Investment policies attractiveness | |
| Pro-investment tax policies | |
| Corruption control | |

0    25    50    75    100

*Source:* Expert Opinion Surveys, AGR I (2005), II (2009) and III (2012).

## Table 1 Overall index of governance trends in Africa, AGR III

| Country | Overall index | Country | Overall index |
|---------|---------------|---------|---------------|
| Rwanda | 72 | Ethiopia | 51 |
| Seychelles | 71 | Kenya | 51 |
| Cape Verde | 69 | Mauritania | 51 |
| Algeria | 66 | Mozambique | 51 |
| South Africa | 65 | São Tomé and Príncipe | 51 |
| Mauritius | 63 | Tanzania | 51 |
| Namibia | 63 | Angola | 50 |
| Botswana | 62 | Congo | 50 |
| Ghana | 62 | Guinea | 50 |
| Liberia | 59 | Uganda | 50 |
| Senegal | 59 | Egypt | 49 |
| Benin | 56 | Zambia | 49 |
| Mali | 56 | Lesotho | 47 |
| Tunisia | 55 | Nigeria | 47 |
| Cameroon | 54 | Burkina Faso | 44 |
| Sierra Leone | 54 | Madagascar | 44 |
| Comoros | 52 | Togo | 44 |
| Gabon | 52 | Gambia | 43 |
| Malawi | 52 | Chad | 42 |
| Djibouti | 51 | Zimbabwe | 38 |

*Source:* AGR III Expert Opinion Survey 2012.

*Note:* The countries cannot be directly compared because of contextual differences in the economic, social and political environment in which the survey was conducted.

---

### Box 1 Africa's elections, 1996–2012

In recent years the following national elections have been held:
- 1996–2006: 44 elections in Sub-Saharan Africa;
- 2005–2007: 26 presidential and 28 parliamentary elections in Africa;
- 2011: 15 presidential and 20 parliamentary elections; and
- 2012: 10 presidential and 13 parliamentary elections.

d'Ivoire, the Democratic Republic of the Congo, Kenya, Nigeria and Zimbabwe.

Rather than unite, elections can divide people, undermining the very essence of elections, which is to peacefully aggregate preferences in the choice of political leadership. Diversity as a resource for governance and development then becomes a political liability among acute electoral deficits. Switching this liability to an asset—so that elections promote social cohesion, grant political legitimacy and manage diversity—requires answers to the following questions, tackled in this report:

- How can elections be sensitive to diversity in ensuring inclusiveness and participation of diverse groups, communities and interests?

- What kind of electoral systems should African countries adopt for democratically managing diversity?

- What are the good practices in Africa in managing diversity in the electoral process?

- How can electoral governance and the quality of elections be enhanced to reduce electoral and political conflict?

- What unique electoral products can Africa develop to promote social cohesion and electoral integrity?

- What legal, political and institutional reforms are necessary to facilitate credible elections and consolidate democracy?

*Chapter 1—Political architecture: State-building and diversity in Africa*
Chapter 1 focuses on diversity in relation to political processes and elections in Africa. It also maps the political geography of Africa and the evolution of Africa's political architecture in the colonial and immediate post-colonial eras.

The main argument is that although African countries are essentially plural societies—of diverse identities, groups, classes and professional interests—state formation and the emergent political architecture exacerbated the challenge of managing diversity in Africa. Diversity is best managed in an enabling democratic framework, in which all people are at liberty to choose their leaders and programmes through free, fair, credible and regular elections. Yet at the time, authoritarian political structures were grafted onto previous policies of ethnic and social fragmentation that had aimed to divide groups and generate antagonism, necessary for colonial economic exploitation and political dominance.

Colonialism did not aim to create a common citizenship—an identity for all. Citizenship was in fact multi-layered and group based: on higher rungs were white colonialists—"first class" citizens of the colonial state; among the "natives" were privileged groups in the "second class"; while the others were lumped as "third class".

The colonial regime's electoral management was rarely impartial. On the contrary, it took great interest in the emergent local political elite and the successor regime, to which political power was to be gradually devolved.

> *Diversity is best managed in an enabling democratic framework, in which all people are at liberty to choose their leaders and programmes*

The gradual introduction of the elective principle under colonial rule (which arose largely as a result of African agitation and resistance) was based on an autocratic and divisive political framework, which produced bitter ethnic politics—embedding the roots of electoral failure in Africa. The colonial heritage and the character of the successor leadership thus framed post-independence politics.

As the successors embarked on the complex task of building their nations, they pursued authoritarian strategies like centralization and single-party systems that stifled democracy and democratic diversity management. They regarded ethno-linguistic diversities or divergent political opinion as detrimental to unity and inimical to the nation-building project, and strangled them under common-identity, single-nation and one-party systems. The successor elites reconfigured liberal democracy and its electoral systems as instruments for themselves and their party's rule—into the foreseeable future.

These strategies stymied any moves to deepen democracy through multi-party systems that would have created the political space in which diverse identity interests could play out. With no alternatives for the smooth transfer of power, military intervention became common, pushing post-colonial states deeper into autocratic rule.

Authoritarianism in Africa generated opposition and struggle, which liberal democratic reforms channelled into democratization in the 1980s. This tide enabled people to exercise their right to organize in associational relations, at last opening the space for diversity aspirations and interests. It also engendered a gradual but significant renegotiation of the political architecture—including issues surrounding the separation of powers (executive, legislative and judicial), decentralization, term limits and horizontal accountability-promoting institutions ("watch-dogs")—geared to entrenching democratic governance and better managing diversity in Africa.

### Chapter 2—Democratic transition, elections and diversity management

Chapter 2 focuses on how democratic transitions—which most African countries have undergone at different periods and to varying degrees—affect democratic diversity management. Elections are central to these transitions and facilitate such management in four main ways: participation, representation, rotation of leaders and fulfilment of local needs and aspirations. Alone they are not enough to address all the demands of diversity management in a plural society, but when backed up by constitutional and political reforms they may ensure efficient and democratic diversity management.

Since the early 1990s, most African countries have witnessed democratic transition in which popular agitation and struggle for political reform have ousted authoritarian and despotic regimes. The process climaxed with North African political

> *Since the early 1990s, most African countries have witnessed democratic transition in which popular agitation and struggle for political reform have ousted authoritarian and despotic regimes*

uprisings that started in Tunis in December 2010, with knock-on effects in Algeria, Egypt and Libya.

Freedom, human rights and economic opportunities were severely constrained in many Sub-Saharan countries and made worse by financial austerity and structural adjustment programmes, which were major factors that triggered political protests for democratic reforms.

Countries differ in the patterns, processes and outcomes of democratic transition, although four modes of transition can be delineated: civil society–inspired; state-led; pacted; and stalled. Hence, while some countries managed to consolidate the democratic process to a degree as elections became more credible, regular and generally accepted by the people, some others used elections only to reinforce autocracy and confirm civilian dictatorships.

Overall, Africa has made progress, with some indicators—such as respect for human rights and the rule of law, legislative capacity, civil society engagement and civil liberties—generally increasing. However, democracy remains vulnerable, and requires greater institutional and procedural certainty to be consolidated.

Almost all democratic transitions have had to navigate serious diversity challenges, including power distribution and the nature of the political structure; ethnicity and religion; citizenship; and marginalized groups of women, youth and people with disabilities. In North Africa, for example, the role of

religion in the state and that of marginalized groups in politics stands out. In addressing the challenge of diversity management, governments have built (or reformed) institutions, passed laws and put in place policies—yet issues linger in many countries.

Central to consolidating the democratic transition are resolving issues like the quality of elections, how the constitution promotes diversity, how deeply embedded diversity is in public and democratic institutions, and the capacity of the state to mediate and rise above sectarian interests.

### Chapter 3—Diversity and the electoral process in Africa

Even at the best of times, elections are hard to organize in societies with deep-rooted diversity, and this chapter argues why diversity in African societies is key to explaining the tensions and conflicts that often accompany elections. Elections on their own do not resolve these issues. The distribution of wealth and power, for example, as well as an end to poverty, cannot be decided in a single election. Indeed, if improperly handled, elections can turn diversity into a tinder box. However, elections can gradually lead to credible processes that resolve contests for power and other resources at national, regional and local levels, transparently.

Drawing on the AGR III country reports, this chapter reviews each stage of the electoral process—boundary delimitation, voter registration and education, campaigning, voting, tallying and adjudication—to see how diversity is ignored or

> *Elections can gradually lead to credible processes that resolve contests for power and other resources*

addressed. At most stages, marginalization of some social groups remains a challenge (although some countries have seen positive results from their efforts).

The debate over which is the most suitable electoral system has not abated. While the chapter avoids a "one size fits all" approach, it weighs the merits of first past the post, proportional representation and mixed-member proportional systems. The trend of expert opinion in Africa favours proportional representation: the majority of respondents in 35 of 40 countries in the AGR III Expert Opinion Survey "agreed or strongly agreed" with the view that "electoral stability and diversity management can be attained through the proportional representation as opposed to majoritarian system."

The extent to which electoral management boards (EMBs)—also called electoral commissions—are sensitive to diversity is crucial, especially how much their composition reflects diversity in wider society. Matters have been gradually improving with the appointment of women as EMB members or chair in Cape Verde, Ethiopia, Ghana, Malawi, South Africa and Zimbabwe, for example, although the number of women and members of other minority groups should also increase among professional staff of EMB secretariats.

Delimitation, voter registration and education should be comprehensive, transparent and fair. The bodies responsible for these processes should be seen to be independent, non-partisan and not manipulative.

Given the high stakes in elections, one of the most contentious issues is deliberately inflating—or undercounting—numbers on registration lists: the majority of experts do not believe that voter registration is credible in Chad, Gambia, Lesotho, Nigeria and Zimbabwe, for example.

Most countries' respondents feel that their countries pay particular attention to voter education, in an attempt to spread information about people's need to claim and exercise the right to vote; to increase voter turnout during elections; and to reduce the number of spoilt ballots. Still, most country reports acknowledge that much ground has to be covered before voter education is accessible to all who require it. This is an area where complementary roles between EMBs and civil society organizations would ensure wider reach.

Few elections are perfect: disputes are common and the adjudication system should deal with them quickly and effectively, especially as even where elections are quite orderly, citizens may have little confidence in the courts to resolve them promptly. In some countries, though, the expert respondents believe that disputes are "usually managed to the satisfaction of the political parties", among them Algeria, Botswana, Cape Verde, Mauritius, Seychelles and South Africa. Encouragingly, in most countries the rule of electoral law is becoming a preferred alternative to resorting to violence.

How do women fare in the electoral process? Although unevenly, they have made real progress in

> *The rule of electoral law is becoming a preferred alternative to resorting to violence*

parliamentary representation (and as seen, in electoral institutions). Countries with more than 20% of female Members of Parliament include Burundi, Ethiopia, Lesotho, Mauritania, Mozambique, Namibia, Rwanda, Senegal, Seychelles, South Africa, Tanzania, Tunisia and Uganda, and women have been elected presiding officers of parliament in Botswana, Gabon, Gambia, Ghana, Lesotho, Rwanda and Zimbabwe. But there is still a long way to go to secure significant female participation, and then consolidate it, in the electoral process. The same can be said about the participation of youth and people with disabilities, which remains paltry.

Religion does not feature as a major factor in most countries. Some exceptions are in West and North Africa as well as the Horn of Africa, including Côte d'Ivoire, Mali, Nigeria and Senegal, and Algeria, Egypt, Sudan and Tunisia (less so in Kenya and Tanzania). Religious diversity represents a challenge to electoral politics that should be sensitively managed in these countries.

Other diversities that electoral systems should address include marginalized indigenous peoples like the Basarwa in Southern Africa and the Batwa in Central and East Africa. They should be enfranchised and represented in parliament and other institutions of state.

### Chapter 4—Electoral management boards

EMBs are central to the electoral process—and thus democratic development in Africa. After

independence, the inherited quasi-autonomous EMBs came under greater control of successor regimes as instruments for retaining power, so that, from the 1960s to the 1990s, a combination of a weak EMB, legislature and judiciary versus a strong executive was fatal for electoral governance and democracy in most countries. However, popular and social movements enabled constitutional and political reforms leading to incremental improvements in EMBs' status and performance.

The challenges that African EMBs encounter are daunting, especially in conditions of diversity where their role becomes even more sensitive as the epicentre of electoral management. Given the history in most African countries of seriously flawed elections—owing mainly to electoral maladministration, manipulations and mismanagement—legitimate, independent and credible EMBs are instrumental for administering free and fair democratic elections. In this guise, they can mitigate electoral violence and deepen democratization, which is crucial to harnessing diversity.

Electoral integrity entails a set of norms and regulations to be established and enforced, in order to ensure professionalism, ethics, accountability and transparency. Concerns remain over the following: EMBs' independence, especially the method of appointing and removing members as well as their funding and costs; involvement of the executive and civil service in elections (and forms of EMB embeddedness in their countries' political processes);

> **Electoral management boards are central to democratic development in Africa**

limited power of EMBs over political parties; professionalization and powers of EMBs; the role of stakeholders as partners; electoral-dispute adjudication; security for elections; and elections' steep costs.

EMBs in Africa have two major models: independent, and "hybrid" or mixed. Whatever the model, EMBs need to be strengthened by ensuring their independence, primarily by entrenching them in constitutions or other statutory provisions and improving their institutional professionalism and operational efficiency.

The perceived lack of independence appears strongly among the respondents, who did not consider 77% of EMBs independent and competent. Most countries' experts did not regard the procedure of appointing and removing electoral commissioners as open, transparent and credible. They pinpointed executives and ruling party–dominated legislatures as the major political forces compromising EMBs' autonomy, underlining the need to review the procedure and guarantee officials' security of tenure, in order to insulate them from undue political influence and interference. An overwhelming number of country reports recommended an independent body be responsible for appointing (and removing) EMB officials in a competitive job-selection process.

Administrative and financial autonomy of EMBs is an issue particularly because, although in most countries these bodies (and the electoral process) should under the constitution

be funded by the state, such financing is inadequate and often delayed, thus promoting dependence on donors and government. This heavily undermines EMBs' performance, which is why most country reports recommended independent budgets for EMBs.

Yet despite these concerns, citizens' perceptions of EMBs have improved in some countries since 1980, and expert respondents rated most EMBs as fair in their performance (and in Ghana, Mauritius, Seychelles and South Africa, good or very good), pointing to sharp gains in democratic institutions since the 1980s' wave of democratization.

### Chapter 5—Competitive elections and conflict

Elections in Africa are not always violent (despite the stereotype): in the past 10 years most elections have improved hugely, with peaceful and satisfactory outcomes the norm, and only about 20% of elections in 1990–2008 involved significant levels of violence. Interestingly, evidence points to greater likelihood of conflict with first past the post than proportional representation, a view backed up by expert panels in Angola, Burkina Faso, Djibouti, Kenya, Lesotho, Namibia, Nigeria, Rwanda, Senegal, South Africa and Zimbabwe, where the majority of respondents believe that electoral stability and diversity management are better promoted through proportional representation.

Electoral systems are entwined with their environments. The causes of election-related violence lie in

*Citizens' perceptions of electoral management boards have improved since 1980*

deep-rooted structural factors and short-term conjunctural "triggers" during the electoral process itself. Structural factors relate to political and economic diversities based on ethnic, regional, racial and class competition for resources, including wealth and power. Triggers relate to conflicts—sometimes serious clashes between parties—throughout the campaign, during balloting and counting, and when results are announced on election day. Conflicts within parties can also break out, especially during party primaries in the run-up to national elections. Such conflicts are an indicator of factionalism and low levels of internal party democracy.

In some countries, the partisanship of state agencies (police, intelligence forces and the army) fuels electoral conflict. The agencies often promote the incumbent party by repressing other parties during elections. Where such state agencies and party-linked militia combine, capacity to deal with electoral violence is further undermined. Election rigging becomes more likely if state agencies support the incumbent party.

Such violence may draw on youth and militia groups during campaigning and post-election periods. Owing to high unemployment, youth are easy to lure into violence, which often goes beyond the parties involved. And women and children are often caught in the melee, and may be displaced.

Countries have tried various approaches to defuse electoral

disputes. These include joint operation committees and party liaison committees in South Africa (which have had marked success), conflict management panels in some countries in Southern Africa and adjudication of disputes through the courts. Unlike other mechanisms, party liaison committees are maintained throughout the electoral cycle. In Sierra Leone, the Political Parties Registration Commission, with members from registered parties, serves as a vehicle for consultation and cooperation between the Independent Election Commission and parties on all electoral matters.

Some good practices for managing electoral conflicts stand out. They include the EISA model (named after the Electoral Institute for the Sustainability of Democracy in Africa), which is based on conflict mediation panels—grass-roots units in the Democratic Republic of the Congo, Lesotho, South Africa and Zambia, among other countries, have been effective. Civil society initiatives, like that in KwaZulu-Natal in South Africa, which helped to heavily cut electoral violence in that province, are others. In Nigeria, the National Campaign on Reduction of Electoral Violence was set up in the 2007 election campaign as an early warning system on violence.

Regional organizations such as the African Union, the Economic Community of West African States (ECOWAS) and the Southern African Development Community (SADC) have mediated to resolve electoral conflicts in several countries including Kenya and Zimbabwe. Other cases include mediation in Togo where a wide range of human rights activities such as training, sensitization, advocacy, capacity building and monitoring programmes for six months before the 2010 election were conducted—and no major violence occurred during the election. In West Africa, the ECOWAS Conflict Prevention Framework and Supplementary Protocol on Democracy and Good Governance have been used to provide technical and financial assistance to member states to organize credible elections. In Southern Africa, SADC has been involved in election-related mediation in Madagascar and Zimbabwe within the framework of the SADC Principles and Guidelines Governing Democratic Elections.

Finally, technical assistance for electoral processes has been fairly effective in providing compliance standards and capacity for EMBs, and should therefore be encouraged. But most countries have yet to fully institutionalize their election dispute settlement mechanisms, and still show a tendency for last-minute attention to conflict prevention. Strategic tools for preventing violence should be woven into each stage of the electoral cycle.

### Chapter 6—The economics of elections

Resources—especially financial—are vital to electoral competition. But while they can enable parties and candidates to be competitive in elections, they can also distort the electoral process. Ruling parties tend to command more resources (than other parties) owing to their access to state resources. Access to campaign resources in parties is also skewed, and women, minorities and youth are usually at a disadvantage. Disparities in electoral resources between parties, candidates, men and women, classes and age groups, as well as within parties, militate against the ability of many citizens to compete fairly for power and leadership.

The new era of competitive politics from the 1990s not only increased the regularity of elections but also their cost—exponentially over the past two decades—making election campaigning affordable mainly to wealthy candidates and well-endowed parties. All types of election resources—money, logistics, campaign paraphernalia and media coverage—are critical to shaping the electoral playing field and ultimately the outcome. Only in 4 of the 40 surveyed countries did half or more of respondents believe that parties have equal access to electoral resources.

In the run-up to elections, ruling parties through their control of government are tempted to splash out on thinly disguised buy-offs that may include new infrastructure (roads, dams, clinics and houses) to attract voters. This is a misuse of incumbency power and tends to corrupt the electoral process.

Electoral risks also slow business and investment, especially in manufacturing, as fear of conflict around elections often makes investors wait

> *Strategic tools for preventing violence should be woven into each stage of the electoral cycle*

and see, discouraging investment (as borne out in Kenya).

Funding for EMBs is largely from the government, for operational expenses (outside election periods) and for elections. EMB allocations in a country often depend on factors like geography and population size, and while some states can fund their EMBs fully, some cannot.

The funding for political parties is critical to their preparedness for elections: a party's presence—nationally, regionally and locally—gives an indication of its capacity to compete. The principal funding sources for most parties are internal party resources as well as public, diaspora and external (donor) funding. While some countries base a party's funding according to the seats it has in parliament, others base it on the proportion of votes that it received in the last election.

Campaign funding shows three major patterns: ruling parties tend to command greater resources; a few opposition parties now also command considerable resources; but most parties in opposition still have few resources (it is also a challenge for them to maintain a national or media presence).

Some countries provide both party and campaign funding, to various degrees and for different elections. Benin, for instance, grants public funding to candidates and parties in presidential and legislative campaigns. On the whole, however, self-funding is the principal resource for election campaigns.

The increasing costs of campaigning mean that only individuals willing to invest large sums of money can become candidates. Another outcome is that, with no rigorous expenditure-monitoring systems in place, candidates with deep pockets can spend far in excess of that allowed by campaign regulations.

Some countries that are not self-sufficient resort to foreign funding for their elections—including the Democratic Republic of the Congo, Liberia, Mozambique, Rwanda, São Tomé and Príncipe, Sierra Leone, South Sudan and Tanzania. This helps to reinforce the authoritarian proclivity that portrays elections as a Western imposition in some political cultures, with the effect of a seemingly half-hearted commitment to elections as integral to democratization. (Some countries, though, ban foreign donations to parties and candidates.)

Political finance remains under-regulated in Africa—and fundraising by parties and candidates is fully unregulated self-help. Two countries have all four constituent elements of a regulatory regime, and 15 others have one to four of the elements—thus slightly fewer than half the AGR III countries have some form of regulation for political finance.

Although resources shape political competition, they do not automatically lead to victory. Ruling parties have sometimes had the greater resources but lost the election. Other variables also have a role, like coalition building among opposition parties, popularity and quality of candidates and organizational capacity of the parties.

## Chapter 7—Electoral, constitutional and political reforms

Born out of pressures for liberal democratic space, reforms in these three interrelated areas have generally made significant progress in Africa—although depth and scope are uneven. Such reforms are embedded in a state–society dynamic in which reform seeks to respond to changes in the relationship and demands by society on the state.

Several countries have undertaken key constitutional reforms (such as Kenya and South Africa) while political reforms have included greater decentralization, establishment of watchdogs like human rights and anti-corruption bodies, and invigoration of democratic institutions like parliament.

With an underlying design to improve and democratize electoral governance in Africa, electoral reforms have centred on the following:

- redesigning EMBs by entrenching them in constitutions and by diminishing the influence of the executive;

- unbundling the powers and functions of the EMBs (in some countries) through creating two (or more) EMBs to undertake the major components of electoral administration and management;

- redesigning the electoral system to achieve a more democratic management of diversity by combining elements of first past the post and proportional representation; and

- making provisions in national constitutions and electoral laws or specific legislation for the regulation and oversight of party activities (including financing).

The country reports and AGR III Expert Opinion Survey suggest that further reforms may be necessary in seven broad areas. First is modifying the electoral system, particularly first past the post: mixed or proportional representation systems are becoming more popular and generally accepted as better for managing and promoting diversity in plural African countries. Second is strengthening the independence of EMBs via constitutional guarantees and transparency (as discussed in chapter 4).

The third area is improving and democratizing the legal framework for election administration, management, EMB accountability and professionalization for increased efficiency. Fourth is strengthening the election-adjudication and dispute-resolution mechanism and providing remedies for electoral irregularities (a reform closely related to judicial independence, which is generally lacking). Fifth is levelling the democratic playing field through guarantees of equitable access to electoral resources by political parties (including the media). Sixth is reforming

*Electoral, constitutional and political reforms have generally made significant progress*

the role of the security forces. Seventh is promoting internal democracy in political parties—a wide deficit in most African countries.

In the areas of constitutional and political reforms, action for marginalized groups of women, youth and the physically challenged should be more affirmative. For women, it has already spawned encouraging results in many countries, but not for youth and the physically challenged: their issues have to be internalized in political and constitutional processes. And even affirmative action for women varies—Rwanda for one stands out for its remarkable progress. Reforms to bring marginalized groups into the governance mainstream require upscaling.

Judicial reform is generally slow, improvised and out of tune with continental democratization, preventing this branch from playing its proper role in regulating and ensuring justice in political and electoral processes. Specifically, institutional capacity, relative autonomy, resources and the quality and integrity of judicial officers need to be addressed in many countries.

Finally, the state's capacity to deliver services is central to promoting citizens' approval and support for democracy—the democratic dividend. But most African countries' service delivery remains abysmal, as the Expert Opinion Survey confirms. African governments should greatly enhance their capacity to deliver services if the democratic project is not to founder.

> *Institutional capacity, relative autonomy, resources and the quality and integrity of judicial officers need to be addressed*

## Chapter 8—Policy recommendations

The concluding chapter synthesizes the policy recommendations flagged in earlier chapters. They are drawn from 40 country reports, views of expert panels, focus group discussions and analysis of these sources. The recommendations are grouped into five categories.

### The political system

Most expert panels did not believe that the constitutions of their countries adequately promote diversity and inclusive governance or protect minority interests, and that at best the constitutional protection of diversity was uneven among countries, engendering two recommendations.

First, constitutions should have specific provisions on the tolerance and protection of diversity as well as a national mechanism to monitor implementation of these provisions. Second, for the constitution to better protect diversity, the voices and aspirations of the people should resonate in the constitution. The best way to achieve this is a bottom-up and people-driven approach in constitutional engineering and reform.

### Electoral institutions, processes and finance

The institutional and financial autonomy of EMBs should be enshrined in national constitutions. Reinforcing this position, most country reports recommended that the appointment of EMB members should not be the prerogative of the national president but should follow either a mechanism of open advertisement or a vetted process in which civil society organizations and parties are involved.

Because most country reports indicated that intra-party democracy was rare, sometimes leading to splits, parties should be required to register and have appropriate democratic governance mechanisms. Other recommendations relate to a more inclusive electoral system—most expert panels believed that proportional representation (or some hybrid) has a clear advantage over other systems, including greater balance in the legislature among ethno-regional parties and among women and other groups. More generally, if democracy is to set down firm roots in Africa, governments must make election funding a priority and reduce dependency on external funding.

### Managing electoral conflicts and disputes

This set of recommendations relates to pre-empting or managing election-related violence, defusing (or fanning) electoral conflicts by state agencies, managing conflict (including early warning systems) and adjudicating election disputes transparently and quickly. The recommendations take on a special resonance given the persistence of election-related violence in some countries—despite the overall declining trend.

### Regional and international organizations and promotion of electoral integrity

Regional and international organizations, as well as development partners, should apply peer pressure on those states that do not respect basic norms of electoral integrity. In particular, the African Union should continue to push for speedy implementation of the African Charter on Democracy, Elections and Governance while the regional economic communities should do the same with their regional protocols on democracy and good governance.

### Policy dialogue, training and research

Given the vacuum in capacity of key stakeholders (such as EMBs, political parties, state institutions and civil society organizations) to administer and shape the election process, countries need to expand EMBs' professional know-how, inculcate internal democratic values and practices in political parties and encourage regular inter-party dialogue and consultations with other key stakeholders. Relevant training and policy-oriented research should be conducted to help further build electoral institutions' capacity, professionalism and effectiveness.

## Note

1. The methodology is outlined in the appendix.

> ❝ *Relevant training and policy-oriented research should be conducted to help further build electoral institutions' capacity, professionalism and effectiveness*

African countries are plural and diverse societies. The continent's political geography has been shaped by its history, and shows diverse groups, communities, regions and societies that were not necessarily coterminous, forcibly merged together, accentuating the plurality of Africa's social formations. Constructed on an authoritarian political infrastructure, the colonial era's model of governance had implications for state–society relations, the management of diversity and the electoral process. This background heavily influenced the character of the immediate post-colonial state and governance, leading to a crisis of identity and disempowerment, of which traces remain today.

In British colonial Africa, for example, the divide-and-rule policy framed state organization, the power structure, intergroup relations, identity and citizenship, the founding of political parties and electoral processes. As Mahmood Mamdani (1996) noted, colonialism created a form of decentralized despotism, in which people were contained in ethnic closets, and their power bases, political identity and allegiance, as well as their electoral horizon, were defined by those ethnic formations. Such closeting largely accounts for the pervasiveness of ethnicity in Africa's political relations and discourse, and in its electoral processes and bargaining. Beyond ethnicity, the way in which other identities, such as gender, youth and disability, were handled during the colonial period shaped the post-independence experience.

African countries have attempted to deal with the legacy of colonialism and re-engineer their nation-building project by renegotiating their political architecture on the basis of liberal-democratic practice, especially in the last three decades. These efforts include promoting the separation of powers among the three arms of government; engaging the issue of term limits in executive political office, especially the presidency; ensuring representation through elections; redesigning institutions to promote inclusiveness and participation; reforming the party system to respect diversity; and establishing horizontal democracy-promoting institutions (or "watchdogs"). These renegotiations have, to a degree, improved the design of Africa's electoral and political systems, and how they function.

Four main conclusions emerge from this chapter. First, an understanding of Africa's electoral crisis in the post-independence era has to be situated in the context of the political geography and architecture of the African state—the colonialists used diversity as an instrument of political manipulation, exacerbating differences and stultifying the subsequent nation-building project in many countries. Second, the largely one-party model in the immediate post-colonial era, though meant to negate political differences and cohere groups in that project, unfortunately reinforced authoritarianism and deepened the pains of diversity. Third, Africa has made tremendous progress in renegotiating its political architecture, reflecting protracted political struggles by different sectors of society, but much remains to be done. Fourth, transformative leadership is required, to finish renegotiating the democratic and diversity-promoting political architecture of Africa.

## Diversity in Africa

Very few countries or societies are completely homogeneous. Their diversity relates to the broad range of associational or group relations that individuals are organized in or the certain identity markers, including ethnicity, language, race and religion, they are classified by.

*Contemporary patterns*
In Africa, diversity refers to the plurality of identity groups that inhabit a country. African states are commonly linguistically, ethnically and religiously divided.[1] The continent has 2,110 living languages, or more than 30% of the world's total. The average number of speakers per language is only 344,291, and African countries' official languages belong not only to the Afro-Asiatic or Niger-Congo language families, but also to English, French and Portuguese. A survey of 40 African countries revealed 14–40 linguistic groups in 21 countries, 41–90 in 11 and 91–134 in 7. For example, 279 languages are spoken in Cameroon, 134 in Sudan, 132 in Chad, 127 in Tanzania, and 79 each in Côte d'Ivoire and Ghana (Lewis 2009). Linguistic diversity usually indicates ethnic diversity, but not always—the Nuba of the Nuba Mountains of Sudan, for example, speak more than 39 languages (Salih 1989).

Africa contains some 3,315 ethnic groups,[2] and Nigeria has the most, with 455. Some African ethnic groups, spread over more than one country, are larger than some countries' populations: about 40–50 million Oromo in Ethiopia and Kenya; 30 million Hausa in Nigeria, Niger, Ghana, Chad, Cameroon, Côte d'Ivoire and Sudan; 30 million Igbo in Cameroon and Nigeria; 20 million Akan in Ghana; 10 million Fulani (Pule or Fulbe) in Guinea, Nigeria, Niger and Senegal; and roughly similar numbers of Shona in Zimbabwe and Mozambique, and of Zulu in South Africa (Lewis 2009).

In no African country is the whole population of only one or even two religions, or only one denomination (for example, Sunni or Shi'a, or Catholic or Protestant). In eight countries—Benin, Cameroon, Central African Republic, the Congo, Côte d'Ivoire, Guinea-Bissau, Liberia and Swaziland—traditional African religions and systems of belief are practised by 25–50% of the population. Christianity and Islam are almost evenly distributed in Côte d'Ivoire, Eritrea and Ethiopia, while 30 countries have Christian majorities and 21 Muslim. In Mauritius, the population is divided into 48% Hindu, 32% Muslim and 17% Christians (Lewis 2009).

Although the markers of identity groups are fluid, they can be classified into primordial and social. Primordial identities themselves fall into two main categories: exclusive (people are born with them), such as race, ethnicity, language, kinship, clan and gender; and non-exclusive

> *Class and income diversities are more than identity markers—they also have a bearing on democracy*

(they can be changed or overlap the exclusive markers), such as religion, region, nationality or citizenship (which distinguish citizens of a given country from those of others, while binding together the diverse identities within that country as a community of citizens; UNECA 2011).

According to this conceptualization, many of the primordial markers of a given identity group overlap with those of other, perhaps linguistic or religious groups, often extending beyond kinship or ethnicity, such that race, ethnic, kinship and clan identities do not necessarily constitute homogeneous groups because such groups may, for example, practise different religions.

The social identity markers are expansive in that they can be formed across primordial identities as well as across national citizenships (UNECA 2011). They are usually acquired, and often based on purposive choices, tactical necessity and common interests or incurred moral obligations (UNECA 2011). Such markers include occupational associations, political affiliation, media groups, business organizations, trade unions, academic associations, human rights bodies and civil society groups.

Other important social identity markers are modes of production and institutional systems of governance. Diversity appears in economic systems (from pastoralism to capitalism) and settlement types (rural or urban). Urban businesses and rural communities have different identities, institutional systems and cultural values, even when they belong to the same ethnic or religious group. Diverse but interlocking modes of production create different economic, political and cultural spaces within countries, as well as within ethnic and religious identities, besides perpetuating diverse institutional systems (UNECA 2011).

Class is another social identity marker, often in successful economies like Botswana and South Africa that have very unequal wealth distributions (AGR III Botswana Country Report 2012; AGR III South Africa Country Report 2012).[3] But class and income diversities are more than identity markers—they also have a bearing on democracy (box 1.1).

The more social identity markers develop, the tighter the interdependence and networks of interaction

## Box 1.1 Examples of identity and politics

Persistent poverty and inequality have potentially deleterious effects on the quality and sustainability of democracy in South Africa (AGR III South Africa Country Report 2012).

In some countries, political parties are more associated with the urban than rural population, reflecting the settlement divide. The AGR III Mozambique Country Report 2012, for instance, reiterates the observation in Sitoe et al. (2005, 20) that with few exceptions, "Mozambique's parties other than Frelimo and Renamo had not yet succeeded in building an organizational structure that covered a significant proportion of the country. Instead, these parties remained largely based on their leadership and in the environs of the city of Maputo".

African societies also embody other identity markers such as those based on gender, age and origin (indigenous and migrants).

among primordial groups grow. Africa is still at an early stage along this trajectory though, and most social markers are weaker than primordial markers—many political parties, for example, are organized along primordial dimensions such as ethnicity, religion or region.

Although pointers of diversity in society, identities generally overlap, allowing individuals to bear more

than one. But they require careful strategic management if they are not to be conflictual. Historical factors like colonialism, as well as geographical and linguistic patterns, have left an indelible imprint of both primordial and social identity markers on most African states and societies.

The labours to build states and cement social cohesion have therefore been Herculean. Organizing elections against a backdrop of ethnic, racial and regional diversities proved very challenging after independence, and the legacies of that challenge persist to the present day. Competition among parties can lead to problems of relations among sectarian identities, fanning the flames of electoral violence and political instability, which are not themselves necessarily caused by ethnic, religious or regional diversities: the socio-economic and political contexts of politics must also be considered.

Table 1.1 summarizes the major factors and their causes that underlie diversity and lead to tension, as identified in the African Peer Review Mechanism.

*Electoral competition*
The essence of electoral competition is that political parties compete for power through the public vote, and are expected to comply with the rules of the "electoral game". Because of the strength of ethnic, religious and other primordial ties, most African societies are at variance with the individualism inherent in liberal-democratic institutions

**Table 1.1 Diversity-related factors for conflicts and tensions in countries that have completed the African Peer Review Mechanism**

| Diversity factors leading to conflicts and tension | Causes of the diversity factors |
|---|---|
| Historical legacy | Pre-colonial and colonial legacies of uneven development<br>Institutional fragmentation left behind by the colonial state |
| Grievances | Uneven access to resources<br>Uneven access to cultural rights like religion and language rights<br>Absence or uneven access to political representation |
| Divisive politics | Manipulation by the elite of primordial identities<br>Organization of political parties along primordial-identity lines |
| State and governance structures | Lack of autonomy of state organs from the executive, and lack of genuine decentralization of power |
| Structural and institutional problems | Fragmented modes of production, marginalizing rural communities<br>Fragmented institutions of governance<br>Poor relations between traditional authorities and government administrators |
| Conflict between indigenous and immigrant populations | Citizenship rights<br>Access to land rights<br>Access to jobs |

*Source:* UNECA 2011.

in which the individual vote takes precedence over group interests. In some African countries, however, the political party is a collective representation of interest groups, which use it—and sometimes abuse it—in electoral and broad political competition to serve their interests. As part of the structure of the governing political institutions, political parties are capable of being guiding beacons for political stability—or major contributors to violence.

Political parties serve as mediating institutions that stimulate and then channel people's political activity. They are therefore central to how electoral competition is organized, conducted and mediated in multicultural societies. In Africa, given the historical formation of parties along ethnic lines, they generate mainly identity-based conflicts (box 1.2). Claims to power, resources and other social goods often seek expression through identity-based mechanisms with serious implications for the nation-building project and for national cohesion and stability.

What these conflicts illustrate is the character of the state as a partisan ethno-hegemonizing entity, an instrument of the dominant ethnic group or groups over other ethnic groups, a function extended—with the electoral process—to using state resources to overwhelm opposition parties and their candidates (Jinadu 2010).

Africa's election context has its own characteristics. Many countries experienced a colonialism that indelibly marked their societies culturally,

economically and politically—perhaps most significant were the attempts to wrench nation-states out of multiple ethnic groups, some of which did not share a common history and culture. After independence, most of the multi-ethnic states displayed diversities that were a challenge to weave into national unity. Elections were contested fiercely as subnational ethnic groups vied for power. It was little surprise that most of these states suffered election-linked conflict, including Côte d'Ivoire, the Democratic Republic of the Congo, Ethiopia, Kenya, Nigeria, Sudan and such small states as Burundi and Rwanda.

The management of social and political diversity proved a colossal challenge that the newly independent states were ill equipped to undertake. They had inherited a political strait-jacket endorsed by the Organization of African Unity, whose founding charter stated that colonially derived territorial boundaries were inviolable. Some analysts have indeed argued that post-independence governance frameworks contributed to what they have termed a "crisis of identity" and disempowerment in much of Africa (Deng 2008). Legal frameworks that stressed unity through suppression of diversity left many Africans feeling disenfranchised.

## Pre-colonial and colonial political systems

*Pre-colonial organizations*
Pre-colonial Africa had a very diverse social and political landscape. Beyond its ethno-linguistic heterogeneity, communities had a variegated landscape of socio-political organizations, at different stages of development.

They ranged from units like extended families, clans, communal and age-set systems at the micro level, to different levels of segmentary, quasi-centralized and centralized polities like chiefdoms, kingdoms, states and empires. Political institutions and systems evolved from various African traditions, drawing on other sources in design and operation (Hodgkin 1961). Organizational architecture varied, as some had fluid structures with adaptability, responsiveness, inclusiveness and accountability (Ayitteh 1991).

Traditional mechanisms for coexistence and interaction, including co-option, assimilation, integration, exchange relations, intermarriage and blood brotherhoods, operated alongside conquest and subjugation through annexation as centralized political entities formed and expanded. By the 16th century, most African societies had come into contact with the outside world during the mercantile era, with plunder for slaves particularly affecting the evolution of most societies.

*Colonial diversity designs and management*
The 19th century witnessed the scramble for Africa, through military conquest, occupation and suzerain treaties that invariably led to loss of sovereignty. Colonialism fundamentally transformed the continent, integrating it with the new world order and interrupting Africa's "natural" processes. It was repressive, undemocratic, divisive and above all extractive, for capitalism's benefit. Of particular concern was the political architecture used to reconfigure and create modern African countries: it balkanized groups, arbitrarily lumping together distinct pre-colonial communities or splitting groups across new borders.[4]

The colonial powers designed these boundaries with utter disregard for the diversities and (some of) the positive traditional institutions and mechanisms for managing diversity, as alien rule and political institutions were superimposed on previously self-governing societies (Ajayi 1969). Pre-colonial societies were

' *Colonialism fundamentally transformed the continent, interrupting Africa's "natural" processes*

realigned to suit the administrative, political and economic interests of the powers, leading to new diversities, including citizenship.

Colonial statecraft managed these diversities by coercion, of course, as well as by manipulation and other subjugating policies. Divide and rule enhanced separation of the different societies or regions to undermine shared experiences and commonality, thus forestalling unity against colonial rule. Indirect rule allowed each society its traditional institutions. And assimilation ground down diversities and (in the colonialists' eyes) "unworthy" systems through association or integration into, for example, French citizenship.

These policies severed some of the inter-ethnic linkages and relations and fostered ethno-regional fragmentation. New territorial confines propelled ethnic consciousness and attendant political mobilization along ethno-parochial platforms and identity lines, nurturing a long-term bias towards ethnic division from common citizenship and social identity markers.

Still, classes like peasants, workers and the elite came into greater visibility through colonial patterns of production, division of labour, distribution and formal education. The elites pushed through the policies of the colonial establishment and supervised those below them. Consistent with divide and rule, Africans were largely confined to producing raw materials, at the bottom of the hierarchy, while groups like

Indians were placed in intermediary administrative positions and in commerce. Yet indirect rule further alienated Indians from traditional institutions and citizenship, and so they were conveniently positioned as "aliens" to forestall integration for a united front against colonialism.

The notion of citizenship was designed to overlap primordial identities, thus reinforcing the new country structures. In settler colonies, a privileged white minority was placed at the top of the hierarchy, which precipitated pre-independence pan-ethnic responses among Africans.

Colonialism often reinforced gender asymmetries in mainly patriarchal systems. Migrant-labour policies, coupled with taxes on men, justified men's pursuit of wage employment and stressed constructs of women as the "weaker" gender, marginalizing them for many years from labour markets and demonetarizing their labour. Women were to play a supportive role of staying at home to cheaply reproduce households of their bread-winning absentee husbands. In peasant economies, subsistence food crops were gendered female and the introduced cash crops male, giving men control of household income.

The colonial state therefore deepened diversity and reified polarization and contradictions in many African countries, heightening ethnic differences, complicating citizenship and preventing national cohesion and identity from emerging.

> *The colonial state deepened diversity and reified polarization and contradictions in many African countries*

## Colonial governance and history of elections

In the colonial period, governance was neither democratic nor participatory, but top-down, centralized or ethnicized (Ndege 2009). Through a hierarchical administrative structure, comprador traditional leaders and appointed warrant chiefs implemented policies and kept law and order. Francophone Africa saw some exceptions, as its assimilation policy occasionally allowed Africans to take part in elections (Golder and Wantchekon 2004). After 1848, the four communes in Senegal were allowed to elect a *député* to the French parliament (Cowen and Laakso 1997; Ellis 2000). It was not until 1914 that the first African, Blaise Diagne, the mayor of Dakar, was elected as Senegal's representative to the French Chamber of Deputies.

The British colonies offered no electoral experience for Africans over much of the period (Wiseman 1990). Keeping major decisions at home, Britain introduced consultative bodies called legislative councils in many colonies between 1900 and the 1920s, but these represented the main non-African interest groups like planters, settlers and businesses. Membership was largely by nomination. The first elections were held in the 1920s in Ghana, Kenya, Nigeria, Sierra Leone and Zambia (Lindberg 2006), exclusive to the small elites in a few major cities (Collier 1982). Although some traditional leaders could be unofficial members, Africans were admitted to the legislative councils usually only after agitation. Greater African representation in the councils in the late 1940s aimed to mollify increasing postwar militant nationalism.

## Nationalist pressure and introduction of liberal democracy, 1945 to mid-1950s

The Second World War accelerated African nationalism, with militancy against a backdrop of war-weary colonial powers and economic recession. The powers were compelled to transfer liberal democracy intended to prepare their colonies for a smooth transition to democratic governance. They introduced some concessions and reforms, including more widely enfranchising electoral systems— Africans increased their representation in legislative councils—and allowed political organizations. They also accelerated formal education for nurturing what they viewed as a "desirable" indigenous successor elite, to defuse radical nationalist elements.

Although the British aimed to transfer power eventually, the French did not, and envisaged continuing to administer their colonies as extensions of France (such as *départements* and *territoires*). They hoped to maintain their influence through a French-dominated federal community (Golder and Wantchekon 2004). In 1945, France increased representation for its West African colonies to 10 seats in the new Constituent Assembly. From 1946, Africans who met tight criteria voted for both the French National Assembly and for local government councils in Africa. The reforms did not, though, fundamentally transform the political landscape, and still reflected colonial control.

## Transition to independence

Facing persistent agitation for self-rule, the colonial powers offered greater democracy in the late 1950s to prepare the transition to self-rule: they widened the African franchise, allowing direct elections to legislative bodies. It was therefore only just before independence that the first African elections with universal suffrage and unrestricted party formation were held (Cowen and Laakso 1997).

Malawi, Tanzania and Uganda in Anglophone Africa held legislative council elections. To manage diversity, they adopted federalism and other decentralization models, intended to protect the interests of ethnic minorities. However, federalism usually had the reverse effect of solidifying ethno-parochialism, as it was within the broader framework of indirect rule.

France arranged a referendum in 1958 for the colonies to approve staying in the newly designed French Community, in which only Guinea voted for full independence (the others voting to stay in). In Lusophone countries, with Portugal undertaking no substantive reforms, unconventional national liberation came to the fore through armed resistance in Angola, Guinea-Bissau and Mozambique. South Africa had already brought in apartheid, ostensibly to preserve identity interests and racial diversity.

Liberal democracy was grafted onto the colonial architecture of fractionalized countries, rendering it complicated to establish democracy for the long term and to manage the diversities. The resultant competitive electoral processes, political parties and electioneering were invariably shaped by ethno-sectarianism that dominated the new citizenship. Liberal-democratic institutions, including political parties, were often reconfigured to serve sectarian interests and preserve identities and aspirations in the new "nation" states.

Further, some of these institutions were foreign to African societies. As Adejumobi (2000, 62) notes on African democratic principles and practices: "Consensus, dialogue and the political collective were emphasized, as opposed to individualism, atomization and the majoritarianism of the Western capitalist political system". Concepts like voting and political majority/minority were foreign (Buijtenhuijs and Rijnierse 1993; Albert 1992; Adejumobi 2000).

Four countries serve to highlight the contradictions in imported liberal democracy on the eve of independence (box 1.3).

## The post-colonial state

Although the contradictions of colonialism ultimately led to independence, the consequences of colonial rule persist. In post-colonial Africa, the state-building project has been particularly challenging, partly explaining the continent's failure to extricate itself from the clutches of poverty and underdevelopment. The complexity largely derives from the dual legacies of colonialism (as seen) and the post-independence, often autocratic, successor leadership.

Post-independence Africa can be divided into two periods. The first—for 25 years after independence to the democratic reforms of the 1980s—was dominated by the twin trajectories of nation-state building and autocratic rule, which both stifled diversity. Together they engendered the struggles and reforms of the 1980s that saw political space open up and democracy gain ground. The second—running until today—marks the reform period (see next section). Although Africa's political landscape shows real progress, a final flowering of democracy and diversity management is a work in progress.

In the earlier period, the first problem confronting the successor leadership was the complexity of the artificial, colonialist-crafted new African state. Independence leaders sought to engineer that fractured entity towards a nation-state, or common-citizenship, project, but their efforts were hampered by the mutual antagonisms and fears of domination among the various social entities. According to Ajayi (1984), the effect of the colonialists' ethnocultural stratification was to diminish "existing intercultural linkages", while strengthening and consolidating "the sense of internal cohesion within the component polities and language group".

Subsequently, the post-independence body politic was punctuated either by attempts to renegotiate and reconstitute the state or by ethnopolitical wars and attempts to secede. Given the interwoven ethnic and citizenship question that was unresolved before independence, Jinadu (2007, 16) notes:

> The departure of the colonial powers was consequently, in several African countries, accompanied by internecine, armed ethno-political conflicts between majority, or "favoured" ethnic groups,

which wanted to maintain control of the inherited state, and "disadvantaged", usually but not always numerically minority ethnic groups, which wanted to capture or reconstitute the inherited state on more favourable terms, or, failing which, to secede from it. This much is clear from the post-colonial histories of Angola, Burundi, Chad, the Democratic Republic of the Congo, Djibouti, Nigeria, Senegal, Somalia, Sudan and Uganda.

The rainbow coalition of ethno-regional nationalist political parties that struggled for independence usually disappeared quite quickly, to be replaced by fragmented and regionally or ethnically anchored parties. At the extreme, colonialism in Rwanda—having exacerbated inter-group diversities—ultimately led to extremism that precipitated refugee outflows and genocide.

The rationale for managing diversity tended to serve as justification for forcing different entities into the nation-state's common citizenship. This approach tried to resolve the diversity question by dissolving it in the myth of common citizenship and individual rights, but it failed in this—generally reinforcing identity-group consciousness—because it raised, then as now, the question of identity in a practical manner that the concept of common citizenship could not adequately answer.

But whose interests among the diverse identity groups—ethnic, political-regional, party-political, racial, religious, rich, poor, urban, rural, women, and youth—does common citizenship promote? Reducing the question further: To whom does the state belong?

Pondering ethnic diversity in post-colonial Africa, Asia and the Middle East, Wimmer (1997, 635) observed that "Ethnic conflicts arise during the process of state formation, when a fight erupts over 'which people' the state should belong to". The state is therefore the primary contested terrain for politically mobilized group demands and conflicts based on identity markers: Who is to control or be excluded from the state and its vast resources and patronage machine?

The second problem facing the successor leadership stemmed from the common citizenship and nation-state project. Across much of the continent, leaders increasingly perceived political pluralism and diversity as inimical to nation building and as potent sources of division and conflict for new-born states, causing them to repress diversity, constrict political space, and consolidate authoritarian and personal rule. Military intervention often became a fashionable remedy to the post-independence nationalist dictatorships, but it usually embedded autocracy, compounding the misrule.

The first 25 years after independence saw many centralizing and control models at work—military or political—which counterproductively sought to dissolve diversity. Very few countries had multi-party politics and opposition parties, and electoral processes were reduced to a sham, leading to a simulacrum of democracy.

*Authoritarianism*

After independence, many nationalist leaders attempted to consolidate their hold on power, usually in one of two ways.

The first entailed consolidating the ruling party's political dominance via development ideology, articulated around notions of nation building and progress. This ideology called for national unity (essentially, unanimity) and silenced dissent of any kind. Under this umbrella, alternative sites and forums for conducting politics, like opposition parties, trade unions, farmers' associations, or student and faculty movements, were silenced or eliminated. In Egypt, for instance, President Nasser dissolved political parties by decree on 16 January 1953 (AGR III Egypt Country Report 2012).

Presidents concentrated power. Although some leaders submitted themselves to periodic elections, these only served as cover for an enduring presidency. Most presidents became elevated above the law and enjoyed unlimited terms of office, as in Algeria, Botswana, Egypt, Kenya, Senegal and Tunisia. They often legitimized this authoritarianism in the name of managing diversity.

The second approach took various forms. Military rule or outright dictatorship appeared in the Central African Republic, Malawi, Nigeria, Uganda and Zaire. Other countries had an absolute monarch (Swaziland) or a constitutional monarchy (Lesotho). Apartheid in South Africa was a unique form of internal colonialism and dictatorship, premised on institutionalized racial segregation and domination. The struggle against apartheid was waged by internal forces, led by the African National Congress, and external forces. It was not only a quest for equality and a non-racial society, but also for a political transition to democracy.

*Electoral processes in authoritarian political systems*

In the post-colonial period, acquiring and monopolizing political power as a force for repressing and eliminating political opponents— and thus the control and redistribution of resources—formed part of electoral politics. This strategy was helped by the inherited first-past-the-post electoral system and its winner-takes-all consequences, which tended to perpetuate the political hegemony of ethno-communal majorities, exacerbating violent majority–minority conflicts (box 1.4). Some countries (including Ethiopia, Nigeria and South Africa) attempted to design political and constitutional measures to assuage fears and protect interests of ethnic minorities through arrangements like proportional representation and federalism, but these measures often threw up new challenges.

After the founding elections at independence in the 1960s, the electoral process in most countries became irregular and opaque, and largely remained so through the 1970s and 1980s (chapter 2). Most polities were either one-party states or military regimes. Other parties were systematically proscribed, generating widespread voter apathy as the utility of the electoral process itself was called into question (Hayward 1987). The only multi-party states were those with smaller populations like Botswana, Mauritius and Senegal.

The absence or proscription of political competition and democratic practices strengthened authoritarian tendencies in civilian regimes but also provoked resistance from other institutions of the state, which explained the bias towards military coups for changing leaders—who rarely left office after elections anyway: out of 101 political successions in 1963–1987, some 57% were fostered by the military, 31% by civilian incumbents and only 8% by elections (Bratton and van de Walle 1997).

The electoral systems under one-party states and military regimes did not encourage or accommodate competitive politics. Most electoral management boards (often called electoral commissions) were subordinated to state structures such as the ministry of home affairs or interior, and lacked adequate funding and staff as well as autonomy. Elections in one-party states consisted of intra-party contests with few choices, generating voter apathy and diminishing interest. The credibility of the electoral process was tarnished, and national or international observation and monitoring of elections before the early 1990s was rare (AGR III Gabon Country Report 2012). One interpretation is that successor regimes began to view

> ### Box 1.4 The tyranny of the majority
>
> Minority ethnic groups—reduced to a perpetual electoral minority; treated as second-class citizens; underrepresented in central and local bureaucracies and in the public services generally; their heartlands neglected, denied of infrastructure development and social services and turned into blighted oases of internal colonialism; and seeing no prospect through the ballot box for capturing political power—have in some countries sought and used various voice and exit options, including non-constitutional ones, to challenge the hegemonic ethnic groups. As Ivo Duchacek observed, commenting on the situation more than 30 years ago:
>
> > The problem for most ethnic minorities is that they are permanent minorities and the ruling group a permanent majority. In inter-ethnic relations therefore, the convenient democratic game of numbers does not work since the unalterable power symmetry between permanent majority and permanent minorities impedes the formation of a consensual community (Duchacek 1977, 23, quoted in Thomas-Woolley and Keller 1994, 414).

democratic elections and competitive politics as a waste of time:

> Before too long, these regimes suspended rules of succession through competitive electoral politics, proscribed oppositional politics and declared the state a one-party state, allegedly or ostensibly for reasons of state, including notably the claims that elections (a) tended to "politicize" ethnicity and related identity differences, in ways that encourage or lead to ethno-political violence, thereby undermining national unity; and (b) were expensive and a drain on scarce resources available for development (Jinadu 2010, 14).

The structures and leadership of one-party states and military regimes may have differed, but they both stifled pluralism, the autonomy of electoral bodies and the institutional mechanisms for political change, as authoritarian rulers weakened parliamentary prerogatives, granted themselves extended terms of office, introduced one-party state constitutions and intimidated or imprisoned opponents.

People disengaged from activist politics, as seen in low voter turn-out, a trend that regimes took advantage of to narrow political space and abet public cynicism. By the 1980s, most authoritarian regimes faced a crisis of legitimacy:

> This crisis was manifest in a loss of faith among African citizens that state elites were capable of solving basic problems of socio-economic and political development. Leaders had damaged their own claim to rule by engaging in nepotism and corruption, which led to popular perceptions that those with access to political office were living high on the hog while ordinary people suffered. The erosion of political legitimacy built on crisis proportions because authoritarian regimes did not provide procedures for citizens to peacefully express such grievances and, especially, to turn unpopular leaders out of office (Bratton and van de Walle 1997, 99).

Any overview of this period must refer to the "strong leaders"—mainly the founding fathers of their countries at independence. Their skills and charisma in holding together ethnic and group interests were crucial in maintaining diversity with some modicum of national unity. Such men included Julius Nyerere in Tanzania, Jomo Kenyatta in Kenya and Houphouet Boigny in Côte d'Ivoire. Nyerere is "still considered by many as not only an icon of national identity but almost a synonym to it. It was under his leadership when the country developed into a unified nation with remarkable achievements in the management of diversity" (AGR III Tanzania Country Report 2012, 112).

*The challenge of pre-reform diversity management*
Authoritarian regimes' iron fist and coercive methods had disastrous consequences. Conflicts in Burundi, Chad, the Democratic Republic of the Congo, Liberia, Rwanda, Sierra Leone and Sudan led to civil wars costing many hundreds of thousands of lives. Conflicts in Ethiopia and Somalia had different origins and affected many tens of thousands of people. Some of these conflicts persisted well into the 1990s, after the democratic wave had swept across the continent.

Because the one-party or military-led unitary projects that became common after independence failed to eradicate ethnic identities (Olukoshi and Laakso 1996), addressing multiple diversities remained a major challenge in most post-colonial states. But this did not stop most of those in power from using inter-ethnic relations, or at times equally diverse linguistic, religious and regional cleavages, for narrow political interests, especially political leaders gaining and retaining political power (box 1.5).

> *The opening of political space and rebirth of multi-party politics ushered in political power struggles*

## Box 1.5  Ethnicity and party support

The opening of political space and rebirth of multi-party politics ushered in political power struggles, with power brokers appealing to their ethnic bases and taking advantage of social inequality and exclusion (Ngenge 1999).

Ethnic mobilization, whether for party formation, electoral campaigns or patronage, was common, and when combined with economic disparity and inequitable access to political power became a source of long-drawn-out conflicts with far-reaching destabilizing effects (Salih and Nordlund 2007).

Research in 12 African states into the impact of ethno-linguistic and ethno-racial characteristics on support for the ruling party confirmed (though with a small sample) a common assumption that ethnic-linguistic cleavages often structure party identification (Norris and Mattes 2003). In national models, ethnicity remained significant in 8 of the 12 sample countries but was not necessarily the primary cleavage.

Other structural factors important for partisanship—if less consistent—included a rural–urban cleavage in Mali, Namibia and Tanzania; age and generation in Botswana, Tanzania and Zambia; and education in Ghana, Nigeria and Zimbabwe. Moreover, in most of the sample countries, support—far from being an automatic expression of group loyalties—also reflected how well governments delivered services to citizens.

Related studies pointed to the continuing significance of religious, regional and linguistic manifestations of identities such as the north–south divide (with variations) in Cameroon, Côte d'Ivoire, Ghana and Nigeria, and a linguistic divide (Amhara and Oromo) in Ethiopia. In addition:

- countries with strong ethnic majorities are not politically more, or less, stable than countries with smaller ethnic groups;

- although elections are fought partly on the basis of the support that traditional authorities such as chiefs lend to a party, after the elections political coalitions are forged without reference to the constituencies; and

- African parties are modern, but their appeal to ethnicity—and to linguistic, religious and regional cleavages—is exploited and mobilized in a classic populist fashion (Salih and Nordlund 2007).

An indispensable first step towards diversity management would be to ensure that the electoral framework in each state was designed in a way sensitive to countries' diversity (Salih and Nordlund 2007). This means creating a framework for greater participation in the political system and decisions, and seriously exploring options like federalism, local administration and proportional representation.

Challenges often arise, as elsewhere in the world, when particular groups face discrimination and when ethnic identities align with patterns of inequality or repression. To deal with what appear to be ethnic disputes therefore requires policy makers to address underlying questions of economic and political marginalization, and to find acceptable ways to redistribute resources.

In view of these embedded and competing identities and loyalties, it is unrealistic to assume that the electoral process on its own can resolve these diversities. Structural reforms combined with electoral reforms are imperative—as one set without the other will fail to resolve the negative features of diversity.

## The reform period: Renegotiated architecture and recurrent issues

Authoritarian rule triggered popular resistance, as African politics descended into violent political succession conflicts and to palace and military coups against "sit-tight" rulers. The 1980s witnessed a wave of democratic reforms across the continent, in the form of debates about redesigning the post-colonial state and of direct struggles against authoritarianism.

A general consensus has now emerged for renegotiating the political architecture of the African state through strengthening democracy as well as promoting and protecting diversity. One aim of these moves is to make it difficult or impossible to abrogate entrenched provisions through ordinary legislation. The debates have focused on recurrent strategic reform in six main areas.

### Electoral representation

Electoral systems, elections and their implications for electoral outcomes and diversity management remain crucial in this consensus, despite recent progress in constitutional provisions for greater inclusiveness and participation in elections and the electoral process in several African countries. The issue has been addressed from different angles, including, first, special constitutional provisions to modify the principle of universal adult suffrage, especially in elections to legislative chambers, and second, reform of the electoral system to make electoral outcomes and thus legislative representation and public political appointments reflect diversity in particular.

Ensuring the second outcome was designed to be achieved through three approaches: making the share of seats won by political parties in parliaments reflect more closely that of the valid votes in parliamentary elections; enhancing female representation in parliaments and public political appointments; and sharing power, especially in central government, among political parties.

### Separation of powers

Constitutional provisions on the separation of powers among the executive, legislative and judicial branches of government, backed by checks and balances, are now essential building blocks in Africa's renegotiated political architecture. The provisions are designed to limit excessive power in the executive and the gross abuse and impunity that typically accompany it. Separation of powers is a compass for rebalancing the relationship among the three branches in the African state, away from the concentration of powers in the executive during the years of authoritarian rule.

This objective has typically taken the form of vesting entrenched countervailing powers in the legislature, judiciary and independent horizontal institutions (the last discussed under *Horizontal democracy-promoting institutions* below).

The extent and forms of separation of powers vary between presidential, semi-presidential and parliamentary

> ❛ **The 1980s witnessed a wave of democratic reforms across the continent**

systems of government; and between unitary, devolved and federal forms. But results have been mixed, so that some commentators still refer to the "imperial" or "monarchical" presidency.

### Legislative independence

Pointing to the importance of the legislature in many African states under the presidential system, Prempeh (2008) concluded that many African countries are yet to be free from executive control, because of poor institutional capacity of the legislature, weak constitutional design and, sometimes, timidity and abdication of responsibility by the legislature.

One target of legislative independence is the enormous power of presidential appointments and patronage disposal, which African presidents have learned to use to strengthen the presidency, despite constitutional powers of appropriation, investigation, oversight, confirmation and impeachment vested in many parliaments. Still, some countries show hopeful trends: parliaments in Ghana, Kenya and South Africa have exercised their wide powers as strategic bargaining ploys to put the executive in check.

Separation of powers under presidential form of government has strengthened the independence of parliaments by making it harder for presidents to dissolve or suspend them, except during emergency rule, and in such cases under constitutional provisions. Another factor buttressing their independence is a forceful parliamentary opposition

and a strong legislative bureaucracy, as in Ghana, Kenya, Nigeria, South Africa and Zambia, although assertions of independence tend to be spasmodic.

The general picture, however, is of historically deep-rooted debilitating capacity and resource deficits, partly due to long years of dissolution, neglect, proscription or suspension of legislatures, and partly due to the structural problem of economic underdevelopment.

### Judicial independence

The renegotiated architecture has typically sought to strengthen judicial independence as part of the separation of powers. Doing this has involved entrenching constitutional provisions, subject to checks and balances, that largely vest judicial powers and functions, including judicial review of the action of the other branches of government, in the judiciary; that grant corresponding fiscal autonomy of the judiciary, usually as a first charge on consolidated revenue funds, to enable it to exercise its powers and perform its functions under the constitution; that guarantee the independence of judicial appointments through the establishment of independent judicial service commissions or judicial councils to vet and process such appointments; and that make it hard to remove judges (to ensure judges' security of tenure until retirement).

If this is the typical constitutional arrangement, the practice varies by country, in an ebb and flow of independence. This back and forth reflects the judiciary's ability

> *Separation of powers is a compass for rebalancing the relationship among the three branches of government in the African state*

to resist encroachments on its powers by other branches of government, to dispense justice fairly, to provide easy access to justice by all, or to protect and provide redress for assault on diversity by the other branches of government or other groups or forces in state and society.

Some African judiciaries, like the legislature, suffer from weak capacity and resources—more so among lower courts—impairing judicial independence and threatening access to justice (and its rapid delivery).

### Federalism, devolution and centralization

Tinged with the residue of precolonial and colonial political systems, debates on renegotiating the political architecture have looked closely at political devolution—transferring power from higher to lower levels—and decentralization—reorganizing into smaller, more independent governance units closer to the people through constitutional provisions for multiple (polycentric) layers of political authority.

Here, the approach of Africa's precolonial federative political systems converges with new global thinking on modes of governance, which emphasizes political devolution and subsidiarity. A landmark development in this new thinking is the African Charter on Human and Peoples' Rights (box 1.6).

### Federalism

Historically, federalism was unpopular in Africa and remains so, as only Ethiopia and Nigeria declare themselves federal. South Africa and Tanzania have federal constitutions, but they are not usually formally referred to as federal. Kenya's 2010 Constitution has federal features in providing entrenched provisions for devolved government, including the Fourth Schedule, which distributes legislative competences between national and county governments that the central government cannot unilaterally take away (except by referendum and under conditions in the constitution).

### Devolution

The continuing unpopularity of federalism has brought into focus the relevance of political devolution—beyond political decentralization—as a constitutional mechanism for managing diversity. Devolution creates new subnational structures and centres of authority that grant limited autonomy and self-government to subnational (regional, district, local) groups and communities, short of creating two sovereign authorities with direct legal impact on citizens. Countries such as Algeria, Benin, Ghana, Sierra Leone and Uganda now have constitutional clauses for political devolution, which provide for—at least in

**Box 1.6 The African Charter on Human and People's Rights**

*Article 20 (1):* All peoples shall have the right to existence. They shall have the unquestionable and inalienable right to self-determination. They shall freely determine their political status and shall pursue their economic and social development according to the policy they have freely chosen.

*Article 22 (1):* All peoples shall have the right to their economic, social and cultural development with due regard to their freedom and identity and in the equal enjoyment of the common heritage of mankind.

theory (box 1.7)—contested terrains and opportunities for redefining the role of local traditional institutions and communities in national governance.

Political devolution offers a halfway house between federalism and unitary government.[5] Although the division of powers under federalism is entrenched and requires special procedures for amendment, which precludes unilateral amendment by either level of government, political devolution involves delegation of powers and functions to lower levels of government from the central government, generally through ordinary legislation, which means that the central government can, again through ordinary legislation, unilaterally recentralize those powers.

### Recentralizing trends

Devolution remains problematic in Africa, and in both unitary and federal states recentralizing moves still provoke public debate. Devolved subnational units of government are typically still under the stranglehold of the central government. The African Peer Review Mechanism country reports of Algeria, Benin, Ghana, Kenya and Rwanda provide detailed illustrations of how power has recentralized, with devolved authorities in practice no more than appendages of central government, which has invasive powers of political, administrative and financial control.

In Ethiopia and Nigeria, where federalism divides or shares sovereignty between federal and regional or state governments, a recurring challenge is how to arrest the recentralizing trend, which may well hinder the states' effectiveness in managing ethno-regional and other forms of diversity. In Tanzania, questions have recurred since the founding Acts of the Union and the 1977 Constitution over the extent and limits of the division of legislative competences between the United Republic and Zanzibar, and over the constitutional dominance of the former over the latter.

In these federal countries, a top-down approach to governance as well as constitutional, fiscal and political asymmetries between the federal and lower governments and among regional or state governments continues to severely diminish federalism as a mechanism for managing diversity. Nigeria and Tanzania are undergoing constitutional reforms to renegotiate the nature of federalism being practised.

---

**Box 1.7  Devolution in practice, Ghana**

The Ghanaian political state, although decentralized administratively, is still very much centralized.

The essence of decentralization is delegation of powers and resources from central government to the district assemblies. The extent to which they have been able to exercise powers is not easy to assess as some ministries and departments in central government do not appreciate the import of true devolution. Merely opening offices of a ministry or department in a district is not devolution, unless they are under the control of the district assembly.

The reluctance of those in central government to let go of power is a potent obstacle to devolution and the success of decentralization in Ghana.

*Source:* AGR III Ghana Country Report 2012, box V.

## Political party systems

### Party reform

Reform of the party system continues to generate interest because of its centrality to democratic politics, and generally to constructively managing diversity. Since the end of the one-party era, the majority of African countries permit multiple political parties and allow them to field candidates for elective office.

In several countries, though, political associations seeking to become political parties have to apply for recognition and registration as political parties, meeting the provisions of national constitutions, the electoral law and regulations handed down by parliaments and electoral management boards. In Uganda, for instance, the formation, registration and general regulation of political parties is governed by the Political Parties and Organisations Act 2005 (AGR III Uganda Country Report 2012). The power to register recognized political parties usually lies with each country's electoral management board, which also has oversight and monitoring powers over party political activities, including their finances.

Party reform has sought to strengthen the party system as a mechanism for constructive diversity management along four main axes: preventing the formation of ethnic-based political parties; writing provisions in national constitutions or electoral laws for internal democracy and for diversity promotion, especially among marginalized groups such as women; ensuring public financing and regulation, including audits of party political financing; and promoting inter-party dialogue and helping to negotiate political parties' codes of conduct to guide inter-party relations and to forestall violence, especially that related to elections.

Countries' requirements revolve essentially around ensuring internal democracy within political parties. They are intended to create an environment of party competition that will mitigate intra- and inter-party violence, reduce pre- and post-election adjudication and strengthen democracy.

> The maintenance of fair and equal procedures in the selection of executive officers as well as its presidential and parliamentary candidates is, therefore, a microcosm of efforts towards enhancing democratic national elections. A political party whose delegates' congress and primaries are characterized by antidemocratic practices or worse still factional violence has already failed in its duty to foster a violence-free election and build a culture of tolerance and peaceful resolution of conflict among its followers (AGR III Ghana Country Report 2012).

### Types of party system

Three main party systems were operating in the early years of this century (table 1.2, and see chapter 5).

## Table 1.2 Party systems in Africa, 2004–2006

| Dominant-party system | Two-party system | Multi-party system |
|---|---|---|
| Angola | Benin | Algeria |
| Botswana | Cape Verde | Burundi |
| Burkina Faso | Ghana | Central African Republic |
| Cameroon | Seychelles | Congo, Dem. Rep. |
| Chad | Sierra Leone | Liberia |
| Côte d'Ivoire | Zimbabwe | Malawi |
| Djibouti | | Mali |
| Equatorial Guinea | | Mauritius |
| Ethiopia | | Niger |
| Gambia | | São Tomé and Príncipe |
| Mozambique | | Senegal |
| Namibia | | Zambia |
| Nigeria | | |
| Rwanda | | |
| South Africa | | |
| Tanzania | | |
| Uganda | | |

*Source:* Based on Salih and Nordlund (2007).

Yet many political parties themselves have failed to live up to hopes, because they lack internal democracy, fail to reflect and promote diversity, and do not reflect democratic governance and diversity management in their constitutions. Other problems are a failure to extend their presence beyond urban areas, a lack of ideological distinctiveness, absence of internal democratic culture and politics, and inadequate resources.

### Political succession and term limits
Despite the forms discussed above, continued abuse of incumbency power to gain unfair political and electoral advantage turned the searchlight on another reform: constitutional entrenchment of presidential term limits.

Afrobarometer surveys conducted in 2000–2006 in West, East and Southern Africa showed that about 90% of about 56,000 surveyed respondents expressed a preference for presidential term limits.[6] They rejected "autocracy in general and perpetual incumbency in particular" (IDASA et al. 2006).

In 2010, national human rights bodies in East Africa proposed a draft regional Bill of Rights, requiring heads of government in the region to serve only two terms of five years each.[7] In Equatorial Guinea, preliminary results from a referendum on a proposal to introduce constitutional change and effect presidential term limits of two consecutive seven-year terms showed that more than 99% of Equatorial Guineans favoured the change.[8]

Thirty-five African countries have adopted presidential term limits, most of them two consecutive terms of four to seven years (table 1.3).

Generally, term limits have been respected, even if reluctantly by presidential incumbents enjoying unlimited tenure. In Cape Verde, for example:

> Given the strong cultural homogeneity and the trajectory of political and administrative elites, and the significant regional representation within the political elite, the rules of electoral [political] succession have been respected and negotiated in an open process of consolidating the institutions of electoral governance (AGR III Cape Verde Country Report 2012).

In countries where term limits have worked fairly well and enjoyed popular support, there have been calls to strengthen them. For instance, "While political succession in Ghana under the current fourth republic has been largely stable and done by the rule, there have been calls for constitutional reforms to extend the term limits

of the president to two five-year terms", from the current four years (AGR III Ghana Country Report 2012). The AGR III Nigeria Country Report 2012 referred to respondents' suggestions to reduce presidential and governorship term limits from two to one. A single term, they argued, would make for faster rotation of power among zones, while eliminating the rancorous politics usually associated with chief executives seeking a second term at the state or federal level.

Strong popular resistance in state and society across Africa now seems to stand against attempts by presidents to extend their tenure though constitutional amendments. In the wake of term limits, presidents cannot, it seems, arbitrarily extend—sometimes for life—their tenure. They now have to go through a rigorous and contested process of amending the constitution if they want to prolong their tenure beyond term limits. This process offers an opportunity for party members or ambitious associates, and for other groups, to drum up support against any such move and defeat it, although some presidents have still managed to extend their term (box 1.8).

Of the 204 African presidents in power over 1960–2004, more than 50% were overthrown. Of the 25 who left office voluntarily, 17 did so in 1990–2004, and 8 did in 2004–2008. Of the presidents who were entitled to serve two consecutive terms, two (Nelson Mandela in South Africa in 1999 and Joaquim Chissano in Mozambique

' **Thirty-five African countries have adopted presidential term limits**

## Table 1.3 Presidential term limits in Africa

| Country | Maximum number of terms | Number of years each term | Country | Maximum number of terms | Number of years each term |
|---|---|---|---|---|---|
| Algeria | Two | Five | Kenya | Two | Five |
| Angola | Three | Five[a] | Liberia | Two | Six |
| Benin | Two | Five | Madagascar | Three | Five |
| Botswana | Two | Five | Malawi | Two | Five |
| Burkina Faso | Two | Seven | Mali | Two | Five |
| Burundi | Two | Five | Mauritania | Two | Five |
| Cameroon | Two | Seven | Mauritius | Two | Five |
| Cape Verde | Two | Five | Mozambique | Two[c] | Five |
| Central Africa Republic | Two | Six | Namibia | Two | Five |
| Comoros | Unlimited non-consecutive | Five | Niger | Two | Five |
| | | | Nigeria | Two | Four |
| Congo | Two | Seven | Rwanda | Two | Seven |
| Dem. Rep. Congo | Two | Five | São Tomé and Príncipe | Two | Five |
| Djibouti | Two | Six | Seychelles | Three | Five |
| Egypt | Two[b] | Four | Sierra Leone | Two | Five |
| Ethiopia | Two | Six | South Africa | Two | Five |
| Ghana | Two | Four | Tanzania | Two | Five |
| Guinea | Two | Five | Zambia | Two | Five |

a. Two further terms of five years each provided for incumbent after first term.

b. From the 2011 presidential election.

c. After two consecutive terms, a former president can stand for election after a five-year break.

*Source:* Compiled from AGR III Country Reports 2012.

in 2005) declined to run for a second time.

More than constitutional provisions for presidential term limits are required to strengthen competitive and credible elections. Constitutional provisions on declarations of emergency, such as those contained in the constitutional amendment by Gabon's parliament in December 2010, might even provide constitutional cover for extending presidential term limits. Some provisions of the electoral law also serve to distort presidential elections, as with those introduced by the Togolese parliament in 2002 to bar the popular opposition leader Gilchrist Olympio from contesting the presidential election against President Gnassingbé Eyadema, on the grounds that he had not lived in Togo in the year before the poll.

making for weak separation of powers; and controversies that trailed attempts to change not only constitutional provisions for presidential term limits in recent years in Cameroon, Gabon, Guinea, Malawi, Mali, Niger, Nigeria, Senegal and Uganda, but also the electoral rules for political succession in presidential and parliamentary elections in some other countries.

All these examples underscore the need to deepen the process of political reforms and address challenges confronting the renegotiated political architecture.

*Horizontal democracy-promoting institutions*

A common feature of that architecture is the introduction of horizontal democracy-promoting institutions (or watchdogs), which, as in effect the fourth branch of government, aim to promote democracy and diversity and to ensure accountability and transparency in political life. These bodies are typically entrenched in constitutions, making it hard to remove them, and are designed to be insulated from the executive in particular (box 1.9 and table 1.4).

The institutions' independence from executive control varies among countries, depending on the means of appointing and removing their members; their sources of finance; the support of critical civil society groups and other key stakeholders; the character of their leadership; and the political will of the national leadership to keep faith with the spirit permeating them.

Other challenges to the effectiveness of provisions for presidential limits include a winner-takes-all or violent psychology that still anchors the approach of the political elite towards elections and competitive parties; docility of parliaments and the judiciary in the face of imperial presidencies in some countries,

**Table 1.4 Horizontal democracy-promoting institutions, selected African countries**

| Country | Institution |
|---|---|
| Algeria | • National Human Rights Commission, Algeria<br>• National Body for Preventing & Combating Corruption<br>• National Commission on Governance |
| Benin | • Independent National Electoral Commission<br>• National Organization Front for the Fight Against Corruption<br>• The Benin Commission for Human Rights |
| Ethiopia | • Human Rights Commission<br>• National Electoral Board of Ethiopia<br>• The Federal Ethics and Anti-Corruption Commission |
| Ghana | • Commission for Human Rights and Administrative Justice<br>• National Commission for Civic Education<br>• National Electoral Commission |
| Kenya | • Kenya Anti-Corruption Commission<br>• Kenya National Human Rights and Equality Commission<br>• Independent Electoral & Boundaries Commission<br>• National Cohesion and Integration Commission |
| Rwanda | • Ombudsman<br>• Electoral Commission<br>• National Human Rights Commission |
| Senegal | • Commission Nationale de Lutte Contre la Non-transparence, la Corruption et la Concussion<br>• Médiateur de la République |
| South Africa | • The South African Human Rights Commission<br>• Commission for the Protection of the Rights of Cultural, Religious and Linguistic Communities<br>• The Independent Electoral Commission |

*Source:* National constitutions and African Peer Review Mechanism country reports.

### Truth and reconciliation

One type of independent body, usually set up ad hoc, is the truth and reconciliation commission. It aims to provide an unusual public forum to air grievances and allegations of historical and current abuses as well as group discrimination and violations of human rights. It is usually designed to provide opportunities for more constructive and democratic management of diversity through reconciliation and restitution. Such commissions have been set up in Chad, the Democratic Republic of the Congo, Ghana, Kenya, Liberia, Nigeria, Sierra Leone, South Africa and Uganda.

### Electoral management boards

Despite handicaps, there is a general perception among the expert panels that electoral management boards are making an impact in many countries. In Benin, Cape Verde, Ghana, Sierra Leone and South Africa, they have helped to engender public confidence in the conduct of elections and in their results.

### Anti-corruption commissions

In some countries, such as Sierra Leone, anti-corruption commissions have been given prosecutorial powers to strengthen their independence, especially from executive branch ministries and departments. In others, such as Ghana, Kenya, Nigeria, Sierra Leone and Tanzania, commissions have secured conviction of high-profile public officers, including ministers, as well as business people. In Ghana, Nigeria, Sierra Leone, South Africa and Tanzania, for example, several ministers have been dismissed for complicity (or suspected complicity) in corruption, in an apparent response by the president to national and international public pressure.

### Constraints

These horizontal institutions are still fragile and often constrained in performing their mandates by cultural, human resource, financial and logistical problems, which may relate to economic underdevelopment and residual, but serious, anti-democratic political tendencies among the political elite. Another constraint stems from weaknesses and ambiguities in their founding statutes, and their overlapping functions among themselves and with other public agencies.

Another problem is that the executive branch and the legislature—made up of politicians—over whom these institutions are to exercise oversight have a conflict of interest in exercising their legislative

functions, so that they may not too readily grant them powers that may then be turned against these same politicians.

It is here that pressures from national stakeholders, African regional and continental institutions—such as regional economic commissions, the African Peer Review Mechanism, the Economic Commission for Africa and the African Union—as well as international donors can force the hand of the executive and legislature to pass laws to bolster these institutions' independence and empower them, so as to better pursue their statutory functions.

## Conclusions

Colonialism fundamentally transformed the African state. The effect was to fractionalize societies, ultimately triggering nationalism and agitation for self-rule and a transfer of liberal democracy. But precisely because the new system was grafted onto a complex architecture of fragmented diversity, it failed to guarantee democratic rule or to manage diversity, as the post-independence successor elite sought to perpetuate their leadership. As military interventions reinforced dictatorship in many countries, suppression of democracy precipitated struggles that ushered in democratic reforms during the 1980s. In the aftermath of the third wave of democratization, Africa has made impressive progress in renegotiating its political architecture.

To manage diversity, the new architecture requires solid foundations:

> *The obstacles along the reform path require deft navigation and determined political will from a transformative leadership*

entrenched constitutional provisions for democratic political succession, in the form of competitive party and electoral politics and free, fair and credible elections, managed by independent electoral management boards; separation of powers, to enable the legislature and judiciary to counterbalance the power of an overbearing executive; term limits for elected heads of state and government; democratic instruments to promote political devolution to multiple centres of power and to ensure cultural, ethno-regional, gender, political-party, religious and other identity-based diversity in representation; and independent, horizontal governance institutions.

The trajectory of each country's renegotiated architecture—varied and complex as it is—has traversed tortuous and difficult terrain, slowing institutional reform as supporters and opponents battle. This is why the obstacles along the reform path—deep-rooted in the colonial and post-colonial inheritance of the African state alongside the overpowering impact of globalization—require deft navigation and determined political will from a transformative leadership. If the unfolding political architecture represents the navigational instruments, the political will to demonstrate such leadership remains its lodestar.

## Notes

1. Somalia has the fewest ethnic groups—the Somali majority and the Bantu minority (Benadiri and Gaboye). See Abby (2005).
2. According to the listing of African ethnic groups per country made by David Barrett, mission report, published in the Africa Mission Resource Centre, 2003.
3. The African Governance Report (AGR) III has 40 project countries. More detail on the background and methodology to the AGR reports can be found in the appendix.
4. Most ethnic groups were split among different countries and colonial powers. A few examples are the Somali who were divided among British, French and Italian colonies; the Yoruba and the Aja each divided among Nigeria, Benin and Togo; the Wolof and the Serers between Senegal and Gambia; the Oromo in Ethiopia and Kenya; and the Banyarwanda in Rwanda, Uganda, Democratic Republic of the Congo, Burundi and others.
5. Federalism deconcentrates powers through the constitutional provision of "legislative lists", and therefore shared sovereignty, which divide legislative competences between two or more levels of public authority within a federation, each with direct legal impact on citizens. The unitary system is characterized by political centralization, with its decentralization of powers to subordinate, lower levels of authority.
6. Surveyed countries include Benin, Cape Verde, Ghana, Nigeria and Senegal; Kenya, Tanzania and Uganda; and Botswana, Lesotho, Madagascar, Malawi, Mozambique, Namibia, South Africa, Zambia and Zimbabwe.
7. See "Regional Rights Bodies Push for Uniform Presidential Term Limits," The East African, www.theeastafrican.co.ke/news/-/2558/848436/-/.../-/index.html, accessed 27 January 2013.

8. See "Equatorial Guinea: A Move to Consolidate Power: Secrecy, Intimidation Ahead of Vote for Constitutional Change," Human Rights Watch, www.hrw.org/news/2011/11/11/equatorial-guinea-move-consolidate-power, accessed 27 January 2013.

## References

Abby, Abdi. 2005. "Field Research Project on Minorities in Somalia." Oxford House, London. http://oxfarmhouse.org.uk/download/Minorities_report/PDF.

Adejumobi, Said. 2000. "Elections in Africa: A Fading Shadow of Democracy." In *Government and Politics in Africa: A Reader*, ed. Okwudiba Nnoli, 242–61. Harare: AAPS Books.

Ajayi, G. B. 1969. *Industrial Development in West Africa*. Ibadan, Nigeria: Economic Research Bureau.

Ajayi, J. F. Ade. 1984. *The Problem of National Integration in Nigeria, No. 11, Distinguished Lecture Series*. Ibadan, Nigeria: Nigerian Institute of Social & Economic Research.

Albert, Isaac O. 1992. "Contemporary Problems of Democracy in Nigeria: The Pre-colonial and Colonial Antecedents." Paper presented to the CODESRIA General Assembly, 10–14 February, Dakar.

Ayitteh, George B. N. 1991. *Indigenous African Institutions*. New York: Transactional Publishers.

Bratton, Michael, and Nicholas van de Walle. 1997. *Democratic Experiments in Africa: Regime Transitions*. Cambridge, UK: Cambridge University Press.

Buijtenhuijs, Rob, and Elly Rijnierse. 1993. *Democratization in Sub-Saharan Africa (1989–1992): An Overview of the Literature*. Research Reports 1993/51. Leiden, the Netherlands: African Studies Centre.

Collier, Ruth. 1982. *Regimes in Tropical Africa: Changing Forms of Supremacy, 1945–1975*. Berkeley, CA: University of California Press.

Cowen, Michael, and Liisa Laakso. 1997. "An Overview of Election Studies in Africa." *Journal of Modern African Studies* 35: 717–44.

Deng, Francis. 2008. *Identity, Diversity and Constitutionalism in Africa*. Washington, DC: United States Institute for Peace.

Duchacek, Ivo. 1977. "Antagonistic Cooperation: Territorial and Ethnic Communities." *PUBLIUS: The Journal of Federalism* 7 (4): 3–29.

Ellis, S. 2000. "Elections in Africa in Historical Context." In *Election Observation and Democratization in Africa*, ed. Jon Abbink and Gerti Hesseling. New York: St. Martin's Press.

Golder, Matt, and Leonard Wantchekon. 2004. "Africa: Dictatorial and Democratic Electoral Systems since 1946." In *Handbook of Electoral System Design*, ed. Colomer Joseph. London: Palgrave.

Hayward, Fred M. 1987. "Introduction." In *Elections in Independent Africa*, ed. Fred M. Hayward, 1–23. Boulder, CO: Westview Press.

Hodgkin, Thomas L. 1961. *African Political Parties: An Introductory Guide*. Penguin African Series No. WA12. London: Penguin Books.

IDASA (Institute for Democracy in South Africa), CDD (Ghana Centre for Democratic Development), and Michigan State University. 2006. "Afrobarometer Research Project, Media Briefing (26 May 2006)." IDASA, Pretoria.

Jinadu, L. Adele. 2007. "Explaining & Managing Ethnic Conflict in

Africa: Towards a Cultural Theory of Democracy." Claude Ake Memorial Paper No.1, Uppsala University, Department of Peace and Conflict Research, Nordica Africa Institute, Uppsala.

———. 2010. "Elections and Management of Diversity in Africa." Concept Paper for United Nations Economic Commission for Africa, Addis Ababa.

Lewis, M. Paul, ed. 2009. *Ethnologue: Languages of the World*, Sixteenth edition. Dallas, TX: SIL International.

Lindberg, Staffan. 2006. *Democracy and Elections in Africa*. Baltimore, MD: Johns Hopkins University Press.

Mamdani, Mahmood. 1996. *Citizen and Subject: Contemporary Africa and the Legacy of Late Colonialism*. Princeton, NJ: Princeton University Press.

Ndege, Peter O. 2009. "Colonialism and Its Legacies in Kenya." Lecture delivered during Fulbright–Hays Group project abroad program, 5 July–6 August, Moi University, Eldoret, Kenya.

Ngenge, T. Simon. 1999. "Ethnicity, Violence and Multi-party Democracy in Africa since 1989." In *Anthropology of Africa and the Challenges of the Third Millennium—Ethnicity and Ethnic Conflicts*. Paris: United Nations Educational, Scientific and Cultural Organization, Ethno-Net Africa.

Norris, Pippa, and Robert Mattes. 2003. "Does Ethnicity Determine Support for the Governing Party?" Afrobarometer Paper 26, Institute for Democracy in South Africa, Cape Town.

Olukoshi, Adebayo, and Liisa Laakso, eds. 1996. *Challenges to the Nation-state in Africa*. Helsinki: Nordiska Afrikainstitutet, in cooperation with the Institute of Development Studies, University of Helsinki.

Prempeh, H. Kwasi. 2008. "Presidents Untamed." *Journal of Democracy* 19 (2): 109–23.

Salih, M. A. 1989. "Africanism and Islamism in the Nuba Mountains." In *Ethnicity, Conflict and National Integration in the Sudan*, ed. Sayed H. A. Hurriez and Elfatih A. Abdelsalam, 208–30. Khartoum: Khartoum University Press.

Salih, M. A., and Per Nordlund. 2007. *Political Parties in Africa: Challenges for Sustainable Multiparty Democracy*. Stockholm: International Institute for Democracy and Electoral Assistance.

Sitoe, Eduardo J., Zefanias Matsimbe, and Amilcar F. Pereira. 2005. *Parties and Political Development in Mozambique*. EISA Research Report No 22. Johannesburg: Electoral Institute for Sustainable Development in Africa.

Thomas-Woolley, Barbara, and Edmond J. Keller. 1994. "Majority Rule and Minority Rights: American Federalism and African Experience." *The Journal of Modern African Studies* 32 (3): 411–27.

UNECA (United Nations Economic Commission for Africa). 2011. *Diversity Management in Africa: Findings from the African Peer Review Mechanism and a Framework for Analysis and Policy-Making*. Addis Ababa.

Wimmer, Andreas. 1997. "Who Owns the State? Understanding Ethnic Conflict in Post-Colonial States." *Nations and Nationalism* 3 (4): 631–65.

Wiseman, John. 1990. *Democracy in Black Africa: Survival and Revival*. New York: Paragon House Publishers.

The recent political uprisings in North Africa manifested a demand for democracy, and seem to have completed the regional trend in the democratic transition, one that began in the 1990s south of the Sahara. But the North African experience—given its profundity, especially in Egypt and Tunisia—may provide renewed impetus for reforms across the continent.

Although democratization differs in many aspects among countries, with push-backs in some such as Guinea-Bissau and Mali, most of Africa shares a consensus on democratic norms and practices, in which regional, subregional and national instruments and frameworks emphasize democracy as the only acceptable mode of governance.

Democratization is a never-finished business. It is a process through which countries—democratic and semi-democratic—seek to build, refine and strengthen their institutions, processes and frameworks. As a contested political project, it is often marked by crises, contours, breakthroughs, reversals and resolutions. It is a process of change characterized by political contestations involving the political leadership, civil society, political organizations and forces as well as other social actors (Adejumobi 2010; Denk and Silander 2012). In short, it is work in progress in Africa, especially among emerging democratic societies.

Democratic transitions have made tremendous gains on the continent. Most have stressed opening the political arena, including legitimizing the political opposition, promoting civil liberties and conducting multi-party elections. The outcomes have been mixed, while broader issues of diversity management—often volatile and controversial—linger or have arisen in the transition. These diversity issues, though germane to consolidating democracy, may not have been planned, expected or incorporated in the transition project, and generate frequent political tension and occasional violence. The issues include the nature of the political structure and power distribution; identity issues of ethnicity, race, religion, citizenship, youth and gender; and diversity management in the electoral process (see chapter 1).

Elections are central to democratic transition and help to democratically manage diversity in four main ways—participation, representation, leadership rotation and fulfilment of local needs and aspirations. But they are not enough to address all the demands of diversity management in a plural society. Also required is structural and constitutional reengineering to promote political and social accommodation and to douse fears of domination by groups previously sidelined (or suppressed) in governing the country.

This chapter raises several critical questions: What is the background to democratic transition in Africa, and what role did the media play in the transition processes? What clear trends in the steps to democracy have emerged? What is the role of leadership? And how have African countries managed key diversity issues in the democratic transition?

It also offers six key messages.

- The struggle for democratic transition has been embedded mainly in domestic economic and political conditions and has taken different trajectories, with different outcomes.

- Sectarian groups (ethnic, racial or religious) continue to hold great leverage over the state and public policy in many countries, limiting the state's autonomy.

- Populations in many countries do not consider their constitution to adequately protect, let alone promote, diversity and minority interests (few countries have revised or rewritten them in a people driven and centred way).

- Elections have become more regular on the continent as has the alternation of power, but the quality of elections differs greatly.

- Elections as a political transition mechanism are relevant to democratically managing diversity, but need to be backed up by legal, institutional and political reforms to ensure consensual politics and inclusive governance.

- Many experiments in Africa are continuing to devise methods for managing diversity in the structure and distribution of power and in sectarian and minority identities as steps to achieving the ideals of equal, non-discriminatory and inclusive democratic systems.

> Africa's context for the democratic renewal has been complex, and firmly rooted in domestic political and economic conditions

## Background to democratic transition

Democratic transition is the process by which a society, nation or state moves from an authoritarian, dictatorial and statist political system to a more inclusive, open and democratic system. It is not a monolithic or teleological process; it is often complex and variegated, in which the interplay of social forces influences trajectories and outcomes.

Africa's context for the democratic renewal has been complex, and firmly rooted in domestic political and economic conditions. Demands for democratic reform were grounded in the system of rule of the immediate post-independence leadership, where the centralizing tendency was strong, bordering on civil autocracy or military and quasi-military dictatorships, as political space was closed, basic rights were denied and living conditions stayed unimpressive. These domestic dynamics continued after the end of the Cold War, which provided dictatorships with a basis for political manoeuvres. Internal struggles blended with the structural adjustment reforms that favoured entrenching liberal democracy.

The worsening economic situation in many countries was a major contributor to mass agitation that drove popular demands for democracy both in the 1990s in Sub-Saharan Africa and from 2010 in North Africa. In the former, matters were not helped by donor pressure as many foreign countries began to demand austerity measures. They gelled in the demand for neo-liberal structural adjustment programmes. With time, many donor institutions and countries made the implementation of these programmes a condition for further disbursement of bilateral and multilateral aid. The austerity measures hit the core of the survival needs of many people.

The programmes were designed to put in place cost-cutting measures for many African governments (Mkandawire and Olukoshi 1995; Adejumobi 1995). The aim was to rescue African economic and governance policies from the neopatrimonial networks that limited the free operation of the market, skewed development towards favoured clients, sanctioned authoritarianism that silenced peoples' voices and manipulated elections to defeat the people's right to freely choose their leaders. But the measures weighed heavily on the weak and vulnerable. In their wake, unemployment rose and the costs of basic commodities rose, and when exchange rate and price controls were removed, inflation skyrocketed. Even those aspiring to middle-class status were hit. In public universities, for example, students were required to pay school fees for the first time.

The all too predictable consequences were seen in several countries (Adejumobi 1996): riots over youth joblessness, evictions from informal city dwellings, peasant demands for lower prices for farm inputs and better prices for their products. In Kenya and Nigeria, the middle classes, such as doctors, nurses, teachers and university lecturers, went on strike demanding better terms of service. In Zambia, the gains from copper had begun to dwindle, giving vent to pro-democracy movements organized around the labour unions.

More recently, before the uprisings in North Africa average unemployment for those ages 15–24 was about 30% against a world average of 14%, and worse still in Egypt and Tunisia—in the latter, unemployment among young university graduates was 40% in 2007 (AfDB 2012). High commodity prices, rising costs of housing and hunger and crime in many countries generated popular calls for reform, expressed in Algeria in food and bread riots.

The essence of the struggle for democratic transition over the years is well captured in the recent North African experience and in citizens' demands for "bread, freedom and dignity". It is a quest for political and economic freedom, a process of renegotiating the social pact between leaders and led.

## Patterns of democratic transition

The patterns of democratic transition (in the 1990s in Sub-Saharan Africa and from 2010 in North Africa) are diverse, as are their driving social forces (box 2.1).[1] Political opposition to authoritarian rule was at times organized from exile or underground, aimed at subverting the regime through armed struggle or other militant acts. Where authoritarian regimes were less oppressive, opposition was organized internally, as pro-democracy civil society organizations (CSOs).[2]

> **The patterns of democratic transition are diverse, as are their driving social forces**

These bodies mounted opposition to the one-party state, demanding political concessions. Regimes reacted differently—immediate concession, procrastination, firm guidance or outright resistance to change—usually leading to protracted struggles. The struggles were fought on the streets, in courtrooms and at work. It is these struggles that culminated in demands for the second *uhuru* (freedom),[3] a call made louder by recourse to modern media.

### Impact of modern media

The information technology revolution has had a profound effect on the democratic transition in Africa. The abundance of information sources—initially radio, then television, mobile phones, the Internet and now social media—have provided new platforms for expanding the frontiers of democratic change. In 2000–2006, the number of licensed commercial radio stations in Africa shot up by 360%, while in 2000–2009 access to mobile phones surged from 2% of the population to 39% (ACSS 2011). Modern tools like mobile phones and text messaging, and social media networks including Facebook and Twitter, offer new channels to spread information fast, and are catalysts for political action among young people, as seen in the Arab Spring. Social media platforms based in or focused on Africa, like Indaba Ziyafika, Ushahidi and Sahara Reporters have assumed a powerful role in demanding accountability, assuaging political violence and politically mobilizing young people as they report in a more critical, open and fearless way than the traditional print and electronic media.

Social media networks have introduced what is now called "citizens' journalism" into political discourse and media practice. Citizen journalists use a range of tools such as mobile phones, cameras, computers and audio recorders as well as pen and paper to monitor events and report quickly to a social network (Sarrazin 2011). This system has enabled young people to monitor elections in Kenya, Nigeria (box 2.2), and Sierra Leone.

### Relationship between modern media and democracy

Media support for democratization has not been without costs. In some countries, social media networks (and even traditional media) have been frequently intercepted online, jammed, monitored or outright banned by the government to censor them, limiting political interaction and people's mobilization. Governments' attempts to suppress social media is obviously a race against time—and facing an ever-changing global information space they will need to waste more resources to cage new media forms.

Thus the media are not just a vehicle for disseminating democratic ideas, they are also a marker of democratic progress, as quantified in the 2012 Expert Opinion Survey of the 40 African Governance Report (AGR) III project countries.[4] Of the countries where 70% or more of the respondents rated the mass media free (figure 2.1), Ghana, Sierra Leone, South Africa, Cape Verde and Mali had alternations of presidential power in 2007–2012 (annex 2.1) and Ghana, South Africa, Cape Verde and Algeria were rated by 50% and more of the respondents both as observing human rights (see figure 2.3 below) and as respecting due process and the rule of law (see figure 2.4 below).

In 17 of the 40 countries, more than half the respondents considered the media to be operating in a relatively free environment, showing the progress Africa has made in promoting media rights and freedom, which feeds back into the democratic loop.

## Democratizing trends

Over the last decade and a half, Africa has shown political gains in the governance landscape: one-party regimes are becoming outmoded, elections are becoming more regular, presidential power alternates

---

**Box 2.2  Social media promoting democratic change in Nigeria**

Two months before the 2007 general election, a group of young professionals, the Human Emancipation Lead Project, sought to increase citizens' participation, especially of young people, in the elections and to promote transparent, free and fair elections. It formed a network of mobile election monitors, aiming to democratize the monitoring, gathering, collation and tallying of election results so as to reduce the fraud often associated with the process in Nigeria (and some other African countries).

These practical steps may not have radically reduced election rigging, but they undoubtedly had an impact, broadcasting the powerful message that young people will no longer accept "business as usual" in Nigeria's elections.

---

frequently, legislative authority is asserted more, respect for human rights and the rule of law are ascending, CSOs are gaining more influence and the separation of powers among the three branches of government is gradually being entrenched (UNECA 2009; Lynch and Crawford 2011; ACSS 2011).

In 1991–1994, legally mandated one-party states shrank from 38 to zero (ACSS 2011). In 1996–2006, 44 elections were held in Sub-Saharan Africa. In 2005–2007, 26 presidential and 28 parliamentary elections were held (UNECA 2009); in 2011, 15 and 20, and in 2012, 10 and 13, respectively.[5]

The alternation of presidential power through elections has now become fairly common. Presidential power alternated in no less than 27 African countries in 2007–2012 (annex 2.1), voluntarily or not. It is perhaps in the Central African sub-region that the alternation of power remains most a challenge.

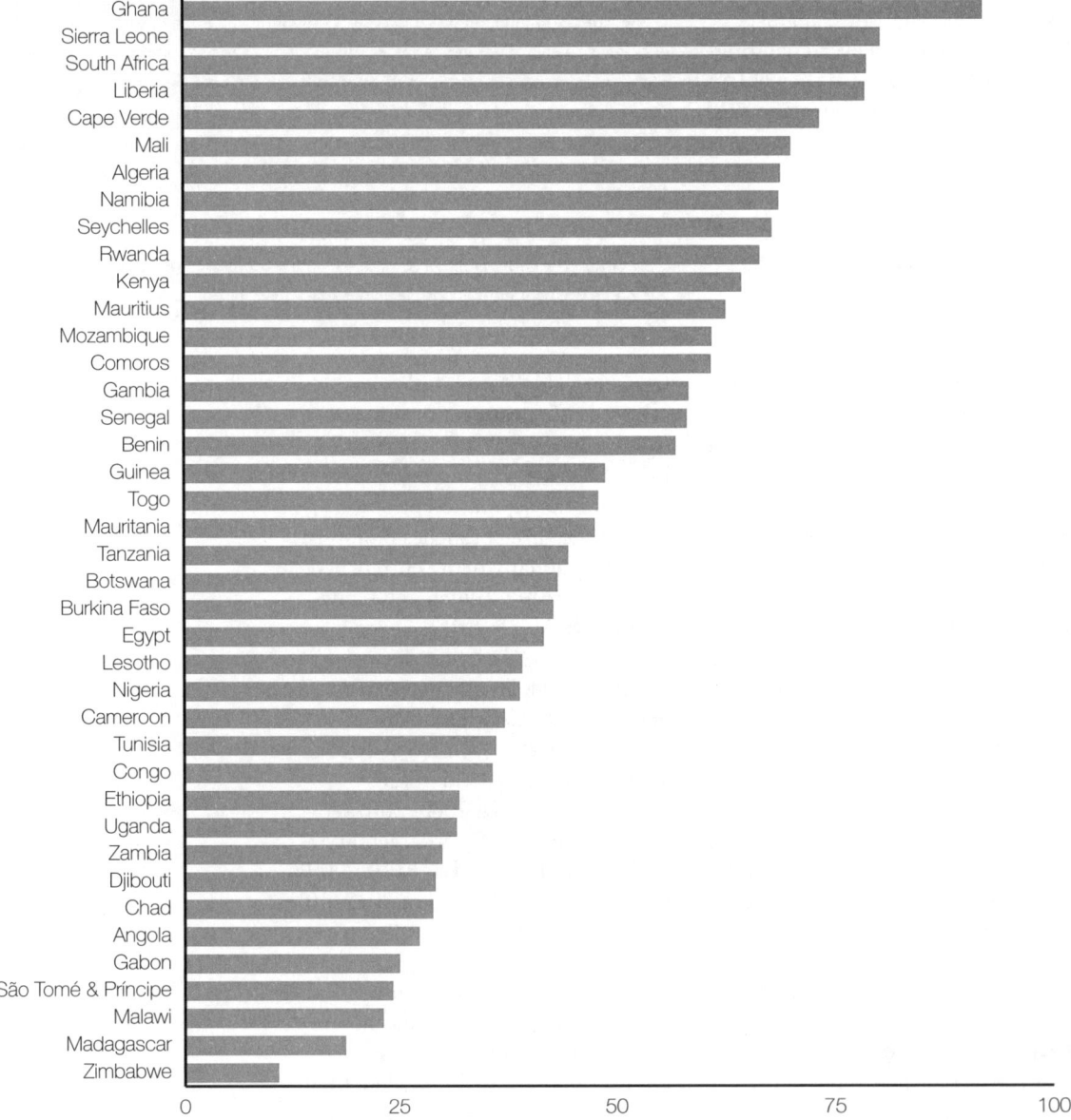

**Figure 2.1 Mass media—completely free or only infrequently violated by the government or ruling party**

Share of experts surveyed agreeing with the statement, by country (%)

*Source:* AGR III Expert Opinion Survey 2012.

The 40 country survey shows that, although the legislature may still be weak in several countries, parliaments seem to be showing greater capacity and commitment to have a law-making and oversight role over the executive arm. The major problem is when the legislature is dominated by the ruling party, which tends to weaken its capacity to control the executive. Barkan (2008), in a case study of six African countries, noted that the legislature was increasingly emerging as important in governance, a point largely corroborated by the AGR III country surveys (figure 2.2): more than half the expert respondents in eight countries consider their parliament to have (usually or always) effective legislative control of the executive.

Respect for human rights is on the rise in Africa, but there is still a way to go: in only 11 countries did more than half the respondents consider that their governments usually or always respected human rights (figure 2.3).

A similar picture emerges on government respect for due process and the rule of law: in only 10 countries did the majority of expert respondents consider that their governments mostly or fully respected due process and the rule of law (figure 2.4).

The civil society has been a major driver of democratic change in many African countries, continuing to insist on transparency and accountability. In 18 countries, more than half the respondents considered civil society to moderately or effectively help to promote transparency and accountability in governance the most (figure 2.5). Cape Verde, for example, had around 13 non-governmental organizations in 1990 but has about 80 today, not to mention more than 600 local organizations (AGR III Cape Verde Country Report 2012). Mauritius has shown similar sharp growth of CSOs, but they "remain weak in governance advocacy except with respect to gender equality activism, and growing on environmental concerns. Certain high political governance advocacy concerns such as the fight against corruption or human rights have been spearheaded by branches of foreign [non-governmental organizations] such as Transparency International" (AGR III Mauritius Country Report 2012, 46).

Liberia still needs to build governance based on democratic elections and to provide socio-economic programmes that benefit all the population. The knowledge that political parties and other CSOs play an effective role in governance is critical for developing democracy, and the country has made incremental achievements, including an increase in the number of opposition political parties, the birth of CSOs and a more vibrant press corps. Also, the character of political parties is changing from passivity to engagement, making it virtually impossible for the government to ignore the interests of the people and rendering the government more responsive to these needs, for which its officials are accountable (AGR III Liberia Country Report 2012).

> **The civil society has been a major driver of democratic change**

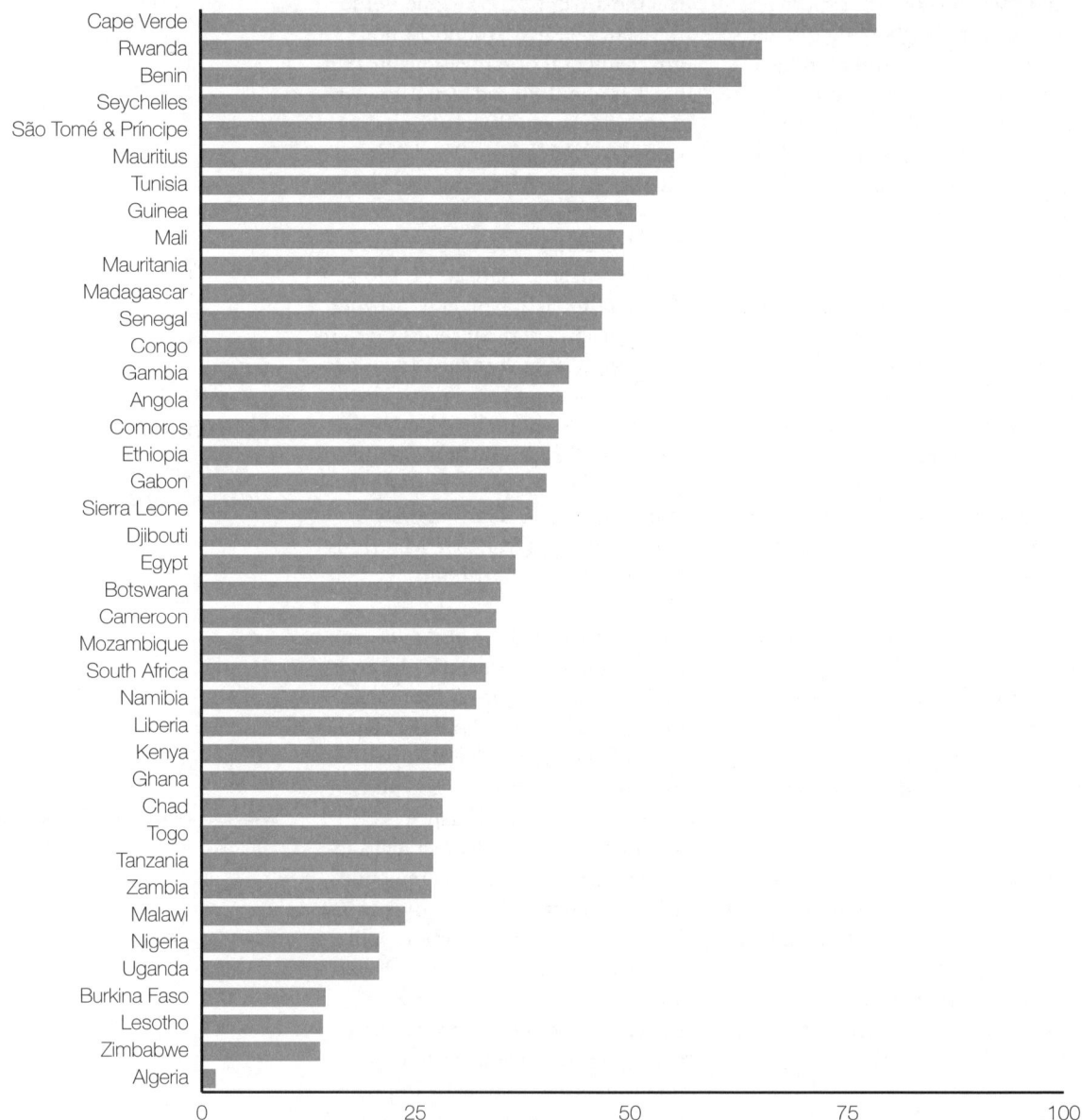

**Figure 2.2 Legislative control of the executive branch—usually or always effective**

Share of experts surveyed agreeing with the statement, by country (%)

*Source:* AGR III Expert Opinion Survey 2012.

## Figure 2.3 Respect for human rights

Share of experts surveyed, by country (%)

- ▓ Usually or always respected
- ░ Sometimes respected
- █ Never or rarely respected

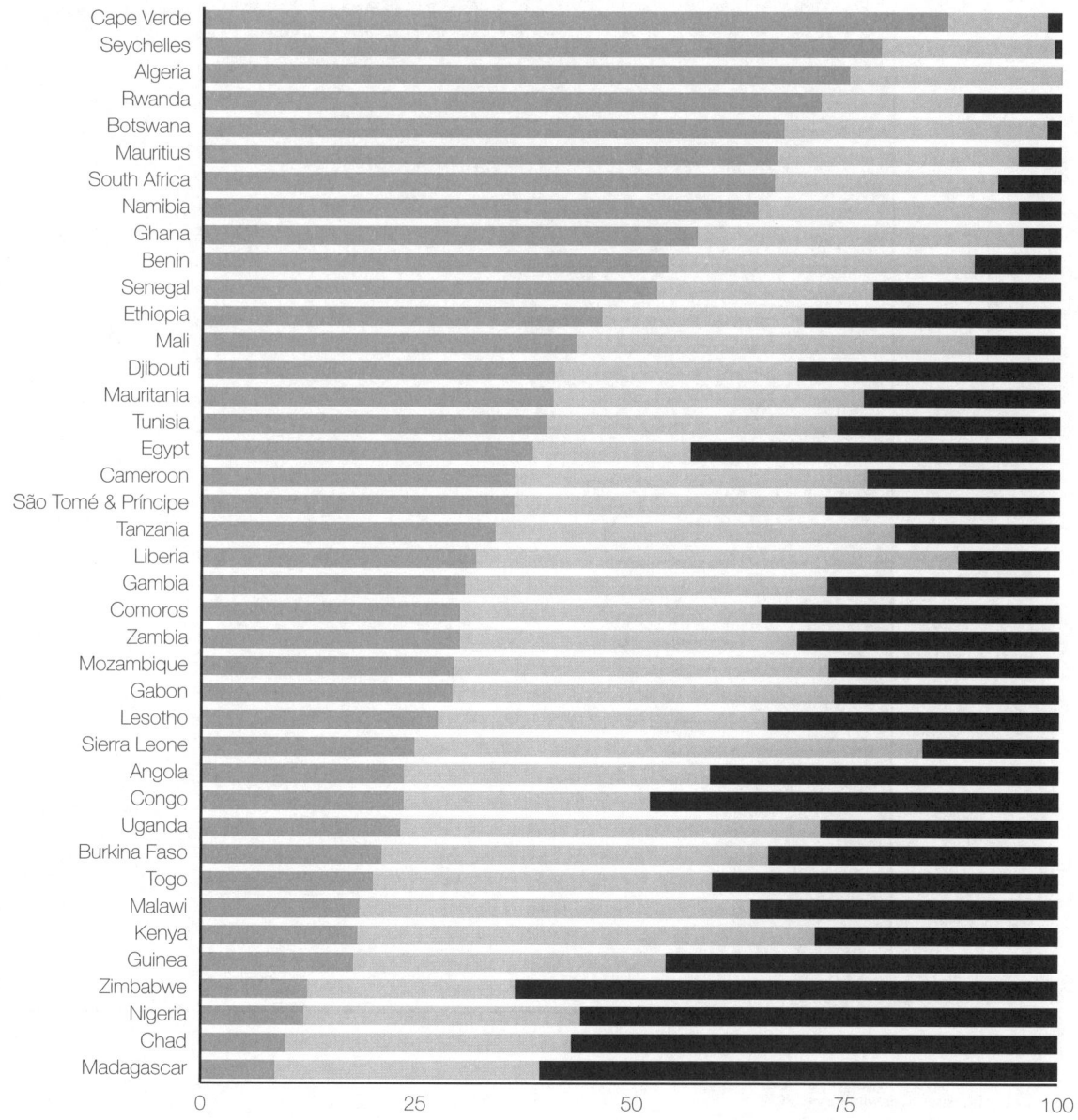

*Source:* AGR III Expert Opinion Survey 2012.

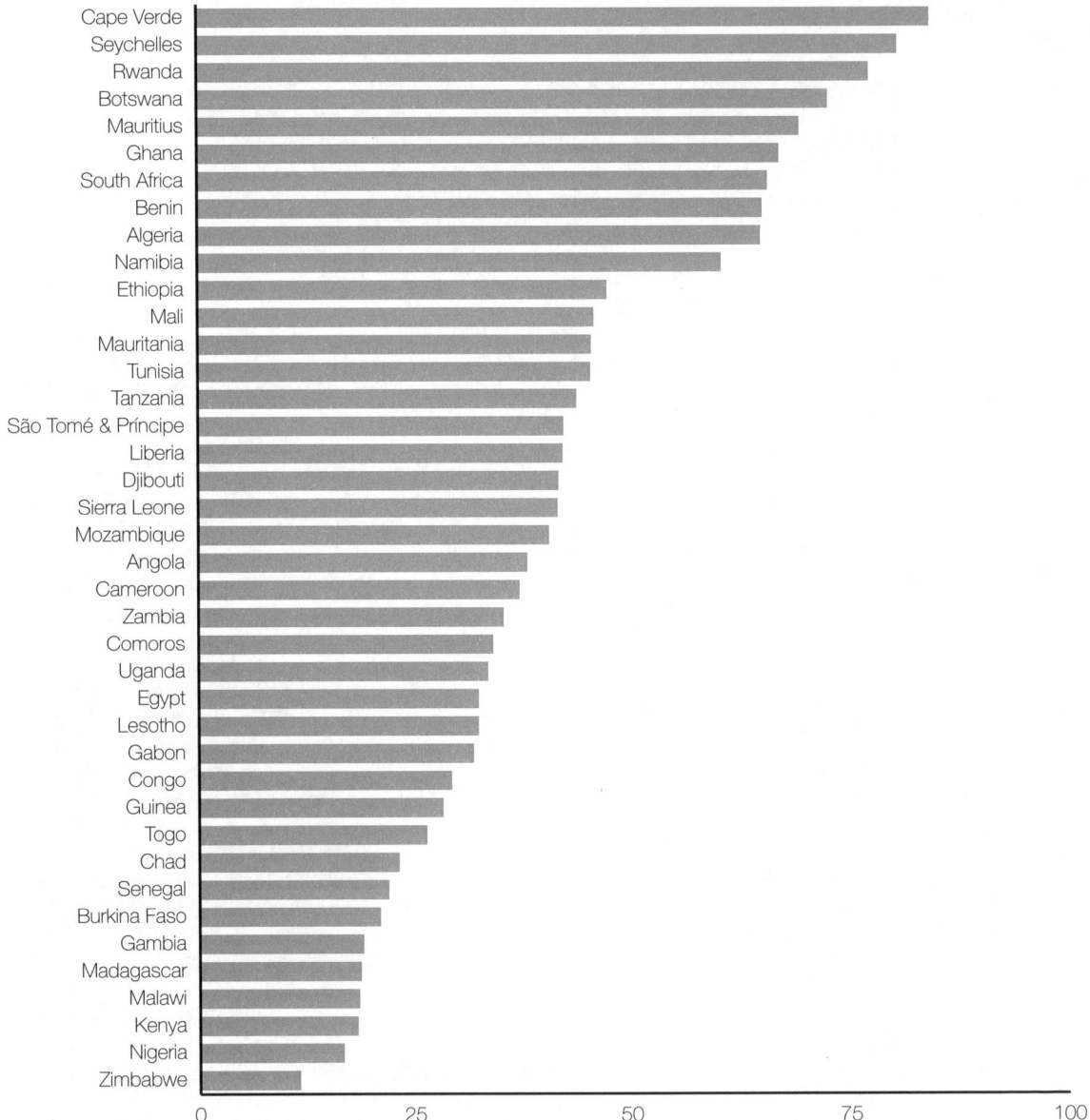

**Figure 2.4 Government respect for due process and the rule of law—mostly or fully**

Share of experts surveyed agreeing with the statement, by country (%)

*Source:* AGR III Expert Opinion Survey 2012.

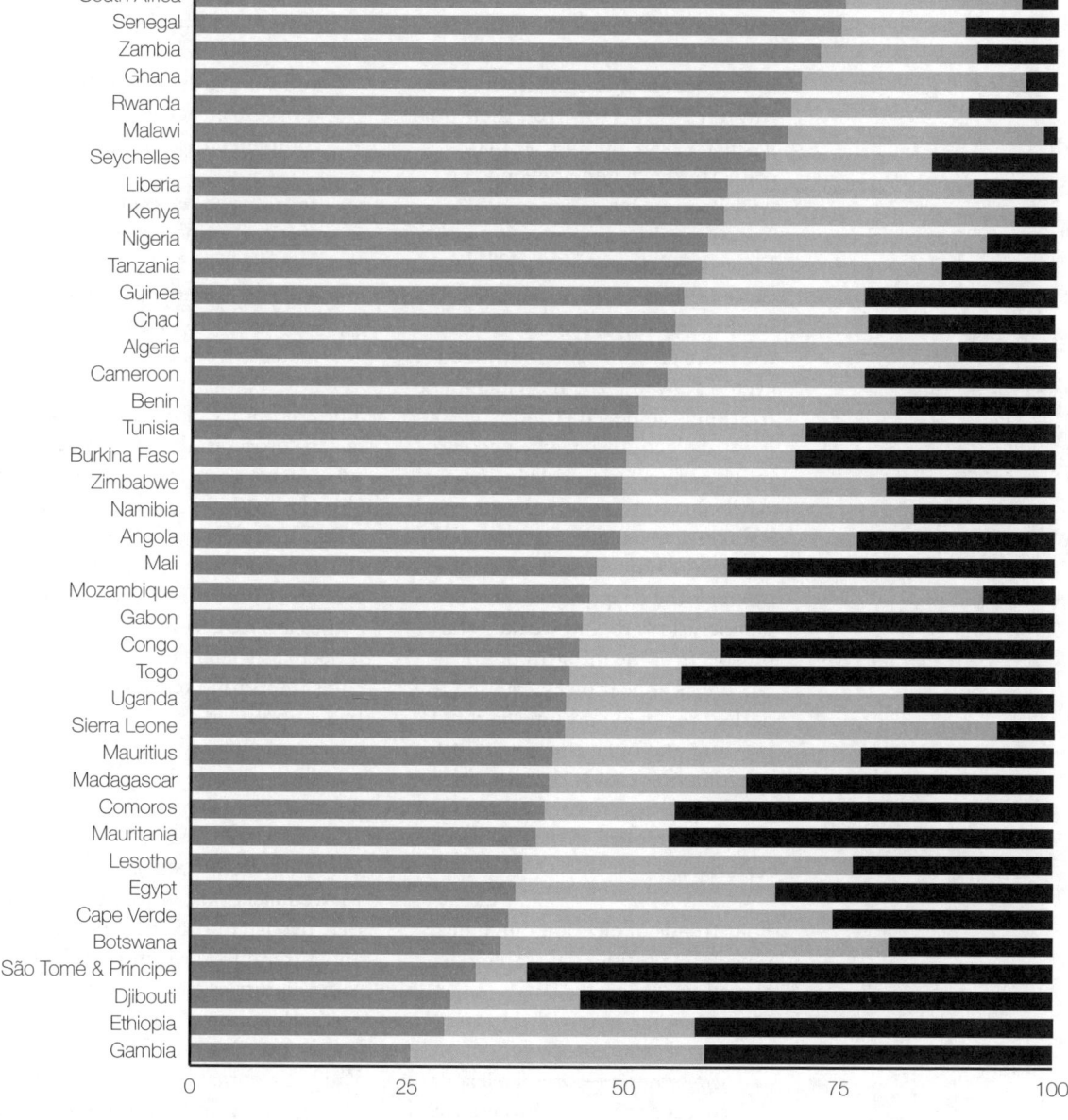

**Figure 2.5 Role of civil society organizations in promoting transparency and accountability**

Share of experts surveyed, by country (%)

- Moderately or effectively contributes
- Fairly contributes
- Does not contribute or rarely contributes

South Africa
Senegal
Zambia
Ghana
Rwanda
Malawi
Seychelles
Liberia
Kenya
Nigeria
Tanzania
Guinea
Chad
Algeria
Cameroon
Benin
Tunisia
Burkina Faso
Zimbabwe
Namibia
Angola
Mali
Mozambique
Gabon
Congo
Togo
Uganda
Sierra Leone
Mauritius
Madagascar
Comoros
Mauritania
Lesotho
Egypt
Cape Verde
Botswana
São Tomé & Príncipe
Djibouti
Ethiopia
Gambia

0   25   50   75   100

*Source:* AGR III Expert Opinion Survey 2012.

### Elections

Despite overall progress, countries are at different stages—elections are a case in point. Elections have often become "routinized" and woven into the political culture, with many countries passing Samuel Huntington's criterion of the "two elections" test necessary for democratic growth and passage of the democratic transition (Huntington 1991). However, their quality often casts doubt that many countries have gone beyond the transition phase.

Flawed elections rarely advance the cause of democratization, undermining Staffan Lindberg's thesis that the more elections are routinized—even if flawed—the more democratization is achieved (Lindberg 2009). Flawed elections have helped legitimize authoritarian rule in some African countries, which some analysts refer to as "autocratization by elections". Indeed, such elections often clothe despotic regimes in democratic garb and weaken the prospects of meaningful political change as appearances are used to deflect regional and international pressure and open the possibility of repressing CSOs that are agitating for political reforms, some of which the regime cynically brands as terrorists.

Four trends of election outcomes, especially presidential, can be discerned in Africa:

- *illegitimate/unpopular self-succession*—when a leader succeeds himself through rough election tactics;

- *proxy succession*—when a leader manipulates the internal party and electoral processes to install his successor in power, often against the wishes of the people;

- *hereditary trends*—when the offspring of the leader assumes power, usually after the death of the leader, in which the norms and standards of credible elections are either sidestepped or completed distorted; and

- *emerging regimes of free and fair elections*—where free, fair and transparent elections are held and the leadership and regime are considered legal and legitimate (Nwosu 2012).

The credibility of elections, which lies in "procedural certainty and the substantive uncertainty of outcomes" (Jinadu 2010, 8), are often compromised in the first three trends as the chances of electoral manipulation and predetermination of outcomes are real. When this happens, it deepens social fault lines, exacerbates intergroup tensions and may trigger political and electoral conflicts and violence in society, compounding the challenge of managing political diversity in plural societies.

### Grouping countries' progress

Flawed elections, weak political parties, persistent executive dominance and a trend towards militarism in some countries (such as the Democratic Republic of the Congo, Gambia, Kenya, Nigeria, Uganda and Zimbabwe) make it impossible to offer general findings on how much countries are moving to democracy.

Some analysts have sought to dis-aggregate outcomes by classifying countries into three groups—strong democratizers, hybrid and defective democratizers. Strong democratizers conduct regular free and fair elections, grant considerable civil and political rights and largely observe the rule of law; hybrid regimes oscillate between democratic and authoritarian tendencies; and the defective democratizers are democratizing in name only—they are pure civil dictatorships.

This classification and a similar tripartite breakdown for governance trends—showing more democracies and intermediate regimes, and fewer autocracies (figure 2.6)—are at best indicative, and must necessarily fail to capture nuances. The figure shows progress along Africa's path to democracy, but also that formidable challenges remain, requiring institutional reforms and norms to be reset for a solid democratic foundation to be laid.

## Leadership

The role of leadership underscores the interface between structures and agency in democratic transition.[6] Leadership may be conceived as a "reciprocal process of mobilizing, by persons with certain motives and values, various economic, political and other resources, in the context of competition and conflict, in order to realize the goals independently or mutually held by both leaders and followers" (Burns 1978, 425). Democratic leadership is not seen as creating a "big man" syndrome or personalizing political power, but deploying power in a rational way to influence political outcomes based on rules, procedures and democratic values.

In uncertain periods, leadership is central to democratization in Africa, projecting the needs of the electorate into a clearly defined vision and respecting the rules of the democratic game. It entails growth in the structures and institutions of accountability, responsiveness, norms of political tolerance, consociational politics and the rule of law.

Yet some African countries have seen leadership deficits in the transition, and even when civil society and democratic forces have waged political struggles for democratic change, the new leaders differ little from the former set.

The trends in electoral outcomes outlined in the preceding section are largely related to the nature of political leadership. In some countries, political leaders have respected the rules of the electoral process, the outcome of elections and term limits, as in South Africa (Nelson Mandela refused to run for a second term) and Tanzania. These two countries stand in sharp contrast to Senegal, with a frantic but botched attempt by the former leadership to change the constitutional provision on presidential elections,[7] and Nigeria, with a failed attempt to change the constitutional provision on presidential term limits.[8]

Because leadership is grounded in a social context, one challenge for Africa's transition is to enhance the

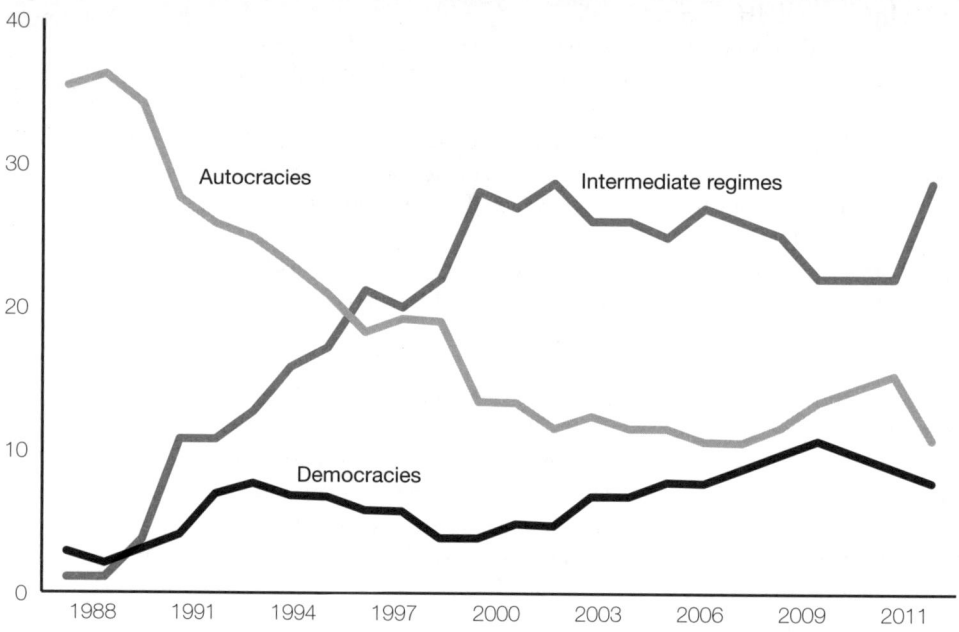

**Figure 2.6 Tripartite breakdown of governance in Sub-Saharan Africa, 1988–2011**

Number of states

*Source:* ACSS 2011.

## Diversity issues in the democratic transition

African countries are essentially plural societies, and so diversity presents ubiquitous challenges for political governance and management of society. Under authoritarian regimes, most diversity issues were suppressed and contained by force of arms. But the move to democracy prised loose the lid, giving vent to social and political differences and letting diversities—even brinksmanship—play out during political discourse and bargaining. Some of these challenges—old, new and often interrelated—are now discussed.

social and political milieu for leadership recruitment and training, including the party system and civil society.

*Power distribution, political structure and diversity*

It is a major undertaking to reconfigure power among elites and other groups so as to achieve social cohesion, inclusiveness and political stability. It requires a move from the concentrated power system of the old authoritarian order to a diffused structure, and democratizing societies have addressed it in three approaches.

First, the structural approach real-locates power among the tiers of government either through a federal arrangement or decentralization. Although Ethiopia, Kenya, Nigeria, South Africa and Tanzania have opted for federal or quasi-federal political formulas, others like Ghana, Mali, Senegal and Uganda have somewhat decentralized power to local authorities (see chapter 1). The objective for both groups is the same—creating avenues of participation, power and pressure to manage diversity sustainably.

Second, using the institutional approach, some countries, including Kenya, Nigeria (box 2.3) and South Africa, have passed laws and regulations on equal representation of groups in national institutions like the national public service, police and military forces, parastatals and government agencies in an attempt to create national cohesion and a sense of national belonging.

Such steps have had some success: respondents in more than half the 40 countries in the Expert Opinion Survey felt that their government's composition represented all segments and diverse interests of the country (figure 2.7).

Third, the circumstantial temporary arrangement is an elite-based approach for managing power in a politically expedient way, especially during political and electoral conflict. This is the formula of power sharing, which is put in place either to forestall political conflicts by dousing fear of sectional elite-group domination or as a result of a major

> **Box 2.3 Guaranteeing Nigeria's federal character**
>
> The "federal character principle", part of the constitution, requires that every state should be represented in all federal establishments.
>
> To manage the spatial diversity of the federation, every federal government in the country's recent history has appointed at least one minister from each state of the federation.

political conflict, which countries then have to manage.

*Power sharing*

Most arrangements to share power have emerged from the dynamics of crisis, tension and conflict that are usually associated with the aftermath of peace agreements by warring parties, with post-election political deadlock and with part of a political pact in a structural political transition. Whatever the background, power sharing is a formula for managing diversity, and usually for moving to democracy.

Power sharing as a temporary consociational arrangement can succeed in three situations: when the political elite shows some consensus and commitment to making things work—the "politics of trust" (Cheeseman 2011; Mehler 2009); when the goals of the arrangement are clear and accepted by all; and when external, including foreign, interference and mediation do not override and dictate the terms and conditions of the power-sharing formula. But it has rarely been successful in midwifing the transition to democracy because it is too often marred by deep-seated animosities and suspicion, irreconcilable interests and

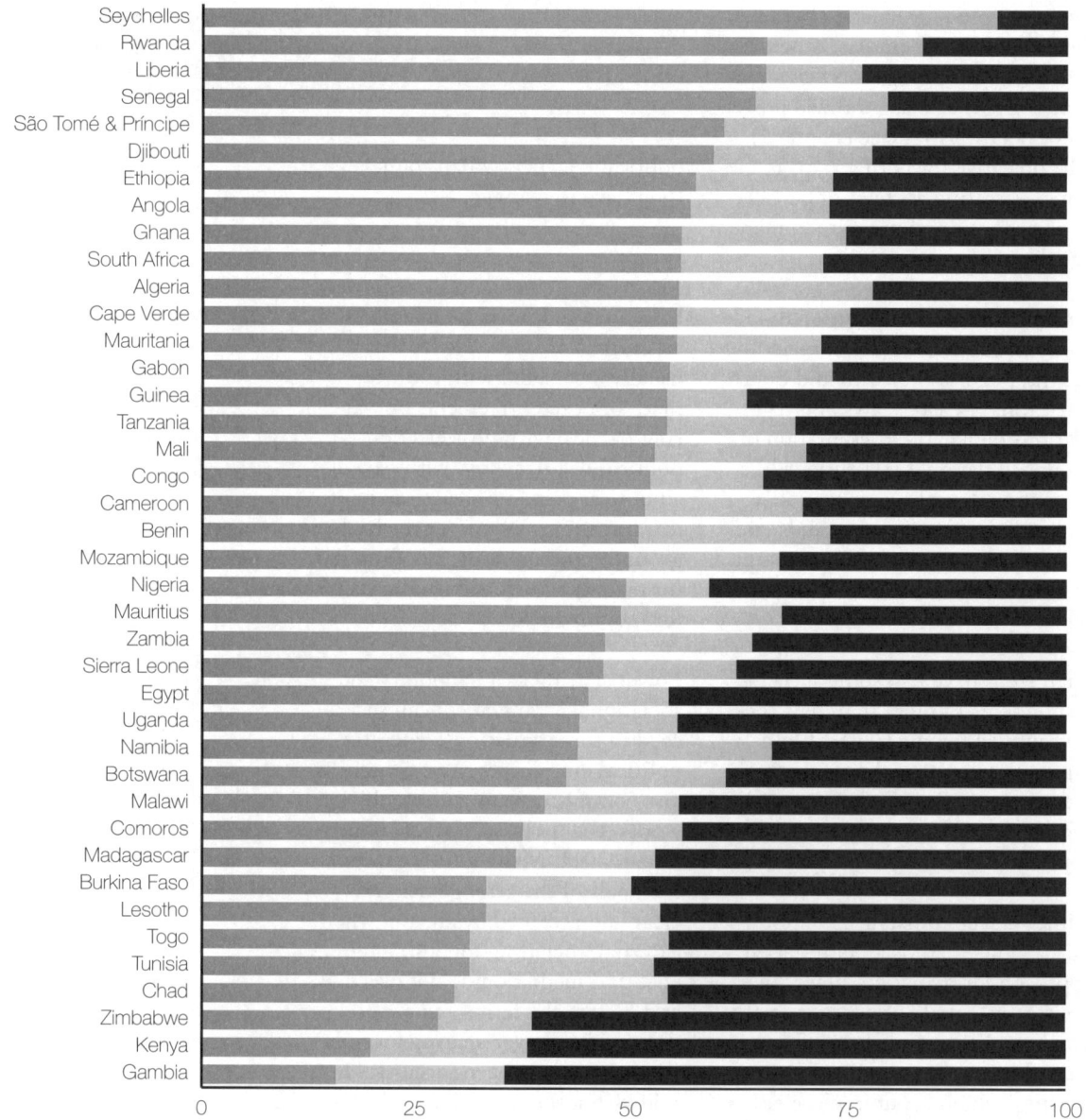

## Figure 2.7 The government and leadership represent all segments and diverse interests

Share of experts surveyed, by country (%)

■ Agree or strongly agree
■ Neither agree nor disagree
■ Strongly disagree or disagree

*Source:* AGR III Expert Opinion Survey 2012.

excessive external (but covert) control of negotiations.

South Africa presents a fairly successful case of power sharing in its transition from apartheid to democracy, partly because it treated power sharing as a process, not an event. Also, the burden placed on the arrangement was limited and short term. The stability of the state resulting from the process did not depend on the fact that power was shared, but on an inclusive governance process. Power sharing was a practical strategy to midwife a transition and with luck to deliver a new South Africa in which institutions of governance would be imbued with a tolerant and inclusive culture. Acknowledging the terrible past, the task of power sharing was to prevent total collapse of the state and society when majority rule came in—in a sense, it entailed sacrificing justice for peace by persuading the minority whites that they could coexist in a multiracial society. This has so far worked well.

Similarly, the Kenyan National Accord and Reconciliation of 2008 was modelled on a limited and short-term power-sharing mandate. Côte d'Ivoire and Zimbabwe also illustrate the range of possible outcomes: power sharing did not work in Côte d'Ivoire and paved way to serious electoral conflicts in 2011, but in Zimbabwe, despite all the challenges, it has prevented systemic breakdown and possible large-scale political violence and even civil war.

### Ethnicity and religion
Ethnicity and religion are two sociopolitical identities manifested very strongly in the political process and affecting the trajectory of democratic transitions (see chapter 1).

### Ethnicity
The importance of ethnicity is historically rooted in the colonial policy of state bifurcation based on ethnic ideology (Adejumobi 2001; Mamdani 1996). Colonialism reified ethnic identities, constructed "ethnic citizens" and intensified ethnic competition and rivalry in many countries. Post-colonial Africa has been shaped by its colonial inheritance such that the formation of political parties, electioneering and political mobilization have been heavily tainted with ethnic colours. Many countries' political parties, for example, have a "home base" or domicile in an ethnic group, even if they have some support in other ethnic bases (box 2.4).

### Religion
In many North African countries, religion is the fault line that has dogged the recent transition. Political discourse has centred on what the role of Islam should be in the state and governance, and what kind of political parties should be allowed to exist and govern. The role of the Islamic Brotherhood as a social movement that has transformed itself into a political party has come under so much scrutiny, particularly in Egypt, that it almost borders on Islamophobia. The arguments over the Egyptian constitution between the forces of secularism and of Islamism, as well as the country's identity with Africa, remain unresolved. The final draft of the Egyptian Constitution of

> *Ethnicity and religion are two sociopolitical identities manifested very strongly in the political process*

2012 (Part 1, Article 1) noted that, while "The Egyptian people are part of the Arab world and Islamic nations", they are "proud of belonging to the Nile Valley and Africa".

Religion in Sudan fuelled a civil war along an ethno-regional line that led to an independent South Sudan in 2011. Nigeria's Boko Haram sect, claiming that its mission is to reconstitute the Nigerian state as an Islamic entity, has been waging a terrorist insurgency against the government. Radical groups in Mali's north, especially among the Tuareg, seek to Islamicize the whole country through force of arms, puncturing the country's much-celebrated steps to democracy.

### Ethnicity and religion—drain or gain?

Ethnic and religious diversity should be rich political resources for any society or nation as they elicit multiple perspectives on governance (box 2.5). And as Beissinger (2008) observed, history offers examples of democracy blooming amid ethnic variety. But ethnic diversity may affect democratization when it interacts with poor government performance, state capture, corruption, lopsided economic growth, skewed income distribution and poor institutional and constitutional design, bringing closer the potential for ethnic (and religious) diversity to become a tool of social and political conflict.

### Perceptions of sectarianism

The response to sectarian pressures (ethnic, racial or religious) has been a challenge for many countries transitioning to democracy, and is a large part of the contestation among social forces in influencing the trajectory and form of the evolving political regime. Most countries have adopted a constitutional approach, which insists on non-discrimination among these identities, and attempts to protect minority identity groups. But the outcomes have not been uniform, with varying degrees of success (figure 2.8). The perception in most AGR III project countries is that sectarian identity groups have considerable influence on the political process—reflecting the limited autonomy of the state for political action—and that they are a likely source of political conflict.

Prominence of sectarian identity is also related to protecting and promoting diversity. In only a few countries did more than half the expert respondents consider that their country's constitution protected and promoted diversity and minority interests (figure 2.9), and in some countries a large majority of respondents felt that their constitution rarely did that.

There are indications of a correlation between the views encapsulated in figures 2.7–2.9 (table 2.1). Among the nine countries where the majority of respondents felt the constitution did not protect and promote diversity and minority interests, the majority also maintained that the composition of government and leadership failed to represent all segments and diverse interests in five of them; also in those five countries, sectarian identity had considerable influence on the country's political process.

### Citizenship

In the democratic transition, citizenship has been used to deny the franchise to individuals and groups and so exclude them from the political

> **Box 2.5 Ethnic diversity as an asset rather than a liability**
>
> Ethnic affiliation by human communities is a natural condition and not a social pathology, and can provide a sense of community in the face of a globalizing marketplace.
>
> Yet it becomes a challenge to broader societal harmony when it becomes mobilized in hostile confrontation with the "other". In such moments of ethnic crisis, the collective psyche is prone to dehumanize that other in ways that produce singular conflict intensities and brutalities.
>
> Conflict—class, interest and ethnic—is a natural aspect of social existence; the heart of the matter is that it is conducted by civil process, by equitable rules, through dialogue and bargaining, in a framework of governance facilitating cooperation and reconciliation.
>
> *Source:* UNRISD 1994.

process.[9] In South Africa, citizenship politics centres on the deadly trend of xenophobia in which those regarded as non–South Africans (blacks from other African countries) are blamed, vilified and even attacked for all the country's ills, economic and political.

The general problem arises because citizenship is usually defined not by birth or residence but by ancestry and heredity. It often also has a gender bias, where women married to nationals do not automatically enjoy citizenship in the country of marriage (but men do, the other way round). Discrimination can also extend to immigrants who, no matter how long they have been domiciled and paying taxes, do not enjoy citizenship rights (Adejumobi 2001, 2004; Manby 2009). (Some of these issues are not peculiar to Africa of course. They are global, seen not only in the West, particularly

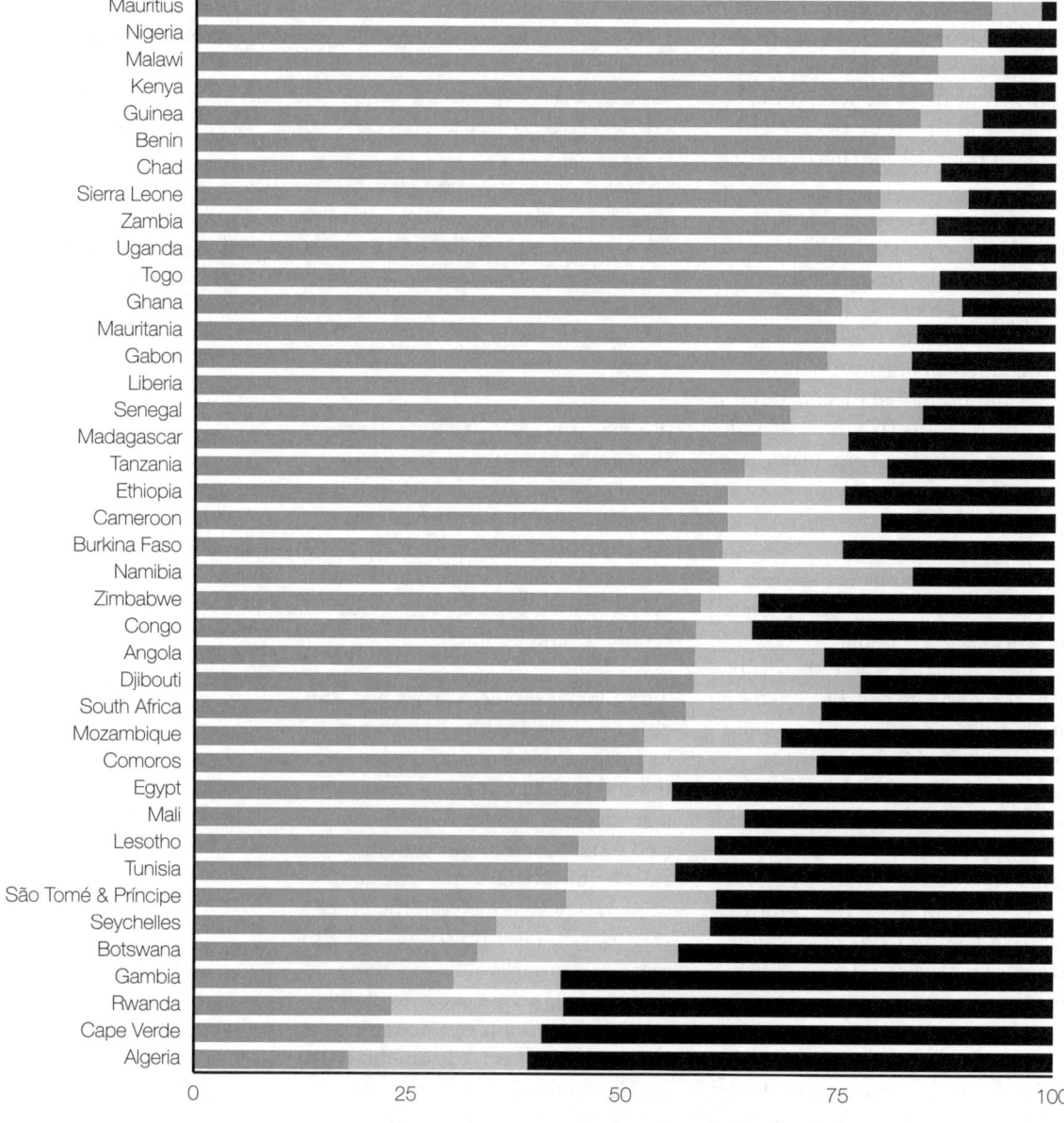

**Figure 2.8 Sectarian groups have a heavy influence on a country's political process**

Share of experts surveyed, by country (%)

- Agree or strongly agree
- Neither agree nor disagree
- Strongly disagree or disagree

Mauritius
Nigeria
Malawi
Kenya
Guinea
Benin
Chad
Sierra Leone
Zambia
Uganda
Togo
Ghana
Mauritania
Gabon
Liberia
Senegal
Madagascar
Tanzania
Ethiopia
Cameroon
Burkina Faso
Namibia
Zimbabwe
Congo
Angola
Djibouti
South Africa
Mozambique
Comoros
Egypt
Mali
Lesotho
Tunisia
São Tomé & Príncipe
Seychelles
Botswana
Gambia
Rwanda
Cape Verde
Algeria

0    25    50    75    100

*Source:* AGR III Expert Opinion Survey 2012.

## Figure 2.9 The constitution promotes diversity and minority interests

Share of experts surveyed, by country (%)

- Protects diversity and mostly or always respects it
- Protects diversity and sometimes respects it
- Does not protect diversity at all or protects diversity and rarely respects it

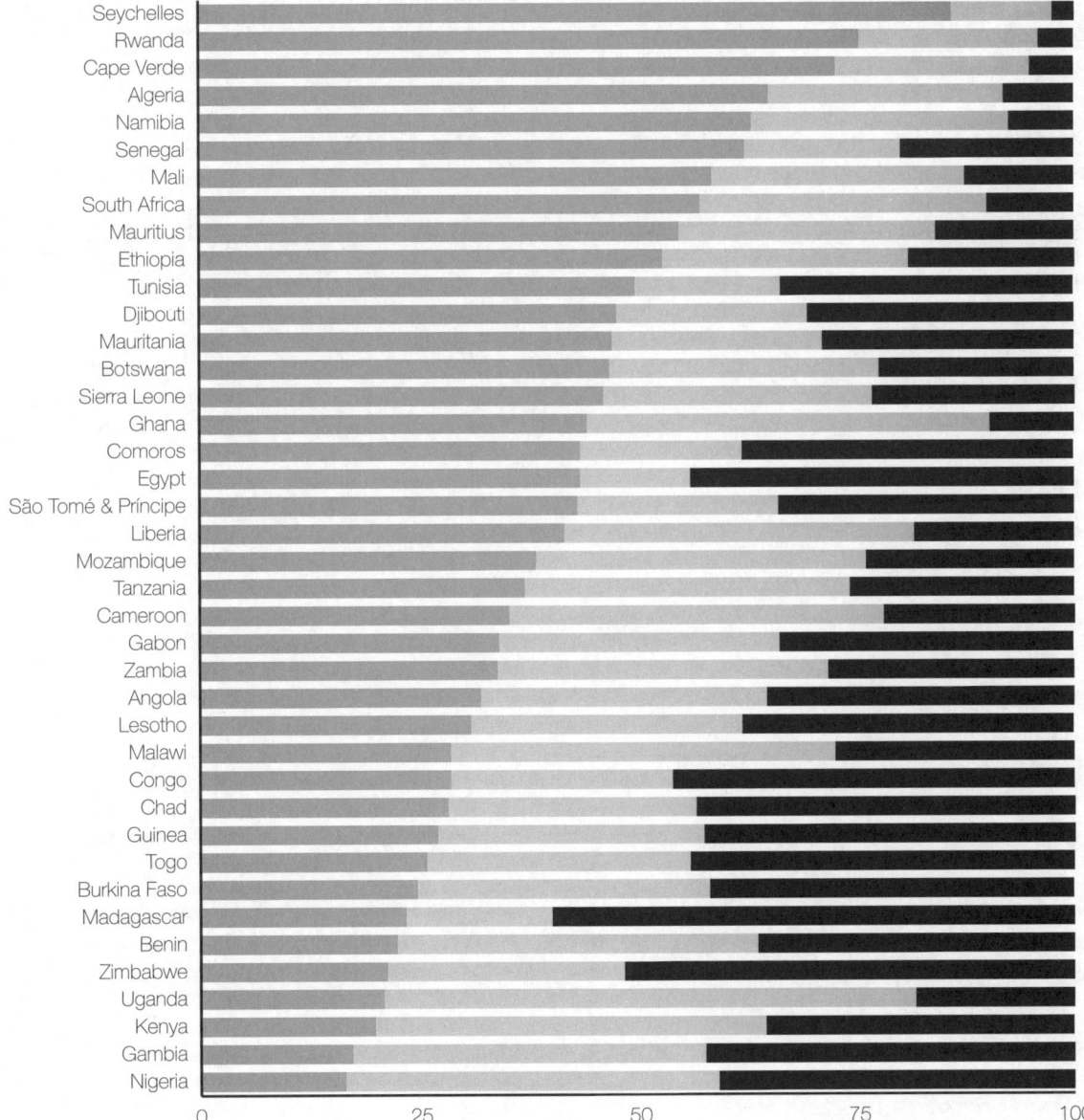

*Source:* AGR III Expert Opinion Survey 2012.

Table 2.1 Relationship among constitutional diversity guarantees, composition of government and sectarian identity

| Country | Constitution does not protect and promote diversity and minority interests (more than 40% of respondents) | Composition of government and leadership not representative of diversity (more than 40% of respondents) | Sectarian identity has considerable influence on the country's political process (more than 60% of respondents) |
|---|:---:|:---:|:---:|
| **Category A** | | | |
| Burkina Faso | ✔ | ✔ | ✔ |
| Chad | ✔ | ✔ | ✔ |
| Madagascar | ✔ | ✔ | ✔ |
| Togo | ✔ | ✔ | ✔ |
| Zimbabwe | ✔ | ✔ | ✔ |
| **Category B** | | | |
| Nigeria | ✔ | ✔ | |
| Egypt | ✔ | ✔ | |
| Gambia | ✔ | ✔ | |
| **Category C** | | | |
| Kenya | | ✔ | ✔ |
| Malawi | | ✔ | ✔ |
| Uganda | | ✔ | ✔ |
| **Category D** | | | |
| Benin | | | ✔ |
| Cameroon | | | ✔ |
| Comoros | | ✔ | |
| Congo | ✔ | | |
| Ethiopia | | | ✔ |
| Gabon | | | ✔ |
| Ghana | | | ✔ |
| Guinea | | | ✔ |
| Lesotho | | ✔ | |
| Liberia | | | ✔ |
| Mauritania | | | ✔ |
| Namibia | | | ✔ |
| Nigeria | | | ✔ |
| Senegal | | | ✔ |
| Sierra Leone | | | ✔ |
| Tanzania | | | ✔ |
| Tunisia | | ✔ | |
| Zambia | | | ✔ |

*Source:* AGR III Country Reports 2012.

Europe, spurred by the global economic crisis, but also in South America and parts of Asia.)

The citizenship challenge in Africa's democratic transition lies in how it has been made hostage to politics, shrinking the political space, silencing or marginalizing political opponents and compromising the electoral process (box 2.6).

Thus instead of harnessing the diverse human and spatial resources of the country, the politics of citizenship usually comes down to the contest for power and access to resources, deepening exclusion, aggravating social discord and promoting political conflicts.

*Marginalized groups of women*
Several countries have evolved political frameworks to accommodate marginalized groups, especially women.

As a means to enable women to fully participate in a country's political life, female representation in legislatures has prompted animated debate, frequently between supporters of the majoritarian/plurality system and proportional representation. Its conclusion seems to be that the latter ensures greater female representation given that it has a higher possibility of district representation with gender inclusion (Tripp et al. 2009).

Most African countries have taken steps towards writing affirmative action clauses into their constitutions, including quotas, and fall into several main groupings. In the lead are countries with reserved quotas

---

**Box 2.6  Shifting citizenships**

In Zambia, a founding father of the country and its former president, Kenneth Kaunda, was declared persona non grata and suddenly classified as a "foreigner" (Malawian) during the 1996 presidential election and so disqualified from running for president.

In Côte d'Ivoire, a former prime minister, Alassane Ouattara (now president), was redefined as a non-Ivorian (allegedly Burkinabe) and disqualified from running for the presidency in 1995, for which the electoral law was changed so that only individuals whose parents are of "Ivorian origin" can stand for the presidency. This law was eventually overturned, but at a great cost of protracted political conflicts and civil war.

In the Democratic Republic of the Congo, the Bayarwanda remain an enduring part of the citizenship politics in the country. Although generations of them have lived in the country, their citizenship remains unsettled, seemingly unresolved by the 2004 citizenship law.

In some East and Southern African countries, the citizenship rights of the "settler" population (whites and Asians) are often contested and even denied either on the grounds that the state does not recognize dual citizenship or that the claimants do not fulfil the ancestry requirement.

---

like Burundi, Rwanda, Tanzania and Uganda.

Second are constitutionalized requirements in Angola, Djibouti, Liberia, Kenya, Niger and Seychelles for all political parties to nominate a certain share of women for the national assembly and related public office. In Kenya, for instance, the next Senate (upper house), to be elected in March 2013, is to have 67 members with one elected representative for each of the newly created 47 counties, two youth representatives, two representatives of people living with disabilities and 16 women (*Saturday Nation Newspaper* 2012). (Compare this with Botswana—box 2.7.)

In Seychelles, the state has long given attention to pro-women policies. Apart from a clear affirmative action policy in governance, the rights of women to land, property and protection against violence have been legally affirmed. In the current National Assembly, 8 of the 34 members are women. A 2011 Royal Commonwealth Society Survey ranked Seychelles fourth of 50 Commonwealth countries for gender equality and support to women (AGR III Seychelles Country Report 2012).

Third, some countries leave it to political parties to decide, while others leave it to executive prerogative to appoint women to legislative seats. Nigeria is an example of this category (Tripp et al. 2009).

Yet despite these measures, the language in the constitution may be subdued to ensure that women parliamentarians are not seen to represent women's interests (Tamale 1999). In South Africa, one upshot of such descriptive—not substantive—representation is female representatives eventually acknowledging that they have numbers but lack the power to make any major difference for women.

In many other cases, as in Burkina Faso, Cameroon and Gabon, the old constitution has remained in force and is thus a stumbling block to inclusive government. In other words, while the political system has been reformed, the content of reform and the substantive outcome for women are still minimal, and contested by patriarchal forces.

## Conclusions and recommendations

Diversity is about difference, in the social, economic and political spheres. Political diversity is about political pluralism—groups, individuals and communities being part of the political process, contesting and competing with ideas, visions and spaces, and respecting the rules of the game. Diversity interacts with the democratic transition in a symmetrical way: the pressures for expressing diversity often give rise to the transition—and the transition has to deal, practically, with managing diversity in a way that promotes peace, inclusiveness and social cohesion.

Elections as a mechanism and a component of the democratic transition support the democratic management of diversity in four important respects: through participation, representation, rotation of leaders and meeting local needs and aspirations. But the architectural design of elections and its processes must be inclusive and participatory, and complemented by diversity-sensitive legal, institutional and policy reforms.

Africa's democratic transition has had mixed results, and the evolving institutions and processes have responded in different ways, also with varying degrees of success. However, deep political changes, as Widner (2005) observed, do not happen overnight. Africa is in an ambiguous transition period with signs of optimism and grounds for concern. Sectarian pressures, despite good constitutional frameworks, continue to undermine democratization. Moves to mainstream voices and create political space for marginalized groups are still contested in many countries.

Leadership is central to the democratic transition in promoting consociational politics, in upholding ethics and morality in governance and in respecting constitutional provisions on diversity. Regrettably, some leaders have reneged on their earlier democratic commitments, attempting to amend the constitution (or circumvent it) to cement their hold on power. The political costs have often been heavy for their countries.

Africa's democratic transition and its diversity challenges should be viewed as part of state formation and political engineering, in which the quest for democratic accommodation

and political consensus is still being navigated.

*Elections*
Elections are a major feature of the democratic transition and are central to its success. Where they are well organized, free, fair and credible, the transition may well succeed. But where they fail, transitions are likely to falter. Thus electoral processes in the transition must be accompanied by strong electoral administration and management and close involvement of civil society.

*Media freedom*
Media freedom is an integral part of civil liberties that should accompany the transition. Where they are free and people can gather and spread information quickly and accurately, a fruitful exchange of ideas becomes possible between leaders and led—necessary for political renewal and government legitimacy.

*Transformative leadership*
Leadership is central to the course of the democratic transition, as demonstrated by the case of Nelson Mandela's government in South Africa. Good leadership seeks not only to build democratic institutions, but also to create opportunities for all interest groups in society. A leadership that inspires, guides and governs by the rule of law is fundamental to managing the uncertainties of the democratic transition.

*Constitutional reforms*
The democratic transition should be paced by inclusive and people-driven constitutional reforms to accommodate the interests of diverse groups,

communities and social categories, and to create space for political and economic freedom where democracy can thrive. Citizenship should be redefined to emphasize birth, residency, tax obligations and civic and national values rather than ancestry and ethnicity.

### Institutional changes
Institutional reengineering is central to the democratic transition.

Authoritarian structures have to be dismantled to give way to institutions that will safeguard the interests and aspirations of the people. These new structures will no doubt constitute sites of political contestation by groups and social forces, but the more independent they are, the better they will be able to represent, accommodate and mediate between society's different interest groups.

## Annex 2.1 Alternation of presidential power in Africa, 2007–2012

| Country | Current president | Former president | Date of accession | Remarks on the current president |
|---|---|---|---|---|
| Mauritius | Kailash Purryag | Sir Anerood Jugnauth | July 2012 | |
| Egypt | Mohamed Morsi Isa al-Ayyat | Hosni Mubarak | June 2012 | His accession to power was preceded by the ousting of former President Hosni Mubarak, through popular protests in February 2011, leaving the office vacant. His election followed an extended period of transition |
| Lesotho | Tom Thabane | Pakalitha Mosisili | June 2012 | |
| Guinea-Bissau | Manuel Serifo Nhamadjo | Mamadu Ture Kuruma | May 2012 | Following an April 2012 military coup, he was designated acting president in a transitional arrangement |
| Malawi | Joyce Banda | Bingu wa Mutharika | April 2012 | The vice-president became president on 7 April in a constitutional succession following the death in office of the former president |
| Senegal | Abdoulaye Wade | Macky Sall | February 2012 | Macky Sall won the election after an aborted attempt by the former president Abdoulaye Wade to amend the constitution on provisions for presidential elections |
| Tunisia | Moncef Marzouki | Fouad Mebazaa (served as President from January 2011 to December 2011) | December 2011 | Following the ousting of Zine El Abidine Ben Ali in January 2011, Mohamed Ghannouchi and Fouad Mebazaa served terms as acting president. On 12 December 2011, Moncef Marzouki was elected by the Constituent Assembly as the interim president |
| Morocco | Abdelilah Benkirane | Abbas El Fassi | November 2011 | The prime minister is the head of government, and is appointed by the King of Morocco, Mohammed VI |
| Zambia | Michael Sata | Rupiah Banda | September 2011 | |
| Cape Verde | Jorge Carlos Fonseca | Pedro Pires | September 2011 | |
| São Tomé and Príncipe | Manuel Pinto da Costa | Fradique de Menezes | September 2011 | |

| Country | Current president | Former president | Date of accession | Remarks on the current president |
|---|---|---|---|---|
| South Sudan | Salva Kiir | | July 2011 | The first president of the new country |
| Comoros | Ikililou Dhoinine | Ahmed Abdallah Mohamed Sambi | May 2011 | |
| Niger | Mahamadou Issoufou | Mamadou Tandja, overthrown in a military coup and succeeded by Salou Djibo, the de facto leader from 19 February 2010 to 7 April 2011 | April 2011 | The election followed a military coup in February 2010 that removed President Mamadou Tandja. Salou Djibo became head of the Supreme Council for the Restoration of Democracy. Presidential elections were later held, resulting in the victory and accession to power of President Issoufou |
| Nigeria | Goodluck Jonathan | Umaru Musa Yar'Adua | April 2011 | The former president died on 5 May 2010, and Goodluck Jonathan (then vice-president) was sworn in as his successor the following day. He was elected in April 2011 as president |
| Côte d'Ivoire | Alassane Dramane Ouattara | Laurent Gbagbo | December 2010 | |
| Guinea | Alpha Condé | Sékouba Konaté (Acting President between December 2009 and December 2010, following the attempted assassination of Moussa Dadis Camara) | December 2010 | He was elected president in a second round of voting. The 2010 election was widely considered the first credible election in Guinea |
| Mali | Dioncounda Traoré (acting president) | Amadou Toumani Touré (deposed in a coup by Amadou Sanogo) | April 2010 | He assumed the presidency in an interim capacity, until an election to be held in 2012 (under the 1992 Constitution, which has a four-year cycle). However, the election schedule is uncertain |
| Gabon | Ali-ben Bongo | Rose Francine Rogombé | October 2009 | Rogombé was interim president from June 2009 to October 2009, following the death of President Omar Bongo. She constitutionally succeeded Bongo due to her role as Senate president. Presidential elections were held, which Ali Bongo won |

| Country | Current president | Former president | Date of accession | Remarks on the current president |
|---------|-------------------|------------------|-------------------|----------------------------------|
| Mauritania | Mohamed Ould Abdel Aziz | Ba Mamadou Mbaré (interim president from April 2009 to August 2009) | August 2009 | Abdel Aziz was a leading figure in the August 2005 coup that deposed President Maaouya Ould Sid'Ahmed Taya, and in August 2008 he led another coup, that toppled President Sidi Ould Cheikh Abdallahi. Following the latter coup, Abdel Aziz became President of the High Council of State as part of a political transition leading to a new election. He resigned from that post in April 2009 to stand as a candidate in the July 2009 presidential election, which he won |
| South Africa | Jacob Zuma | Thabo Mbebi | May 2009 | He was elected by parliament following his party's victory in the 2009 general election. Like his predecessor, he headed the African National Congress |
| Madagascar | Andry Rajoelina | Marc Ravalomanana | March 2009 | He became president on 21 March 2009 during the 2009 political crisis that saw the resignation of President Ravalomanana and his installation as President of the High Transitional Authority of Madagascar |
| Ghana | John Atta Mills | John Kufuor | January 2009 | |
| Swaziland | Barnabas Sibusiso Dlamini | Bheki Dlamini (acting prime minister from 18 September to 23 October 2008) | October 2008 | He was reappointed prime minister by King Mswati III |
| Botswana | Ian Khama | Festus Mogae | April 2008 | Khama and his predecessor were members of the Botswana Democratic Party |
| Sierra Leone | Ernest Bai Koroma | Ahmad Tejan Kabbah | September 2007 | Ernest Koroma was re-elected as president in December 2012 |

## Notes

1. Although the transition's pattern is important in the electoral process in the nascent democratic era, other factors include the nature of political parties, the quality of leadership in the transition phase, commitment to institution building and consensus among the political elite for democratic practices.

2. These included trade unions, professional associations, student and women's movements, faith-based groups, farmers' associations and non-governmental organizations.

3. The first freedom struggles were during decolonization. *Uhuru* means freedom in Khiswahili, a language widely spoken in Eastern Africa.

4. Discussed further in the appendix on background, methodology and calculating the indices.

5. For information on elections in 2011 and 2012, see "Tentative Elections Calendar," African Union, http://pa.au.int/en/sites/default/files/Tentative_Elections_Calender_2012+[1]_0.pdf, accessed January 2013.

6. Agency in this case means actors especially in the political process.

7. In June 2011, President Abdoulaye Wade of Senegal tried to change the constitutional provision on presidential elections but was resisted through violent mass protests and demonstrations organized by civil society and opposition political parties.

8. In Nigeria in 2006, President Olusegun Obasanjo wanted to change the constitutional provisions on term limits in order to run for a third term, but failed.

9. As in Côte d'Ivoire, the Democratic Republic of the Congo, Nigeria, Sudan, Uganda and Zambia, among others.

## References

ACSS (African Centre for Strategic Studies). 2011. *Africa and the Arab Spring: A New Era of Democratic Expectations*. ACSS Special Report 1. Washington, DC.

Adejumobi, Said. 1995. "Structural Reform and Its Impact of State and Society." In *The Political Economy of Nigeria under Military Rule: 1983–1993* ed. Said Adejumobi and Abubakar Momoh. Harare: SAPES Trust.

———. 1996. "The Structural Adjustment Programme and Democratic Transition in Africa." *Verfassung Und Recht in Ubersee. Law and Politics in Africa, Asia and Latin America* 29 (4): 415–33.

———. 2000. "Elections in Africa: A Fading Shadow of Democracy?" *International Political Science Review* 21 (1): 59–73.

———. 2001. "Citizenship, Rights and the Problem of Conflicts and Civil Wars in Africa." *Human Rights Quarterly* 23 (1): 148–69.

———. 2004. "Antinomy of Citizenship: Negotiating Power or Social Existence?" *Development and Democracy—Journal of West African Affairs* 4 (1): 3–8.

———. 2010. "Democracy and Governance in Nigeria: Between Consolidation and Reversal." In *Governance and Politics in Post-Military Nigeria: Changes and Challenges*, ed. Said Adejumobi. New York: Palgrave Macmillan.

AfDB (African Development Bank). 2012. *Job, Justice and the Arab Spring: Inclusive Growth in North Africa*. Tunis.

Agbaje, Adigun, and Said Adejumobi. 2006. "Do Votes Count? The Travails of Electoral Politics in Nigeria." *Africa Development* 31 (3): 25–44.

Barkan, Joel D. 2008. "Legislature on the Rise?" *Journal of Democracy* 19: 124–37.

———. 2012. "Ethnic Fractionalisation and the Propensity for Conflict in Uganda, Kenya and Tanzania." In *On the Fault Line: Managing Tensions and Divisions within Societies*, ed. Jeffrey Herbst, Terence McNamee, and Greg Mills. London: Profile Books.

Basedau, Matthias. 2011. "How Ethnic are African Parties Really? Evidence from Four Francophone Countries." *International Political Science Review* 33 (1): 5–24.

Beissinger, Mark. 2008. "A New Look at Ethnicity and Democratization." *Journal of Democracy* 19 (3): 85–97.

Burns, James M. 1978. *Leadership*. New York: Harper Torchbooks.

Cheeseman, Nic. 2011. "The Internal Dynamics of Power Sharing in Africa." *Democratization* 18 (2): 336–65.

Denk, Thomas, and Daniel Silander. 2012. "Problems in Paradise? Challenges to Future Democratization in Democratic States." *International Political Science Review* 33 (1): 25–40.

Huntington, Samuel. 1991. *The Third Wave Democratization in the Late Twentieth Century*. Norman, OK: University of Oklahoma.

Jinadu, L. Adele. 2010. "Managing Elections: The Winner-Take-All Rule, Democracy and Development." Ghana Speaks Lecture Series No. 2, Institute of Democratic Governance, Accra.

Lindberg, Staffan. 2009. "Democratization by Elections?" *Journal of Democracy* 20 (3): 86–92.

Lynch, Gabrielle, and Gordon Crawford. 2011. "Democratization in Africa 1990–2010: An Assessment." *Democratization* 18 (2): 275–310.

Mamdani, Mahmood. 1996. *Citizens and Subjects: Contemporary Africa and the Legacy of Late Colonialism*. Princeton, NJ: Princeton University Press.

Manby, Bronwen. 2009. *Struggles for Citizenship in Africa*. London: Zed Books.

Mehler, Andreas. 2009. "Introduction: Power Sharing in Africa." *Africa Spectrum* 44 (3): 2–10.

Mkandawire, P. Thandika, and Adebayo O. Olukoshi, eds. 1995. *Between Liberalisation and Oppression: The Politics of Structural Adjustment in Africa*. Dakar: CODESRIA.

Nwosu, Bernard U. 2012. "Tracks of the Third Wave: Democracy Theory, Democratisation and the Dilemma of Political Succession in Africa." *Review of African Political Economy* 39 (131): 11–25.

Parliamentary Development Unit. 2009. "Report on the African Charter on Democracy, Governance and Elections: A Case Study of 12 African Countries." AusAid, Canberra.

Sarrazin, Tom. 2011. *Texting, Tweeting, Mobile Internet: New Platforms for Democratic Debate in Africa*. Nambia: Fesmedia Africa, Friedrich Ebert-Stiftung.

*Saturday Nation Newspaper*. 2012. "At a Glance: Parliament by Numbers." Nairobi, 11 August 2012, p. 17.

Tamale, Sylvia. 1999. *When Hens Begin to Crow: Gender and Parliamentary Politics in Uganda*. Kampala: Fountain Publishers.

Tripp, Aili M., Isabel Casimiro, Joy Kwesiga, and Alice Mungwa. 2009. *African Women's Movements: Changing Political Landscape*. Cambridge, UK: Cambridge University Press.

UNECA (United Nations Economic Commission for Africa). 2009.

*African Governance Report II.* Addis Ababa.

UNRISD (United Nations Research Institute for Social Development). 1994. *Ethnic Diversity and Public Policy: An Overview.* Geneva.

Wanyande, Peter. 2006. "Electoral Politics and Election Outcome in Kenya." *African Development* 31 (3): 62–80.

Widner, Jennifer. 2005. "Africa's Democratization: A Work in Progress." *Current History* 104 (682): 216–21.

*While one can have elections without democracy, it is not possible to have genuine democracy without elections* (Kadima 2009, 2)

*Elections are the principal and necessary condition of democracy, the first step without which democracy cannot otherwise be born* (Bratton and van de Walle 1997, 13)

*Elections are not straightforward as tools for conflict resolution. . . . An election can bring to a head the very conflict that it is supposed to sort out* (Leonard 2010, 37)

Managing politics in a society with deep-rooted diversity is complicated at the best of times. Organizing elections in such a social and national context is more complex still. Most countries in Africa are characterized by various forms of diversities ranging from ethnicity to language, race to religion, culture to class, and gender to generation. Diversity poses both an opportunity and a challenge to a society and a country. It can be valuable asset—as in development and "unity in diversity". But it can also be threat to a society's stability and prosperity, especially where unity is imposed for the sake of "unity in conformity".

Developing societies, such as most in Africa, experience greater challenges and tensions than in most developed societies in forging a strong sense of cohesive nationhood. Post-colonial states shoulder the Herculean task and responsibility of forging a new collective consciousness and identity out of a welter of various primordial and social identities in polities that were arbitrarily carved out during the colonial era.

This chapter explores the issue of diversity in the electoral process in Africa. It underlines how African countries have sought to accommodate diversity and pluralism in their electoral institutions, processes and electoral cycle to promote integrity and public confidence, and how the electoral process in its interface with diversity generates tension and conflicts in some contexts.

This chapter also shows that elections require sensitive, efficient and timely management of diversity-related challenges. Where these are missing, the consequences have been bad, even disastrous. Elections on their own, however, do not resolve the issues that arise from diversity, because it is often deeply rooted historically. Structural issues relating to social inequalities, discrimination and marginalization, for instance, cannot be settled through a single election—nor can the distribution of wealth and power. Indeed, improperly handled, elections can turn diversity into a tinder box.

Several key messages emerge. Although elections on their own do not fully resolve issues that arise from diversity, over time, fair and transparent elections can mitigate and help resolve diversity-based contests for power and resources at national, regional and local levels. Mixed forms of proportional representation are generally considered more accommodative of diversity management than other electoral systems, but every stage of the electoral process, including constituency delimitation, voter registration and education, the voting process, and dispute handling and adjudication, need their diversity to be managed. This entails making the electoral process sensitive to the interests and concerns of marginalized social groups, drawing on those good practices already followed by African countries.

Finally, leaders need to eradicate the structural roots of diversity-related conflicts, strengthen the ability of electoral institutions and political parties to address diversity in the electoral process, and manage and defuse conflicts before they get out of hand.

## Managing diversity

From the conceptual discussion in chapter 1, it might appear that diversity is an unfortunate inheritance. Yet although a source of tension, it need not lead to violent conflict. Nearly all countries worldwide are marked by diversity, and most of them do not experience diversity-related violent conflict.

In fact, diversity can be an enriching asset, especially if harnessed for development, innovation and unity. There are plentiful examples of diverse societies that have reaped large gains from the dynamism and creativity from interactions of different cultural, social and ethnic groups, including Ghana, Mauritius, Tanzania and Zambia (UNDP 2004). These effects are sometimes not easy to capture but are more visible internationally, where

benefits accrue from trade and other exchanges. It was the revered statesman Nelson Mandela who said that "once we won power, we chose to regard the diversity of colours and languages that had once been used against us as a source of strength". The stability that South Africa has experienced since its democratic transition in 1994 disproved the stereotype that a region or continent rich in diversity experiences political and development challenges simply as a consequence of that diversity.

Challenges arise not because diverse groups live together, or share the same national territory. They arise when tensions among groups lead to inefficient political decision making as well as to disproportionate access to material resources and patronage (UNDP 2004). So, if ethnic groups are to coexist peacefully with each other, they need to know that their views are fairly represented in national decision making, usually through systems of power sharing (UNRISD 1995).

Challenges also appear when groups are discriminated against, and when ethnic identities align with patterns of inequality or repression. For dealing with what appear to be ethnic disputes, state institutions therefore need to address underlying questions of economic and political marginalization, and to find acceptable ways to redistribute resources.

Diversity, then, cannot be ignored, and must be addressed squarely and managed innovatively (box 3.1). Force or assimilation has proved inadequate. This chapter focuses on

> ' *Diversity can be an enriching asset, especially if harnessed for development, innovation and unity*

how to positively manage diversity to achieve a transparent, free and fair electoral process.

In assessing how diversity impinges on the electoral process, one should bear in mind that structural economic and social conditions and access to power shape both the actions and perceptions of political leaders and voters. These conditions mould attitudes towards elections in particular, and to the electoral system in general. Thus structural issues of wealth, poverty and power distribution determine the orientation of the political system and electoral agenda. Experiences and perceptions of unfairness and discrimination can become conflict triggers around election time, allowing some politicians and parties to exploit diversity for their own ends. Historical and structural factors that have exacerbated inequality, insecurity or suspicion throw fuel on the fire.

## Elections

The administration of elections and tone of election campaigns assume a special resonance where diversity is based on ethnic, racial, religious, regional or class lines. They become highly charged "do or die" affairs for a host of reasons.

### Structure

How wealth is created and distributed between groups, as well as the level of development, influence the country's politics. Massive inequalities and marginalized or excluded groups can let a sense of grievance fester, which can explode, often around elections. This danger has

---

**Box 3.1  Managing diversity in Africa**

Managing diversity has become a public policy issue partly owing to the need to resolve conflicts from two sources: the demand of historically marginalized or excluded cultural, political, regional and socio-economic groups in the state for participation in governance; and internal migration and resulting issues of citizenship and identity.

These conflicts place democratic management of diversity at the centre of recent debates over national identity and the range of permissible cultural diversity, as well as the best way to combine the needs of these two aspects.

Framed this way, public policy concerns with such management rest on the realization that diversity can be a source of strength as well as a problem for the African state. How the state is designed and constructed, as well as how it stands on the questions of diversity, is at the heart of diversity-related conflicts—and how to diminish them.

*Source:* Jinadu 2010.

---

a historical dimension, in that the crisis of identity is not a product of contemporary events but rather one with deep roots (Deng 2008). The African state was carved out of diverse entities that gave the state a pluralistic configuration, making it a composite of distinct ethnic units, many of which would likely describe themselves at the time of colonization as nations in their own right (Deng 2008).

A legacy remains of the former colonial powers' preferential treatment of some indigenous groups and regions in political and economic policies (which led to wide disparities among ethnic groups in power, wealth, social services and development opportunities), sowing the seeds of intergroup conflict. At independence, most states failed to address these disparities, choosing instead to adopt wholesale constitutional and governance models prescribed by their colonizers. This uncritical borrowing haunts many countries' political and electoral systems.

### Inter-ethnic competition and mistrust

Large and small African states face this issue. Larger states such as the Democratic Republic of the Congo, Ethiopia, Nigeria and Sudan have suffered from civil wars partly caused by ethno-regional conflicts. Smaller countries have not been spared either, notably Burundi, Lesotho and Rwanda. More recently, states such as Côte d'Ivoire and Kenya have suffered considerable election-related violence that fed on ethnic grievances and competition for power. During elections, the ethnic and regional factors provided combustion to long-festering inter-ethnic and interregional tensions (box 3.2).

### Religion and race

These can be potent factors in politics, especially around elections. Sudan before partition in 2011 was, for example, mired in one of the longest civil wars in memory in Africa, based on religion and race between the north and south. In the end, self-determination of South Sudan was the solution. Before that, elections had not been meaningful in a polity with sharp disparities, regional differences and tensions.

In Algeria in 1992, the election debacle in which Islamic fundamentalists seemed poised to gain victory triggered a vicious internal conflict, while in Nigeria the religious factor remains potent, sometimes flaring up around election time.

Race and culture underlay the tensions that periodically broke out in Mauritania. Its society has been described as "not homogeneous but relatively compartmentalized, at least among people of African descent and those of Arab-Berber descent" (AGR III Mauritania Country Report 2012). This racial and ethnic cleavage has created conflict over how the "national question" should be addressed. Fortunately, however, competition between political parties in recent years has not been influenced by sectarianism because the parties take into account "the diversity factor and ensure balanced representation, especially during the preparation of lists of candidates" (AGR III Mauritania Country Report 2012).

In South Africa, apartheid had barred voting to the majority for many decades, leading to armed insurrection until the democratic transition in 1994. Although the racial factor is somewhat downplayed these days, a residue of race remains in voting patterns at local and provincial elections. Wealth distribution, too, is still racially skewed, raising the prospect of political and social tensions in the future.

### Geography

Remote areas tend to be marginalized during elections. Communities in the Niger Delta in Nigeria and swathes of the Democratic Republic of the Congo and Ethiopia, for example, are vulnerable to electoral manipulation. Weak infrastructure and communications are a disadvantage to peripheral communities in most African countries.

### Failure to grant citizenship

Citizenship is important for access to voting rights. As in Côte d'Ivoire, some citizens do not have access to this right because they are not original citizens of a particular region or area (see box 3.2). Autochthons versus settlers and migrants is a fault-line in most African countries, limiting access to political participation and especially the right to vote. Internal and external varieties of xenophobia persist in some states— only a few countries have granted the right to vote to migrants (and to those in the diaspora).

### Identity and access to resources

Identity and access to resources have fanned conflicts in at least three countries. In Senegal, owing to a separatist feelings stemming from marginalization, the Casamance region has long been a thorn in the side of the state. In Burkina Faso, latent social and political tensions, underpinned by ethnicity, relate to access to land and other natural resources as well as to economic opportunities. Mali, touted as a model of an emergent democracy in the past decade, saw long-simmering separatism among the Tuareg in the north come to a head in early 2012, when, after coup in Bamako, the separatists and the Maghreb branch of Al Qaeda exploited the power vacuum to declare a separate state of "Azawad", which has, however, failed to win international recognition (box 3.3). French military intervention, together with Malian forces and various countries of the Economic Community of West African States, beat back the rebel forces in February 2013. It is now possible that the next elections in Mali will be conducted during the second half of 2013.

### Marginalized women and youth

These two groups are politically sidelined in most of Africa. Although there are more women than men, their participation as election candidates is generally lower. But because political participation is often discussed in general terms, the absence or low visibility of women often goes unnoticed (Poluha 2002). Similarly, youth face conditions that discourage them from registering as voters and standing as election candidates.[1] Peoples with disabilities are another marginalized social group in the electoral process.

### Civil society organizations' reflection of society

Mirroring society's diversities, civil society organizations (CSOs) are not homogeneous but rooted in a range of backgrounds, and are thus not immune to the wider political and social currents in society. They can play a constructive role in moderating diversity-based conflict, but they can also be accomplices in inciting them.

### Incoherent role of state institutions in elections

State institutions could play a strategic role in addressing issues concerning diversity-related matters. If they have effective checks and balances, their accountability and credibility will improve, but they need to be coherent and autonomous enough in planning and administering elections. Bodies charged with running and supervising the electoral process, for example, should be independent of the executive and from state security institutions like the police and military. State institutions should at most play a limited facilitative role, rather than a direct one.

## Electoral systems' strengths and weaknesses

Africa has seen intense debate on the nature of an electoral system that is more representative and accommodating of diversity. The debate centres on which of the principal systems—first past the post (FPTP), proportional representation or a hybrid model of the two—is more suitable to better promote democratic management of diversity in the electoral process (annex 3.1). Lewis (1965, 71) noted that:

> The surest way to kill the idea of democracy in a plural society is to adopt the Anglo-American system of first past the post. If you belong to a minority in a new state, and are being asked to accept parliamentary democracy, you can hardly build much faith in the system if you win 30% of those votes and only 20% of the seats, or no seats at all. If minorities are to accept Parliament, they must be adequately represented in Parliament.

To correct distortions by FPTP, Lesotho and South Africa have adopted alternative systems that combine FPTP features with those of variants of proportional representation. For the same reason, Nigeria's Electoral Reform Committee recommended in 2008 that the country adopt a combination of the two systems' variants (although this approach has yet to be adopted).

What comes clear in the African Governance Report (AGR) III country reports is the preference for proportional representation: the overwhelming majority of respondents in 34 of the 40 countries surveyed in the AGR III Expert Opinion Survey agreed or strongly agreed with the view that electoral stability and diversity management can be attained through proportional representation as opposed to the majoritarian electoral system.

The reform of the electoral system, particularly to promote diversity through affirmative action to favour women in the legislature and public appointments, has also featured in the wider discourse on diversity (discussed in *Representation of women and minorities* below).

### First past the post

The FPTP system, especially in former British colonies in Africa, has come under close scrutiny. African countries that use the system divide the country into single-member electoral districts. The winner in each district is the candidate with the most votes (a plurality). The name comes from the analogy to a horse race in which the winner merely needs to edge out the next closest competitor.

This system has several advantages. The voters directly choose their representatives, which helps to make representatives' more accountable to their voters. The voting process is simple, because voters are required to choose only one candidate in each electoral district. Another benefit is that the system ensures that all geographical areas of a country are represented, which works against the party system and government fragmentation (ACE Electoral Knowledge Network 2011). FPTP also gives independent candidates the opportunity to get elected, and pressures political parties to broaden their scope beyond ethnic and other cleavages, especially in presidential elections.

The main disadvantage is that the winning candidate does not need to receive the majority of votes, so that his or her mandate could come from the minority—as Navrat (2003, 6) notes "The winning party bases its support on the biggest minority among the voters". A related drawback is that the number of seats a party has in parliament may not reflect its share of votes cast. Malawi's 2004 parliamentary elections, for example, "yielded parliamentary results that [were] not in tandem with the share of the national votes received by the parties. . . . The landscape could have been very different if the country had used a different electoral system, such as proportional representation" (AGR III Malawi Country Report 2012, 50).

FPTP also tends to create a system dominated by two parties, marginalizing third parties, and cannot easily

> *Africa has seen intense debate on the nature of an electoral system that is more representative and accommodating of diversity*

ensure ethnic and female representation in parliament, as it is prone to creating disincentives for accommodation and inclusiveness.

On this ground, Ghanaian participants in the focus group discussions felt that the country's FPTP system gives too much power to the winning candidate, thus failing to promote diversity in parliament. In the Expert Opinion Survey, however, two-thirds of respondents held the opposite view—that Ghana's electoral system promoted inclusion and representation of diverse groups (AGR III Ghana Country Report 2012).

*Proportional representation*
Proportional representation is anchored on the "concept of numbers", and when executed well, every vote counts (Testa 2011). Operationally, African systems (excluding South Africa's) have established thresholds for determining the minimum share of the votes a party needs to win a seat in parliament. The system has open or closed party lists: in the former, the party reveals its ranking of candidates to voters, but not in the latter.

Proportional representation offers several benefits, primarily that the number of seats a party has in parliament is proportional to the support (share of votes) it receives in an election (Drogus and Orvis 2008). Another advantage, in theory at least, is that smaller parties have a chance to be represented in parliament, but given the ruling parties' domination in Africa, it is hard for smaller parties to garner the votes to cross the representation threshold.

This system allows representation across the political, ethnic and gender spectra (especially women in parliament). In Burundi, for example, the system is based on ethnic quotas: the Hutus are allotted 60% of the seats, the Tutsis get 40% and the Twas receive three seats. Women should receive a minimum of 30% of the seats. In addition, 6 of the 100 seats in the parliament are reserved for ethnic balancing.

Proportional representation has two major disadvantages in Africa. It makes political parties rather than voters the political centre, rendering parliamentarians more accountable to their party than to their constituencies (because they know that their political fortunes depend on pleasing their party leader).

*Two-round system*
The winner must garner 50% plus one of the votes in the two-round system. If no candidate achieves this, a run-off (second round) is held between the two candidates with the most votes in the first round.

The two-round system has several benefits. It provides voters with a second choice after the first round. Linked to this is the opportunity for voters to change their minds about their choice of candidate. It also encourages bargaining, accommodation and coalescing among political parties, especially when the top two candidates seek support in the second round.

Some of the system's drawbacks are that it increases the cost of an election in holding a second round of

> *Proportional representation is anchored on the "concept of numbers", and when executed well, every vote counts*

voting, it places an extra burden on people to vote for a second time (lowering voter turnout) and its election results may not fully reflect parties' support among the electorate.

### Party block voting

The party block voting system (as with block voting) is based on multi-member electoral districts, although voters have a single vote and choose between party lists of candidates rather than individual candidates. The party that wins the most votes takes all seats in the district, and its entire list of candidates is elected (ACE Electoral Knowledge Network 2011).

It has many benefits, and is quite suitable for Cameroon, Chad and Djibouti, given their history of ethnic and regional tensions. Well executed, it can help address ethnic and regional problems by providing parliamentary balance, although the ruling-party hegemony in Cameroon and Chad makes that hard there. Another benefit is that the system encourages political parties in the three countries to broaden their membership beyond ethnic and regional constituencies. If this is done, political parties in these countries could then field candidates from divergent backgrounds (Navrat 2003).

The three countries' experience points to some major drawbacks. Because the party that wins takes all votes in a district, election results have been disproportional. Equally, because the system restricts voters to voting for parties only, it favours the ruling parties.

### Parallel voting

Parallel voting is based on the notion of two elections for parliament—that is, the seats in the parliaments of the African states that use it are grouped. Some seats are based on single-member constituencies through FPTP while the rest are based on the list proportional representation system. However, the proportion of seats a party wins is limited to the listed seats, not the overall share of the votes it wins nationally.

The system has some potential benefits. Smaller and opposition parties could gain from the proportional representation dimension, but given the suzerainty of the ruling parties in the countries that use it, the benefits are small. The system is well suited to minimize party fragmentation (ACE Electoral Knowledge Network 2011).

The core weakness is that the system does not guarantee overall proportionality (ACE Electoral Knowledge Network 2011). Consequently, some parties are usually shut out of representation, and smaller parties can at most only garner small shares of seats. Moreover, the ruling parties can use the power of incumbency to "gerrymander" the electoral districts in their favour. It is also a complex electoral system that leaves voters confused about its aims and operation (ACE Electoral Knowledge Network 2011), exposing them to manipulation by the ruling party.

### Mixed-member proportional system

This combines features of FPTP and proportional representation, and parliamentary seats are

> ❛ *The parallel voting system is well suited to minimize party fragmentation*

apportioned based on the two systems. In Lesotho—the only African state using it—80 of the 120 seats are based on FPTP and 40 on proportional representation.[2]

As used in Lesotho, the system has two major advantages. It allows for geographical representation, thus partly facilitating vertical accountability between some of the parliamentarians and their constituents. And it gives voters essentially two votes—party and locality, the former for political parties and the latter for representatives.

The disadvantages are that it creates two classes of parliamentarians— one accountable to political parties (those elected by proportional representation) and the other to voters (those elected under FPTP)—and that FPTP is constrained because the votes cast under it are not major determinants of the seats a party gets.

### Block voting

In Mauritius—the only African country with the block voting system—62 of the 70 parliamentary seats are allotted on the basis of block votes. The remaining eight are assigned by the election commission following a complex formula to "best losers" to ensure "fair and adequate" representation of each community.[3] Each electoral district has multiple members, and voters have as many votes as there are parliamentarians in each district. Candidates with the most votes (a plurality) win the seats in an electoral district.

The advantages are that voters can vote for candidates from various parties in each district, that the system rewards well-organized political parties (ACE Electoral Knowledge Network 2011) and that small parties can play important roles, especially if no party wins an overall majority of seats.

Two disadvantages stand out. One is that many votes can be wasted, particularly if they are not relevant to determining the election of a candidate or party. Another is that in the 1982 and 1995 elections, the party in opposition won every seat in the legislature with only 64% and 65% of the votes, creating difficulties for effective parliamentary functioning. Even the "best loser" formula has only partly addressed this weakness (ACE Electoral Knowledge Network 2011).

## Tackling diversity issues in the electoral process

### Constitutional provisions

Most African states are aware of the challenges in the political system and electoral process, and most constitutions have provisions to address diversity-related issues in governance, especially on representation in decision-making bodies, parliament and electoral institutions (box 3.4).

States are concerned about diversity and potential harmful consequences, which can make the electoral process even more highly contested than usual. Electoral campaigns can take on a special but negative resonance where diversity draws on ethnic, racial, regional or religious divisions, underlining the importance of sensitivity to diversity in electoral

*Electoral campaigns can take on a special but negative resonance where diversity draws on ethnic, racial, regional or religious divisions*

management boards and at each stage of the electoral process.

*Strengthening diversity sensitivity in electoral management boards*
The pivotal institution in the electoral process is the electoral management board (EMB).[4] How alert it is to diversity issues is crucial, and this often reflects its composition, which in turn should mirror wider society (box 3.5).

Before the democratic transitions in the 1990s, most EMBs were predominantly male and most appointees were selected by the head of state—and so they did not reflect diversity in society. This has gradually changed in the past decade. For instance, women's representation is no longer ignored: in Ghana, the Electoral Commission is made up of three women and four men, all with college and university education and from a variety of professional and ethnic backgrounds (AGR III Ghana Country Report 2012).

African countries have also tried to reflect significant national diversities in the composition of EMB members, as part of the wider governance processes of managing diversity, even when, as in the rare case of South Africa, members' positions at the EMB are open to competition based on merit, through public advertisements.

Some countries' constitutional provisions—Ethiopia, Kenya, Nigeria, South Africa and Tanzania, for example—require appointments to public political office to reflect diversity. However, countries with no specific constitutional or statutory provisions for diversity in EMB membership reflect it in appointing members, more as conventions than the law.

Women form half of Malawi's Electoral Commission (box 3.6), and similar female representation can be found in EMBs in Cape Verde, Mauritius and South Africa. Women have chaired EMBs in Malawi, Sierra Leone and South Africa in recent years. The same progress cannot be claimed for ethnic and racial minority groups, youth and the disabled, however.

### Managing diversity in the electoral cycle

Delimiting constituencies
One element in the transparency and fairness of the electoral process is how constituencies are delimited. Since that entails creating constituencies or redrawing boundaries, it should be done transparently, to prevent political manipulation and controversy. The Electoral Commission of Kenya, for instance, was believed to have gerrymandered constituency boundaries to the disadvantage of communities it saw as opposing the Kenya African National Union in the 1997 election (AGR III Kenya Country Report 2012). This allowed it, with 38% of the votes, to secure 107 seats to the opposition's 103—with 62% of the votes. Gerrymandering has also been recorded in Cameroon, Nigeria and Uganda.

Safeguards are needed to prohibit or pre-empt manipulative delimitation, and underline why the body charged with this task should be guaranteed its independence, and why it should be non-partisan. It should also be sensitive to the interests of minorities and social groups such as the poor, youth and smaller linguistic groups. The latter groups include the poor who live in slums on the margins of cities—they risk being excluded when boundaries are drawn or redrawn, as are pastoralists, who move their livestock for sustenance for part of the year.

In Sierra Leone, constituency demarcations have produced different election results even if the underlying voting patterns remain the same, ruining the credibility of the delimitation process (AGR III Sierra Leone Country Report 2012).

A consensus is needed on the minimum and maximum numbers of voters per constituency. But unless that draws on a recent population census or official estimates, delimitation can become guesswork, even sparking controversy by reducing, maintaining or increasing the number of constituencies. Ghana, for instance, had 200 constituencies in 1987 based on a population estimate of 13.5 million; the 2004 demarcation was based on a population of about 18.9 million (AGR III Ghana Country Report 2012). Indeed, the decision of the Election Commission to add 30 more constituencies to reflect this greater population generated much interest and even controversy over the criteria used, but given the transparency of the exercise, expert opinion was positive on how the commission handled the matter.

## Registering voters

Registering voters is one of the most contentious in Africa, given the high stakes in elections. It, too, can be manipulated and abused.

Deliberately inflating voter registration lists or undercounting numbers registered are common practices, and some authorities make it hard for certain sections of the population to register at all, such as people in remote areas and slums, the displaced and refugees. Opposition and youth parties often struggle to overcome the antics of incumbents and register.

Incumbents in some countries such as Cameroon, Kenya, Malawi and Uganda have twisted voter registration in various ways. Cameroon, for example, saw a steep increase in voters in the 2002 election, largely owing to a voter-registration campaign undertaken by the ruling party, which offered to waive the fee for people's voting cards in (largely rural) supportive regions (Albaugh 2011).

Other challenges include multiple registrations and dead people ("ghost voters") on the rolls. The Uganda country report noted that it is complicated to update and display registers, quoting an expert respondent who observed that in areas with widespread support for the ruling party, many new people are registered and the registers are not properly cleaned. Thus for any party to "rig" the rolls, "it does it properly where it has an upper hand and the people to rig for it" (AGR III Uganda Country Report 2012, 66). And in only 22 countries did most expert respondents believe that voter registration was "mostly or always" credible and accepted, pointing to widespread scepticism (figure 3.1).

> *Electoral management boards should be sensitive to the interests of minorities and social groups*

# Figure 3.1 Voter registration is credible and accepted

Share of experts surveyed, by country (%)

- Mostly or always
- Sometimes
- Not at all or rarely

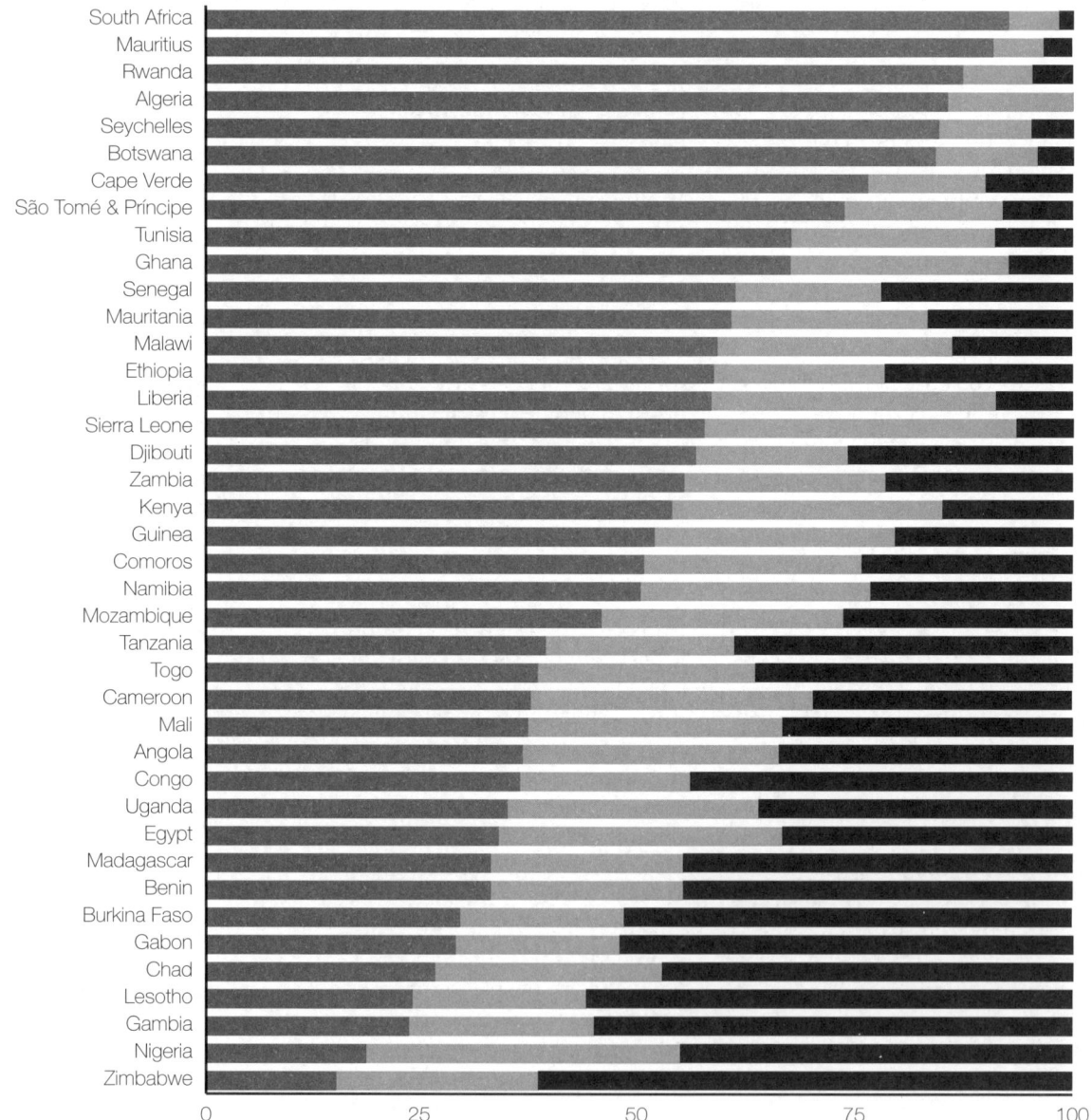

*Source:* AGR III Expert Opinion Survey 2012.

More than 90% of expert respondents in Mauritius considered the exercise credible, transparent and well conducted (AGR III Mauritius Country Report 2012). This view may well come from good practices: voter registration is a continuous process open to anyone qualified at any time. The voters' list should be first advertised in the Government Gazette and at least three recognized daily journals before being published at the time and places mentioned in the advertisement (AGR III Mauritius Country Report 2012). This secures the widest publicity, and objections can be brought by any member of the public on names and other information in the list.

Turnout in the Tunisian election in 2011 was impressive. For the first time, the diaspora, accounting for 10% of the country's population, could vote (AGR III Tunisia Country Report 2012). And countries that do not give a vote to diaspora members should, as well as to internally displaced people and refugees of long-time residence. A denial of the vote is a denial of the right to diversity.

The technology for voter registration has opened new avenues. For instance, since 2010 voter registration in Rwanda has been conducted electronically via mobile phone and the Internet. Registration and correction of errors are preceded and accompanied by mass communication methods such as radio and TV shows, debates and public announcements, as well as many field visits by officials of the National Election Commission (AGR III Rwanda Country Report 2012). These technologies are positive for extensive voter registration, but the reach towards rural and disadvantaged communities will remain a longer journey for some time.

### Educating voters

Beyond the construction of effective and transparent electoral systems, democracy building entails inculcation of democratic values, which rests on a strong civic culture. Voter education is an attempt to spread the message of the need to claim and exercise the right to vote, and so contribute to governance by selecting representatives. It also aims to increase turnout during elections and to reduce spoilt ballots.

EMBs bear the responsibility for voter education in most states, often backed by CSOs. The Malawi Electoral Commission admits that it has too few resources and so relies heavily on CSOs, while playing a coordinating function (AGR III Malawi Country Report 2012). Yet the CSOs tend to concentrate their programmes in urban centres, which offer better facilities and transport, but it is the rural areas that have greater need for voter education, owing to lower literacy rates there.

The Electoral Commission of Kenya has made a systematic attempt to educate voters among internally displaced people, pastoralist communities, women, youth and religious leaders (AGR III Kenya Country Report 2012), but as elsewhere on the continent, the drive failed to meet the needs of illiterate voters. In Cape Verde, civic

> *Electoral management boards bear the responsibility for voter education in most African states*

education is crucial for rural populations, the elderly and those with little education—they needed to be informed "where and how to vote and why voting is important" (AGR III Cape Verde Country Report 2012). CSOs' efforts were also thinly spread out in Nigeria, and not sustained (AGR III Nigeria Country Report 2012).

Voter education is often conducted too close to an election to have much of an impact. Lack of cooperation can also stymie it: in Ghana, its two major providers are the Electoral Commission and the National Commission for Civic Education, but they have not worked well together, as hinted at by the 2% spoilt and invalid ballots in the 2008 election (AGR III Ghana Country Report 2012).

Campaigning

Campaign rules are usually spelt out in electoral laws or codes, which often stipulate penalties for infringing them as well as the length of the campaign, though not many have provisions on addressing diversity (box 3.7).

As the electorate consists of different groups, campaigning methods necessarily vary, for example, among rural and less literate voters or sophisticated urbanites. Similarly, access to potential women voters may vary according to the wider social and religious context, which may make it hard to reach women, especially outside working hours. How to reach out to youth voters like students may require more innovative approaches.

Still, the public meeting or rally is the most common format in both rural and urban areas, heating parties' competition for venues such as stadiums, halls and urban open spaces. Some ruling parties attempt to deny other parties access to these venues, prompting violence at times. But such meetings (and similar events) do not cater to people living with disabilities, and if held outside working hours they may also discourage women from attending.

Most inter-party violence occurs during campaigning (chapter 5), usually as minor scuffles but potentially becoming an iterative cycle of violence. Politicians may make matters worse with rhetoric to drum up ethnic sentiment in areas with large settler populations, for example.

A party's access to the media is one of its most crucial assets, and electoral law should allow access to publicly owned media especially, which should observe such access in letter and spirit. But because most countries' public media do not provide fair coverage to diverse groups and voices during campaigns, reasonably fair coverage is needed of campaign

## Box 3.7 Educating voters on diversity

Vital as information about the technical aspects of voting can be, there is a compelling need to include the issue of diversity, and political and social tolerance, in voter education programmes.

Not only should efforts be made to reach out to marginalized groups—as country reports advocate—the themes of unity in diversity, responsible citizenship and peaceful conduct of politics should also be infused. This would have an empowering effect on those receiving voter education.

*Source:* AGR III Country Reports 2012.

activities and messages by all registered contending parties. The EMB and inter-party liaison committees should deal with cases that block the "levelling of the campaign playing field", and resolve them before they explode into serious violence.

### Integrity of the voting process

The integrity of voting on election day depends crucially on whether electoral law is followed, and whether procedures are properly carried out (from observing polling-station opening and closing times, opening and sealing ballot boxes, to counting and announcing results). If some stage in this process is compromised, the result is tainted. Most disputes about elections relate to tampering with ballot boxes, and many elections have foundered on these disputes, some of them triggering conflict and violence. Some of the challenges are genuine and not orchestrated to facilitate rigging, but inordinate delays in announcing election results cause suspicions among contenders over the EMB and the incumbent, undermining the election's credibility.

On a positive note, some country reports observe orderly and peaceful voting—in Cape Verde, for example, over four parliamentary and presidential elections (AGR III Cape Verde Country Report 2012).

Common challenges to voting in Kenya include distance and lack of facilities:

> The majority of primary schools, secondary schools and polytechnics gazetted as polling stations lack adequate

space or are located far [away]. The ones in populated areas do not have adequate stream to facilitate the voting process. In the arid and semi-arid areas, voters are forced to walk for long distances to reach polling stations. For the pastoral communities it becomes unpredictable where they would vote from (AGR III Kenya Country Report 2012, 82).

Disabled or illiterate people should also be given assistance to reach the polling station to cast their vote. They should not be influenced or commandeered by electoral authorities or party agents. In some countries, other groups that have access in law to voting include prisoners, and facilities should therefore be available to them.

### Election observation and monitoring

Election observation and monitoring are vital for promoting elections' integrity. In 1990–2005, international election observation became a global norm as the number of missions expanded hugely (Global Commission on Elections, Democracy and Security 2012), and the proportion of authoritarian incumbents who were re-elected fell by almost 40%.

Domestic monitors have a special role. Unlike international observers who tend to come into a country a few days before the election and leave shortly afterwards, they are the real local watchdogs (AGR III Malawi Country Report 2012). In the 2007 election in Kenya, some 24,063 domestic observers were deployed out of suspicion that the

*❛ Election observation and monitoring are vital for promoting elections' integrity*

incumbent regime might manipulate the election outcome (AGR III Kenya Country Report 2012).

Before the advent of new technology and social media, many states had a monopoly on information. This power sometimes restricted or delayed information on vote counting, and helped to rig elections through "stuffed" ballot boxes. Mobile phones and cameras have made it possible to communicate posted results instantly by voice, picture and video. Party agents, observers and monitors can communicate results as fast as state agencies and can report discrepancies immediately. Similarly, information about numbers of voters per voting station is no longer a monopoly of an EMB and incumbent party.

Such technology has gone some way to deter brazen rigging of results. Experiments in Uganda (and Afghanistan) suggest that it could cut electoral fraud by up to 60% (*The Economist* 2012). In those experiments, local researchers were deployed to polling stations, with digital cameras and smart phones to take photographs of the publicly posted election tallies. In the Ugandan experiment, the sample consisted of 1,000 polling stations around the country:

> Letters were again sent to half the sample reminding them about the requirement to display vote tallies and telling them that a photo would be taken of their count. . . . The researchers were able immediately to send their data to a server. . . . Academics there could then check to see if the

voting numbers had been falsified by looking for give-away number-patterns. They found that vote tampering and ballot-box tampering were much lower among polling stations that had received warning that a photo would be taken of their tally than among those that did not (*The Economist* 2012).

These experiments and recent experience in Kenya, Senegal and Zimbabwe show encouraging results of how new technology and social media can quickly spot and disseminate electoral fraud.

## Representation of women and minorities

*Women—commitments still to be met*
Women have greatly increased their representation in electoral institutions, parliaments and governments, including the cabinet. For example, in 2003 Rwanda adopted gender equity in its governance system, and women held 56% of the seats in its Chamber of Deputies, 35% of the Senate and 27% in the government (AGR III Rwanda Country Report 2012). Women also accounted for 35% of permanent secretaries, 61% of supreme court judges and 32% of mayors and deputy mayors, suggesting that gender balance has made progress. Mauritania, too, since 2007 has made progress, through new appointments of women as regional governors, and the creation of a quota for women in public service posts (AGR III Mauritania Country Report 2012).

Burkina Faso's parliament passed a law in 2009 to strengthen women's

---

**'** *Women have greatly increased their representation in electoral institutions, parliaments and governments*

representation by setting quotas for legislative and local elections, requiring any list of candidates submitted by a political party for parliamentary and local elections to be at least 30% for the benefit of one or the other sex. Kenya's constitution, approved a year later, has provisions for affirmative action on representation of women, youth, minorities and people with disabilities, and workers. It specifies, for instance, that the National Assembly of 350 members is to consist of 47 women elected by registered voters of the counties and 12 members nominated by parliamentary political parties, according to their proportion of members of the National Assembly.

The Tunisian electoral system promotes gender participation. Decree 35, Article 16 states that "candidates shall file their candidacy applications on the basis of parity between men and women". Lists that do not follow the principle of gender parity will only be admitted when there is an odd number of seats in the relevant constituency. In addition, women have benefited from the rule of alternation.

Other reform measures include the following:

- the constitutions of Burkina Faso, Rwanda, Senegal, Tanzania and Uganda contain provisions for women's quotas in parliament;

- the electoral laws of Sudan and Tanzania have parliamentary quotas for women; and

- in Côte d'Ivoire, Malawi, Mozambique and South Africa,

some parties' political regulations require them to nominate a proportion of female candidates for parliamentary elections.[5]

The AGR III Sierra Leone Country Report 2012 found that although "there are no affirmative action provisions in the country's laws", 85% of expert survey respondents supported such laws or quotas to enhance women's representation. It also found that a coalition of political-party women's groups has been engaged in advocacy to achieve the 30% legislation for women's parliamentary representation (Sierra Leone Truth & Reconciliation Commission 2004).

Yet despite such commitments, most governments have registered slow progress. In Cape Verde, where indicators point to democratic advances overall, the presence of women in parties' key decision-making bodies is only 15–22%, and their representation in local and national assemblies is 18% (AGR III Cape Verde Country Report 2012). Similarly in Mauritius, the proportion of seats held by women in parliament was only 18% in 2010, although this marked more than a doubling from 7% in 1990 (AGR III Mauritius Country Report 2012).

Tables 3.1–3.3 give recent data on women's representation in parliament and where women serve as presiding officers of parliaments. Only one country has more than half its lower house of parliament filled by women—and none has for the upper house.

Executive branch elections have made women head of state and of

## Table 3.1 Women in African parliaments, lower or single house, October 2012

| Country | Election | Seats[a] | Women | Share of women in national parliaments (%) |
|---|---|---|---|---|
| Rwanda | 2008 | 80 | 45 | 56.3 |
| Senegal | 2012 | 150 | 64 | 42.7 |
| South Africa | 2009 | 400 | 169 | 42.3 |
| Mozambique | 2009 | 250 | 98 | 39.2 |
| Tanzania | 2010 | 350 | 126 | 36.0 |
| Uganda | 2011 | 386 | 135 | 35.0 |
| Angola | 2012 | 220 | 75 | 34.1 |
| Algeria | 2012 | 462 | 146 | 31.6 |
| Burundi | 2010 | 105 | 32 | 30.5 |
| Ethiopia | 2010 | 547 | 152 | 27.8 |
| Tunisia | 2011 | 217 | 58 | 26.7 |
| South Sudan | 2011 | 332 | 88 | 26.5 |
| Sudan | 2010 | 354 | 87 | 24.6 |
| Namibia | 2009 | 78 | 19 | 24.4 |
| Malawi | 2009 | 193 | 43 | 22.3 |
| Mauritania | 2006 | 95 | 21 | 22.1 |
| Eritrea | 1994 | 150 | 33 | 22.0 |
| Cape Verde | 2011 | 72 | 15 | 20.8 |
| Mauritius | 2010 | 69 | 13 | 18.8 |
| Madagascar | 2010 | 365 | 64 | 17.5 |
| Morocco | 2011 | 395 | 67 | 17.0 |
| Libya | 2012 | 200 | 33 | 16.5 |
| Gabon | 2011 | 114 | 18 | 15.8 |
| Burkina Faso | 2007 | 111 | 17 | 15.3 |
| Zimbabwe | 2008 | 214 | 32 | 15.0 |
| Chad | 2011 | 188 | 28 | 14.9 |
| Cameroon | 2007 | 180 | 25 | 13.9 |
| Djibouti | 2008 | 65 | 9 | 13.8 |
| Somalia | 2012 | 275 | 38 | 13.8 |
| Swaziland | 2008 | 66 | 9 | 13.6 |
| Niger | 2011 | 113 | 15 | 13.3 |
| Sierra Leone | 2007 | 124 | 16 | 12.9 |
| Central African Republic | 2011 | 104 | 13 | 12.5 |
| Zambia | 2011 | 157 | 18 | 11.5 |
| Togo | 2007 | 81 | 9 | 11.1 |
| Côte d'Ivoire | 2011 | 254 | 28 | 11.0 |
| Liberia | 2011 | 73 | 8 | 11.0 |
| Mali | 2007 | 147 | 15 | 10.2 |

*(continued)*

**Table 3.1 Women in African parliaments, lower or single house, October 2012 (continued)**

| Country | Election | Seats[a] | Women | Share of women in national parliaments (%) |
|---|---|---|---|---|
| Equatorial Guinea | 2008 | 100 | 10 | 10.0 |
| Guinea-Bissau | 2008 | 100 | 10 | 10.0 |
| Kenya | 2007 | 224 | 22 | 9.8 |
| Dem. Rep. Congo | 2011 | 492 | 44 | 8.9 |
| Benin | 2011 | 83 | 7 | 8.4 |
| Ghana | 2008 | 230 | 19 | 8.3 |
| Botswana | 2009 | 63 | 5 | 7.9 |
| Gambia | 2012 | 53 | 4 | 7.5 |
| Congo | 2012 | 136 | 10 | 7.4 |
| Nigeria | 2011 | 352 | 24 | 6.8 |
| Comoros | 2009 | 33 | 1 | 3.0 |
| Egypt | 2011 | 508 | 10 | 2.0 |

a. Figures correspond to the number of seats currently filled in parliament.

*Source:* "Women in National Parliaments," Inter-Parliamentary Union, http://www.ipu.org/wmn-e/classif.htm, accessed 29 January 2013.

government in Liberia and Malawi, and head of state in Mozambique. Twenty-two countries have more than 20% of women in the cabinet, headed by Cape Verde, São Tomé and Príncipe and South Africa (annex 3.2).

Still, the journey ahead to ensure gender equity in representation is long and much remains to be done. This point was spelt out by recommendations of the Eighth African Governance Forum in 2011 and in the expert panels: in only 14 countries did at least half the respondents believe that women mostly or always played a major role in the electoral process in their country (figure 3.2).

### Youth, people with disabilities and the diaspora

Although most states profess a commitment to upgrading youth participation in the political process,

progress has been slow in practice. In Ghana, exclusion of youth in governance and decision making is deeply rooted in the country's politics and traditional practice (AGR III Ghana Country Report 2012). Yet most parties there, as elsewhere in Africa, identify youth as the nucleus of their support, and have sought to consolidate this support by setting up youth leagues. Rwanda and Uganda have also taken steps to increase youth representation in politics, including affirmation action seats for youth and people with disabilities (AGR III Uganda Country Report 2012). An African Governance Forum workshop made several resolutions on youth participation (box 3.8).

The broad impact of youth in politics goes further than seats in parliament. Events in North Africa

**Table 3.2 Women in African parliaments, upper house or senate, October 2012**

| Country | Elections | Seats[a] | Women | Share of women in national parliaments (%) |
|---|---|---|---|---|
| Burundi | 2010 | 41 | 19 | 46.3 |
| Swaziland | 2008 | 30 | 12 | 40.0 |
| Rwanda | 2011 | 26 | 10 | 38.5 |
| South Africa | 2009 | 53 | 17 | 32.1 |
| Namibia | 2010 | 26 | 7 | 26.9 |
| Zimbabwe | 2008 | 99 | 24 | 24.2 |
| Sudan | 2010 | 28 | 5 | 17.9 |
| Gabon | 2009 | 102 | 18 | 17.6 |
| Ethiopia | 2010 | 135 | 22 | 16.3 |
| Mauritania | 2009 | 56 | 8 | 14.3 |
| Congo | 2011 | 72 | 10 | 13.9 |
| Liberia | 2011 | 30 | 4 | 13.3 |
| Madagascar | 2010 | 164 | 20 | 12.2 |
| South Sudan | 2011 | 50 | 5 | 10.0 |
| Nigeria | 2011 | 109 | 7 | 6.4 |
| Algeria | 2009 | 136 | 7 | 5.1 |
| Dem. Rep. Congo | 2007 | 108 | 5 | 4.6 |
| Egypt | 2012 | 180 | 5 | 2.8 |
| Morocco | 2009 | 270 | 6 | 2.2 |

a. Figures correspond to the number of seats currently filled in parliament.

*Source:* "Women in National Parliaments," Inter-Parliamentary Union, www.ipu.org/wmn-e/classif.htm, accessed 29 January 2013.

**Table 3.3 Female presiding officers in African parliaments, January 2010**

| Country | Women as presiding officers of parliaments |
|---|---|
| Botswana | National Assembly |
| Gabon | Senate |
| Gambia | National Assembly |
| Ghana | Parliament |
| Lesotho | National Assembly |
| Rwanda | Chamber of Deputies |
| Swaziland | Senate |
| Zimbabwe | Senate |

*Source:* "Women in Politics: 2010," United Nations, www.un.org/womenwatch/daw/public/womeninpolitics2010/wmnmap10_en.pdf, accessed 29 January 2013.

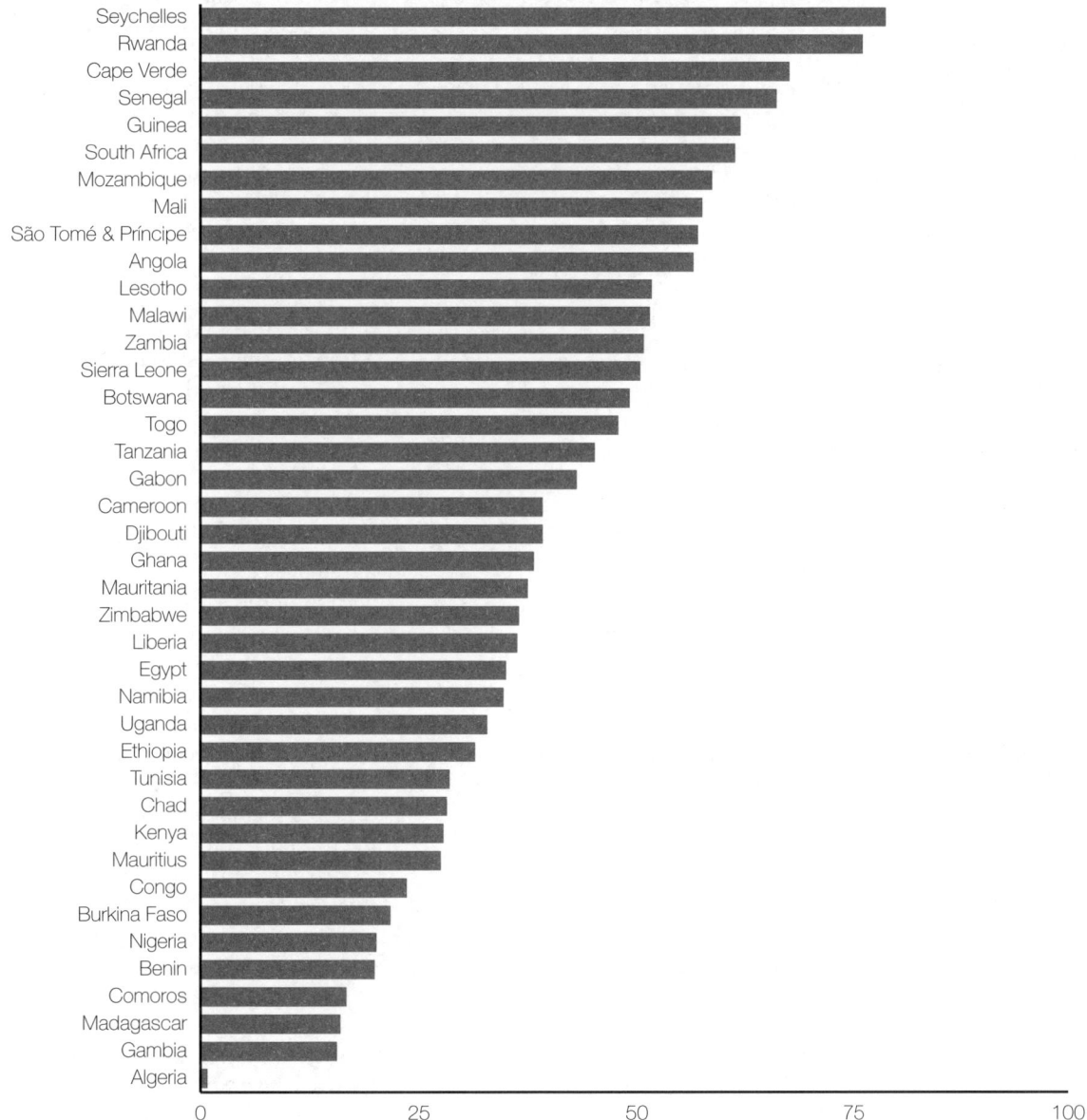

**Figure 3.2 Women play a major role in the electoral process—mostly or always**

Share of experts surveyed agreeing with the statement, by country (%)

|  |
|---|
| Seychelles |
| Rwanda |
| Cape Verde |
| Senegal |
| Guinea |
| South Africa |
| Mozambique |
| Mali |
| São Tomé & Príncipe |
| Angola |
| Lesotho |
| Malawi |
| Zambia |
| Sierra Leone |
| Botswana |
| Togo |
| Tanzania |
| Gabon |
| Cameroon |
| Djibouti |
| Ghana |
| Mauritania |
| Zimbabwe |
| Liberia |
| Egypt |
| Namibia |
| Uganda |
| Ethiopia |
| Tunisia |
| Chad |
| Kenya |
| Mauritius |
| Congo |
| Burkina Faso |
| Nigeria |
| Benin |
| Comoros |
| Madagascar |
| Gambia |
| Algeria |

0    25    50    75    100

*Source:* AGR III Expert Opinion Survey 2012.

and Senegal in 2011 and 2012 demonstrate how youth can be catalysts in the democratic transition and defenders of constitutionalism. Youths were in the forefront of campaigns for change in such countries as Egypt, Libya and Tunisia (see chapter 2). In Senegal, they were the focal points of protests against President Abdoulaye Wade's attempt to change the constitution and run for a third term, and the major force in forming a coalition of CSOs and parties called the June 23 Movement (named after the day when the people of Senegal forced the National Assembly to cancel a proposal to amend the constitution). The movement was also very active in monitoring the electoral process in March and April 2012 that saw Wade's defeat, and the ascendancy of a new president, Macky Sall.

For people with disabilities, opportunities remain very limited. Although some have taken part in electioneering with CSOs, only three people with disabilities have ever contested parliamentary seats in Ghana's Fourth Republic, for example. Sierra Leone, though, provides a stirring example of a country trying to remove electoral barriers for those with disabilities (box 3.9).

Another group that reflects social diversity in Africa is the diaspora. Although its numbers have expanded in the past decade, only a few countries give voting rights to diaspora members. In Cape Verde, the diaspora vote is becoming increasingly influential and their 8 reserved seats (out of 72) can make an impact, especially in a presidential election (AGR III Cape Verde Country Report 2012).

## Religion and diversity management
Religion is not a decisive factor in the politics of many Sub-Saharan countries, but where it is, it can add to tensions and even lead to civil war—as in Sudan, which saw the creation of South Sudan in 2011.

In Somalia, too, religious extremism has contributed to internal divisions and civil war. In Nigeria, the religious factor has underlain the North–South fault-line, and more recently a version of fundamentalist Islam (represented by the Boko Haram sect) has threatened peace and unity. Bombings of Christian churches and property as well as killings of believers heighten the political temperature in that country. And religion cannot be completely ignored in the politics of Cameroon, Chad, Côte d'Ivoire, Ghana, Kenya and Senegal, for instance.

In North Africa, however, religion is a potent force in national politics. After the Arab Spring, Islamic parties such as the Moslem Brotherhood made large parliamentary gains, as in Egypt and Tunisia, which will have major repercussions. These parties will, though, have to coexist with important minorities, such as Coptic Christians in Egypt.

## Challenges for managing diversity

Africa's challenges for managing its diversity cannot be underestimated. Many governments acknowledge its magnitude and complexity, but they still have much to do. Uganda, for example, caters to ethnic and religious diversities with universal adult suffrage but offers no special government positions for ethnic and religious minorities (AGR III Uganda Country Report 2012). Some religious (Moslem) and ethnic (Batwa) minorities are still marginalized.

In Liberia, focus group discussions in 2011 indicated that although the

> **Box 3.9  Some disabilities overcome in Sierra Leone**
>
> Years of civil war, including a campaign by the rebel Revolutionary United Front to amputate the hands and feet of citizens to discourage participation in the 1996 elections, produced a large disabled population. Elections since have seen numerous efforts to include people with disabilities.
>
> Some simple but effective steps include using polling places without stairs or allowing disabled voters to skip lines, which can often be hours long.
>
> Without more efforts like these, people with disabilities in countries around the world will continue to face great difficulties in being part of the electoral process.
>
> *Source:* Global Commission on Elections, Democracy and Security 2012.

political system allows for inclusion and representation in political parties, managing diversity of the different political groups was only partial (AGR III Liberia Country Report 2012). Representatives in parliament had not made sufficient effort to set up a channel for bringing to the fore issues of managing diversity among the different constituencies.

Regionalism in Sierra Leone failed to strengthen diversity management against a background of claims that the ruling party sought to strengthen identity politics that links them to certain ethnic groups (AGR III Sierra Leone Country Report 2012). In Ethiopia, some focus group participants mentioned "unhealthy inter-ethnic relations, disputes over borders and territories, religious issues, competition over scarce resources, group disputes over various issues, and differences on the issue of right to self-determination as factors that often lead to conflicts" (AGR III Ethiopia Country Report 2012, xii).

Encouraging attempts at diversity management came from some other countries, however. In Ghana, major political parties took steps regionally to encourage competitive and inclusive party politics and governance. Both the National Democratic Congress party and the New Patriotic Party have shown a preference for a north–south joint presidential–vice-presidential ticket in an effort to show some balance and have broader appeal (AGR III Ghana Country Report 2012). (The same balancing of regional interests and appeal has characterized the presidential and vice-presidential tickets in Nigeria over the decades.)

Most countries, though, do not have statutory electoral quotas for any diversities. Most attempts are voluntary, lacking coordination and strategy. Three suggestions are to (AGR III Namibia Country Report 2012):

- monitor composition of the public service according to disaggregated data on the basis of race, ethnicity, colour, religion, gender, disability and sexual orientation;

- adopt policies and measures (including staff training) that promote tolerance, and that affirm and celebrate diversity and inclusiveness, such as special days; and

- introduce equal-opportunity and affirmative-action laws

and regulations to ensure that the full scope of diversity is included (for example, disability, race and gender).

## Conclusions and recommendations

How diversity issues are addressed at each stage of the electoral process contributes to its overall quality and thus integrity, underlining the need to address these issues sensitively and comprehensively, and so preempt conflict.

*Addressing structural imbalances*
As the structural factors that shape diversity are varied, the political economy of diversity has to be understood. Uneven development, the rural–urban divide, and centre–periphery relationships create inequalities and grievances, which are often expressed around election time. But a single electoral cycle is not long enough to address the political-economy challenges.

Medium- and long-term policies and programmes are necessary to tackle poverty reduction, move to an equitable distribution of public goods and services such as education, and redress regional and social economic imbalances. They should be sensitive and comprehensive, formulated with groups representing the beneficiaries.

*Attenuating inequitable political representation*
Most studies have shown that women, minority groups and people with disabilities are poorly represented in parliament and electoral institutions. Special measures

> *Medium- and long-term policies and programmes are necessary to tackle poverty reduction and redress regional and social economic imbalances*

should be considered to raise their representation. There is a reasonable case for affirmative action to encourage their members to run for office or to serve in EMBs. These groups need to be empowered economically, to provide a basis for their capacity to enter the political system.

Most of the country reports produced under the auspices of the African Peer Review Mechanism recommend measures such as devolving power from the centre and setting up bodies for minority protection. Most AGR III country reports advocated electoral reforms such as proportional representation. Both these sets of reforms should be buttressed by measures that transform the state to ensure autonomy of its various organs from excessive dominance by the executive.

### Strengthening electoral institutions
Electoral institutions like EMBs and delimitation commissions are frontline institutions providing the "face" of the electoral process. Their credibility hinges on their transparency and accountability. Countries that have promoted and strengthened such institutions appear to have been more successful in addressing diversity than those that have not. They have, among other things, granted their electoral institutions some autonomy, cultivating public trust in them.

Other countries have work to do, so that their EMBs should have enough autonomy to become non-partisan institutions, free from

executive interference. Further, EMBs should be endowed with the necessary power and authority to create mechanisms to promote cooperation among political parties, relevant CSOs and candidates, with the objective of building trust and consensus among those participating in the electoral process, and preventing or defusing electoral disputes.

EMBs' funding and staffing should be strengthened, the latter particularly to ensure that the composition reflects society's wider diversity. Women, members of ethnic groups and various religious faiths with requisite skills and experience should be encouraged to serve.

### Ensuring responsible media
Newspapers and radio sometimes broadcast "hate language," triggering sectarian clashes. The media should be trained to be more sensitive and professional in handling diversity-related conflicts during election periods.

The media should also ventilate issues on voter registration and education as well as diversity, striving to reach beyond a narrow partisan agenda. Many controversies about the electoral process relate to the credibility of voter registration, and the media's handling of this matter can inflame passions. Sober and accurate reporting is therefore imperative.

The public media should grant fair coverage of campaign activities and messages by all registered contending parties.

> **' Countries that have promoted and strengthened electoral institutions have been more successful in addressing diversity than those that have not**

### Building capacity

Just as it is vital to strengthen EMBs to make them more autonomous and effective, so it is imperative that stakeholders in the electoral process increase their monitoring capacity. Political parties, the media, CSOs and other stakeholders should develop a professional approach for inter-party dialogue and consultations with EMBs at all stages of the electoral process.

CSOs can play an important medium- and long-term role as mechanisms for holding governments, parties and relevant stakeholders accountable in the electoral process. Their unfettered development will be fundamentally useful for developing social identities across primordial identities.

### Managing and resolving conflict

Elections cannot hope to avoid disputes or conflict completely, but strong conflict-resolution mechanisms can forestall or manage them. Thus they should be built or strengthened at local, regional and national levels. Electoral institutions should explore and identify such mechanisms, and strengthen them. Traditional institutions of reconciliation can be used, especially locally.

# Annex 3.1 Prevalence of electoral systems

| Country | Presidential election | Parliamentary election |
|---|---|---|
| Algeria | Two-round system | List proportional representation |
| Angola | Two-round system | List proportional representation |
| Benin | Two-round system | List proportional representation |
| Botswana | First past the post | First past the post |
| Burkina Faso | Two-round system | List proportional representation |
| Burundi | Absolute majority (two-round system) | List proportional representation |
| Cameroon | Two-round system | Party block voting |
| Cape Verde | Two-round system | List proportional representation |
| Central African Republic | Two-round system | Two-round system |
| Chad | Two-round system | Party block voting |
| Comoros | First past the post | Two-round system |
| Congo | Two-round system | Two-round system |
| Côte d'Ivoire | Two-round system | Parallel (party block voting and first past the post) |
| Dem. Rep. Congo | Two-round system | Parallel (party block voting and first past the post) |
| Djibouti | Two-round system | Party block voting |
| Egypt | Two-round system | Two-round system |
| Equatorial Guinea | First past the post | List proportional representation |
| Eritrea | Elected by parliament | First past the post |
| Ethiopia | n.a. | First past the post |
| Gabon | Two-round system | Two-round system |
| Gambia | Two-round system | First past the post |
| Ghana | Two-round system | First past the post |
| Guinea | Two-round system | Parallel (party block voting and first past the post) |
| Guinea-Bissau | Two-round system | List proportional representation |
| Kenya | Two-round system | First past the post |
| Lesotho | King (hereditary) | Mixed member proportional |
| Liberia | Two-round system | Two-round system |
| Libya | n.a. | n.a. |
| Madagascar | Two-round system | Mixed member proportional |
| Malawi | First past the post | First past the post |
| Mali | Two-round system | Two-round system |
| Mauritania | Two-round system | Two-round system |
| Mauritius | n.a. | Block voting |
| Morocco | King (hereditary) | List proportional representation |
| Mozambique | Two-round system | List proportional representation |
| Namibia | Two-round system | Mixed member proportional |
| Niger | Two-round system | List proportional representation |
| Nigeria | Two-round system | First past the post |

| Country | Presidential election | Parliamentary election |
|---|---|---|
| Rwanda | First past the post | List proportional representation |
| São Tomé and Príncipe | Two-round system | List proportional representation |
| Senegal | Two-round system | Parallel (party block voting and list proportional representation) |
| Seychelles | Two-round system | Parallel (party block voting and list proportional representation) |
| Sierra Leone | Two-round system | List proportional representation |
| Somalia | n.a. | n.a. |
| South Africa | n.a. | Closed proportional representation |
| Sudan | Two-round system | First past the post |
| Swaziland | King (hereditary) | First past the post |
| Tanzania | Two-round system | First past the post |
| Togo | Two-round system | Two-round system |
| Tunisia | First past the post | Parallel (party block voting and list proportional representation) |
| Uganda | Two-round system | First past the post |
| Zambia | First past the post | First past the post |
| Zimbabwe | Two-round system | First past the post |

n.a. = not applicable.

*Source:* Compiled from Reynolds et al. (1995) and Salih and Norlund (2007).

## Annex 3.2 Women holding cabinet appointments in African countries, January 2010

| Country | Share of women in cabinet (%) |
|---------|-------------------------------|
| Cape Verde | 53.5 |
| São Tomé and Príncipe | 38.5 |
| South Africa | 34.3 |
| Rwanda | 33.3 |
| Uganda | 32.0 |
| Lesotho | 31.6 |
| Gambia | 31.3 |
| Liberia | 30.4 |
| Burundi | 28.6 |
| Angola | 27.8 |
| Malawi | 27.3 |
| Tanzania | 26.9 |
| Swaziland | 26.3 |
| Mozambique | 25.9 |
| Eritrea | 25.0 |
| Namibia | 24.0 |
| Guinea-Bissau | 23.5 |
| Mauritania | 23.1 |
| Niger | 22.6 |
| Ghana | 21.6 |
| Mali | 21.4 |
| Seychelles | 20.0 |

*Source:* "Women in Politics: 2010," United Nations, www.un.org/womenwatch/daw/public/womeninpolitics 2010/wmnmap10_en.pdf, accessed 29 January 2013.

## Notes

1. Some countries define youth as those younger than age 21.
2. "Lesotho: Electoral System," Electoral Institute for Sustainable Democracy in Africa, updated November 2006, www.eisa.org.za/WEP/les4.htm.
3. "Mauritius: Electoral System," Electoral Institute for Sustainable Democracy in Africa, updated May 2010, www.eisa.org.za/WEP/mau4.htm.
4. Chapter 4 analyses EMBs in greater detail.
5. In Côte d'Ivoire, the Ivorian Public Front; in Malawi, the United Democratic Front; in Mozambique, Frelimo; and in South Africa, the African National Congress.

## References

ACE Electoral Knowledge Network. 2011. "Electoral Systems." http://aceproject.org/main/english/st, accessed 20 February 2011.

Albaugh, Ericka A. 2011. "An Autocrat's Toolkit: Adaptation and manipulation in 'democratic' Cameroon." *Democratization* 18 (2): 388–414.

Boas, P. 2011. "Côte d'Ivoire: The Politics of Land, Autochthony and Elections." Paper presented to a conference organized by Christian Michelsen Institute and Makerere University, June 2011, Jinja, Uganda.

Bratton, Michael, and Nicholas van de Walle. 1997. *Democratic Experiments in Africa: Regime Transitions.* Cambridge, UK: Cambridge University Press.

Deng, Francis. 2008. *Identity, Diversity and Constitutionalism in Africa.* Washington, DC: United States Institute for Peace.

Drogus, Carol A., and Stephen Orvis. 2008. *Introducing Comparative Politics: Concepts and Cases in Context.* Washington, DC: Congressional Quarterly Press.

*The Economist.* 2012. "African Elections: How to Save Votes." Baobab Africa blog, 28 February. www.economist.com/blogs/baobab/2012/02/african-elections.

Global Commission on Elections, Democracy and Security. 2012. *Deepening Democracy: A Strategy for Improving the Integrity of Elections Worldwide.* Stockholm: International Institute for Democracy and Electoral Assistance.

IDEA (International Institute Democracy and Electoral Assistance). 2012. *Electoral Management during Transition: Challenges and Opportunities.* Stockholm.

Jinadu, L. Adele. 2010. "Managing Elections: The Winner-Take-All Rule, Democracy and Development." Ghana Speaks Lecture Series No. 2, Institute of Democratic Governance, Accra.

Kadima, Denis. 2009. "Overview." In *Compendium of Elections in Southern Africa 1989–2009,* ed. Denis Kadima and Susan Booysen. Johannesburg: Electoral Institute for Sustainable Development in Africa.

Leonard, David. 2010. "Elections and Conflict Resolution in Africa." In *When Elephants Fight: Preventing and Resolving Election-related Conflicts in Africa,* ed. Khabele Matlosa, Gilbert M. Khadigala, and Victor Shale. Johannesburg: Electoral Institute for Sustainable Development in Africa.

Lewis, W. Arthur. 1965. *Politics in West Africa.* London: George Allen & Unwin.

Navrat, Petr. 2003. "Comparative Study of Electoral Systems and their Features." Working Paper. Lok Satta,

Foundation for Democratic Reforms, Hyderabad, India.

Poluha, Eva. 2002. "Beyond the Silence of Women in Ethiopian Politics." In *Multiparty Elections in Africa*, ed. Michael Cowen and Liisa Laakso. London: Palgrave MacMillan.

Reynolds, Andrew, Ben Reilly, and Andrew Ellis. 1995. *Electoral System Design: The New International IDEA Handbook*. Stockholm: International Institute for Democracy and Electoral Assistance.

Salih, M. A., and Per Norlund. 2007. *Political Parties in Africa: Challenges for Sustainable Multiparty Democracy*. London: International Institute for Democracy and Electoral Assistance.

Sierra Leone Truth & Reconciliation Commission. 2004. *Witness to Truth: Report of the Sierra Leone Truth & Reconciliation Commission*. Accra: Graphic Packaging Ltd.

Testa, R. 2011. "Proportional Representation versus First-Past-the-Post." http://economics.about.com/cs/issues/a/proportionalrep.htm.

UNDP (United Nations Development Programme). 2004. *Human Development Report 2004: Cultural Liberty in Today's Diverse World*. New York.

UNDP (United Nations Development Programme) and UNECA (United Nations Economic Commission for Africa). 2011. "The Eighth African Governance Forum (AGF-VIII) Proceedings Report: Gender Equality, Elections and the Management of Diversity in Africa." Eighth African Governance Forum, 1–2 November 2011, Kigali.

UNRISD (United Nations Research Institute for Social Development). 1995. *Ethnic Diversity and Public Policy: An Overview*. Geneva.

Perhaps no other institution is as pivotal to the electoral process in Africa as the electoral management board (EMB).[1] An independent EMB is the fulcrum of electoral governance—the broad institutional legal and political framework of regulations for competitive party and electoral process in the post-transition modern democratic state. Succinctly: "The key element of the democratic process is the periodic holding of free and fair elections . . . for which the existence of EMBs, which are politically legitimate and technically efficient, is a necessary condition".[2]

As part of the process, electoral administration and management cover the tasks and processes for conducting credible, free and fair elections in accord with domestic, African and international codes. Given the diversity and complexity of African states and the volatility of elections, no other comparable institution plays such a sensitive and front-line role.

This chapter examines the evolution, powers and function of EMBs in Africa, reviews their autonomy and performance and analyses the challenges they face in consolidating democracy. It underlines—as key to credible and transparent elections in Africa—the integrity, impartiality and sheer professionalism of EMBs. Although there is usually a wide gap between precepts and practices, African EMBs are intended to be independent of partisan political control and to ensure that elections serve as strategic mechanisms for democratically managing diversity.

The key messages of the chapter are that performance varies in Africa, but the main pointer to good performance is an EMB's independence from the executive, which requires—ideally stipulated in the constitution—security of tenure for commissioners, adequate volume of assured funding and transparent appointment and removal of commissioners. Also crucial for the democratic outcome of elections are professional, non-partisan staff at EMBs, a good relationship with other institutions, and a composition of commissioners that reflects society.

## Evolution

### The colonial period

EMBs' powers and composition show notable heterogeneity among countries and even from one electoral cycle to another, reflecting the complexities of national and regional culture, history and law (annex 4.1). Senegal, for example, has more than 150 years of parliamentary elections officially dating back to 1848 with the initial electoral system limited to the four communes of Rufisque, Gorée, Saint-Louis and Dakar (Hayward and Grovogui 1987). In the British colonies in West Africa, indirect elections with limited suffrage to legislative councils began in the early 1920s. The period from the mid-1940s saw increased agitation for independence, hence the attempts to prepare the colonies for a smooth transfer of power and democratic self-rule. The decolonization process climaxed in the late 1950s, with wider direct franchises and elections for Africans.

Britain and France, whose own elections were directly administered by their civil services, created electoral commissions during decolonization, which had a weighty impact on the electoral politics of most African countries during the first decades of independence (box 4.1).

Britain established semi-autonomous electoral commissions to administer pre-independence elections in the late 1950s, aiming to moderate internal tensions ignited by the introduction of party politics. The underlying principle was separation of politics and administration: the organization and conduct of elections was delegated either to career civil servants with protected tenure of office (Nigeria, Sierra Leone, Uganda and then Tanganyika) or specially appointed electoral commissioners (Mauritius and the 1956 regional elections in western Nigeria; Smith 1960; Mozaffar 2002).

In contrast, Francophone and Lusophone Africa integrated politics and administration. In Francophone Africa, electoral governance was vested in the ministry of the interior or territorial administration. Multiparty electoral committees sat at the local level, under designated administration officials who supervised routine activities like revision of electoral lists, distribution of voters' cards and poll monitoring. Almost all Francophone countries in Africa inherited these non-autonomous EMBs (Holleaux 1956; Nicholas 1956; Smith 1960; Mozaffar 2002).

To the development of party politics and the electoral process must be added the stunted and fragile electoral machinery, including the EMBs, bequeathed to the independent African countries. The machinery was generally rudimentary and improvised. The franchise had for long been narrow and restrictive, and progressively enlarged. Colonial electoral processes, including elections, were not necessarily devoid of fraudulent manipulation because in most cases they were intended to

## Box 4.1  Origins of electoral management boards in Africa

The idea that electoral management should be carried out by honest and competent public servants, outside the influence of politics, dates from the colonial period. But there were different trajectories.

In some cases, the public servants were recruited from among the colonial administration itself; in others, eminent personalities independent from the administration led the process. In the Francophone countries during the last years of colonialism, elections were carried out within the framework of the colonial project, with the aim of consolidating its legitimacy (as in Benin and Senegal). In the Anglophone countries, elections took place within the context of challenging colonization and preparing the elites for independent government (as in Ghana, Nigeria and Sierra Leone, among others).

These differences partly explain how in the Francophone countries the electoral management systems in place during colonization were maintained after independence, consolidating the new regimes. In the Anglophone countries, the role of electoral management boards was among the issues contested in the political turmoil of the first decade of independence.

They may also account for the different levels of electoral violence along language lines. Elections just before independence were part of the decolonizing process in Anglophone countries, partly explaining the violence there, while in Benin and Senegal, elections bordered on a routine administrative formality and contests were for colonial offices among African candidates who were already part of the colonial elite. Violence in most Francophone countries is a relatively recent phenomenon that came with the wave of democratization in the early 1990s.

*Source:* Kambale 2011.

serve specific interests, like ensuring succession of the favourable elite to the colonial administration. This objective was not always achieved, however, as seen with the victory of the Nkrumah-led Convention People's Party in the Gold Coast (now Ghana) and Jomo Kenyatta's Kenya African National Union party in Kenya.

In Francophone Africa, Fred M. Hayward (1987, 8) points out that:

> Elections . . . were much less open [than in the British colonies] and were frequently subject to extensive manipulation by colonial officials. Elections in both Guinea and Senegal, for example, were sometimes rigged by the colonial authorities. In this respect, the French colonial electoral experience created a legacy of abuse that lived on after independence.

### The post-colonial era
In the immediate post-colonial period, the general tendency was for successor governments to replicate the electoral manipulation of former colonial administrations, through the power of incumbency. Notably, the inherited EMB—where they already existed as part of the executive branch or were newly created— were subject to outright control or intimidation by these successors. This was part of their bid to retain power, thus they had no need for strong, independent boards that would serve to strengthen competitive party politics and open the possibility of their being voted out of power in free and fair elections.

Indeed, such politicization was symptomatic of a wider process of a grave assault on democratic institutions and of the narrowing of political space, which whittled away the separation of politics from administration, allowed a strong executive to emerge and weakened the countervailing powers of the legislature, judiciary and civil society (Jinadu 1997).

While quasi-autonomous electoral commissions have been the tradition since independence in most African Anglophone countries, they are relatively new in the Francophone and Lusophone states (Kambale 2011). The fate of EMBs over 1960–1990 was largely tied to constitutional and political reforms. The combination of weak EMBs, legislatures and judiciaries was fatal to electoral governance in most African countries in this period. This combination endures in some African countries and constitutes the less wholesome residue of the political legacy of Africa's colonial and immediate post-colonial period.

Since the 1960s, electoral administration and management have featured protracted ethnic-related violent political conflicts, fuelled by the political mobilization of ethnicity and "a combination of potent identity-based factors with wider perceptions of economic and social injustice" over access to and distribution of the state's economic and political resources (Harris and Reilly 1998, 9).[3] Elections thus accentuated ethnic differences and proved ineffective as mechanisms for democratic governance. Drowning in the cauldron of political ethnicity and related primordial identities, EMBs became ineffectual mechanisms for democratically managing diversity (Ake 1976, 2001).

Successor regimes began to view democratic elections and competitive electoral politics as a threat to their power (Hayward 1987). They also came to regard independent judiciaries and the rule of law the same way—as encumbrances worth eliminating. This view had dangerous implications for electoral administration and management, which on the contrary needed successor regimes to build confidence in electoral governance among the citizens that their votes would count, to ensure the "ex ante indeterminacy" of elections and to ensure fair and non-partisan adjudication of election-related disputes (Jinadu 2010).

If elections became a charade under the single-party dominant state, EMBs and the judiciary were used as pawns that also generated a backlash and fuelled agitational politics. The pressures so released precipitated military rule but also, in the medium term, contributed to the rebounding or deepening of social movements as well as the politics of re-democratization (see chapters 1 and 2). These pressures were an important factor in convoking several African countries' national sovereign conferences or constituent assemblies, as critical milestones in democratic transitions from the 1980s.

The third wave of democratization sweeping through Africa and the rest of the world in the 1990s brought a strong revival of interest in democratically managing diversity in the African state. The revival took the form of heated debate and struggle over how competitive party and electoral politics, as well as the rules of electoral governance—particularly constitutional provisions and legislation—should be structured and institutionalized.

## Powers and functions

The powers and functions vested in African EMBs underscore their design as democracy-promoting institutions. They typically include voter registration; voter education; constituency delimitation; registration of political parties; monitoring, oversight and supervision of party activities and financing; ballot design; design, procurement and securing of ballot boxes; printing and securing of ballot papers; conduct of elections; and declaration of election results. Of course they vary from country to country. Some EMBs have restricted functions, others have far-ranging powers.

Since the late 1980s, constitutional, electoral and political reforms have been increasingly designed to strengthen African EMBs, not only to improve election management but also to insulate them from party political or government interference. The reforms have sought to professionalize and remove the EMBs from the ambit of their historical location within the civil service and to make some of them horizontal institutions, or the fourth branch of government, with varying degrees of autonomy.

> ‘ **Since the late 1980s, constitutional, electoral and political reforms have been increasingly designed to strengthen African electoral boards**

## Models

The different models of EMBs reflect the country's history, these bodies' relationship with the executive, their powers and functions and their autonomy (table 4.1). Four broad trends in the constitutional or legal design of EMBs in Africa have emerged: independent single track, independent multi-pronged, hybrid/ mixed and government-controlled models.

### Independent single track

There has been a trend towards establishing one (or more) independent EMB. This has turned EMBs into horizontal institutions, as implied in "independent". This designation is important, especially in countries where national constitutions provide for them to be set up this way. It involves making a distinction between, on the one hand, the EMB as a permanent institution whose existence is guaranteed by the constitution and that cannot be dissolved through the ordinary process of legislation, and on the other, some members of the commission are political appointees tasked with policy making.

With administrative independence also comes the imperative of financial independence. Accordingly, the independent EMBs are also generally endowed with constitutional or

**Table 4.1 Models of African electoral management boards**

| Model | Characteristics | Country examples |
|---|---|---|
| Independent single track | Independent of the executive. Full responsibility for administration and management of elections, with members chosen on personal merit and integrity, professional background and party political affiliation | Angola, Botswana, Central African Republic, Ethiopia, Gambia, Ghana, Kenya, Lesotho, Malawi, Mozambique, Nigeria, South Africa, Uganda and Zimbabwe |
| Independent multi-pronged | Two (occasionally more) bodies, independent of the executive, responsible for administration and management of elections. Usually one body responsible for administration and management, one serving as a regulatory and supervisory body | Sierra Leone and Tanzania |
| Hybrid/mixed | Government manages the election under the supervision of an independent body comprising judges, members of the legal and other professions, and party representatives | Cape Verde, Côte d'Ivoire, Democratic Republic of the Congo, Guinea and Senegal |
| Government controlled—full | Management and administration of elections are solely under the control of government | — |
| Government controlled— decentralized | Limited control, coordination and supervision by a national authority, independent of government | — |

— = not available.

*Source:* Abstracted from Lopez-Pintor (2000), Hounkpe and Fall (2011) and Kambale (2011).

other statutory guarantees of separate budgetary appropriations, in some cases (Nigeria, for instance) as a first charge on their country's consolidated revenue fund.

Their enabling legislation, in other words, grants them powers to hire and fire their own permanent bureaucracy based at national headquarters, but also in the regions or provinces, and usually at district and local government levels. For example, Sierra Leone's National Electoral Commission Act 2002 vests the commission with powers to recruit its own staff, with a view to professionalizing its bureaucracy and activities. Since the act, the commission has gradually moved to detach itself from its inherited civil service apron-strings by establishing its own secretariat headed by an executive secretary. Other electoral commissions under this EMB model have similarly established their own secretariats with their own head.

An atypical administrative structure among independent EMBs is that of Ghana's electoral commission where its chairman and two deputy chairmen perform the "managerial functions" assisted by coordinating directors, one for each of the commission's organizational divisions.

In most of the EMBs with this model, the heads of secretariat are appointed by the EMB, and they serve as the EMBs' chief accounting officers (as in South Africa). The designation of the head of the independent EMBs' secretariat as chief accounting officer can lead to

conflict, between the chairperson of the EMB and the head of the secretariat, as to where the ultimate authority and final accountability lie over the deployment of election-related resources and logistics, unless clearly spelt out in the enabling legislation, as the experience of Nigeria's Independent National Electoral Commission (INEC) has shown (Jinadu 2011a).

Independent multi-pronged
The multi-pronged model stemmed from the complexity and enormity of the powers and functions of the independent single-track model. Some African countries shared these duties between two (sometimes more) bodies, to make for more effective and streamlined operations.

In Sierra Leone, the country's 1991 Constitution and the Political Parties Act 2002 unbundled the National Electoral Commission by transferring the party registration and regulation to the Political Parties Registration Commission, a regulatory and supervisory body with oversight powers and functions for party political activities financial issues under Section 34 of the Constitution of 1991 (box 4.2). The National Electoral Commission performs only election-related functions like registering voters, delimiting constituencies and conducting elections. Tanzania has the same arrangement in which the Registrar of Political Parties is separate from the electoral commission. However, unlike Sierra Leone, it is not a body established by the constitution, but by legislation. Still, given interlocking responsibilities, they are forced to work with each other and with other bodies.

Although categorized as different independent models, Nigeria and Tanzania have two levels of electoral administration. In Nigeria, the INEC conducts elections at national and state levels, and the Independent State Electoral Commission at the local level. In Tanzania, Mainland Tanzania and Zanzibar both have their own electoral commission (for historical reasons, reflecting the merger of the two separate territories—Tanganyika and Zanzibar). Dual electoral administration can raise coordination issues, however.

What both the independent models show is the need to turn a critical searchlight on the powers and functions of the electoral body—including the mode of appointing and removing its members—and its fiscal empowerment. The aim would be to turn EMBs into a horizontal branch of government, restructured to make it independent of political influence. This is critical for EMBs where the same party controls the executive and the legislature, where the legislature and judiciary are weak, and where countervailing pressures from other actors have little impact.

### Hybrid/mixed

The third trend has been towards establishing "hybrid" or "mixed" EMBs, in which the main or core electoral functions are performed by a ministry or department or agency within the executive, supervised by an independent body.[4] With this model, the executive branch

| Box 4.2 Interlocking electoral management board responsibilities, Sierra Leone |
| --- |

The National Electoral Commission and the Political Parties Registration Commission have interlocking electoral responsibilities, compelling them to cooperate. Thus the Chief Electoral Commissioner (of the electoral commission) is a member of the registration commission, which in turn is represented on the Electoral Commission's Political Party Liaison Committee, a forum for consultation and communication between the electoral commission and political parties.

The operational areas in which the two bodies collaborate include meetings with political parties on strategies for credible and violence-free elections, on declarations of political parties' pre-election assets and liabilities and post-election expenditures, and on campaign schedules. They also collaborate with the Anti-Corruption Commission, the National Human Rights Commission, the Law Reform Commission and the National Commission for Democracy, all constitutionally established bodies. These other commissions supplement funding from the electoral commission and registration commission through their own budgeted democracy-promotion activities.

The registration commission has poorer funding, staffing and logistical support than the electoral commission.

The dominant perception among the people is that the registration commission is a suitable complement to the electoral commission, although there is no consensus whether their functions had to be unbundled.

*Source:* Jinadu 2011b.

ministry, department or agency vested with the core electoral functions also serves as the secretariat, which is tasked with implementation. But the independent EMB, vested with oversight powers over the elections, has its own secretariat.

### Government controlled—full and decentralized

Africa has seen movement from both full and decentralized government-controlled variants, to different degrees. This trend reflects new African and global thinking, but is also informed by the sad African experience of the fully government-controlled model that was inherited at independence. The post-independence conflation of politics with administration in many African countries gave rise to the view that the state bureaucracy was unreliable for conducting free and fair elections, which explains the current trend in Africa "almost invariably in the direction of establishing independent electoral commissions independently of historical political traditions" (Mozaffar and Schedler 2002, 15).

Whichever form the design takes, the objective is to strengthen the EMBs by entrenching them in constitutions (as is generally the case in Anglophone Africa) or in other statutory provisions (such as electoral laws as in much of Francophone Africa) and to provide them with an independent administrative structure or secretariat. This would insulate them from executive control or to minimize such control over them.

### Legal foundations

The constitution, legislation or a combination usually provides the legal basis for founding an EMB. The relevant item often specifies the EMB's duties, powers, functions and funding—in short (ideally) providing a basis for autonomy. Drafting should be as consultative as possible, reflecting society's diverse interests.

The African Governance Report (AGR) III country reports show that, while some countries[5] have entrenched their EMBs in their constitutions as democracy-promoting institutions, others[6] have created them through ordinary laws. The advantage of the former is that it is much harder to amend the constitution than laws, which buttresses the EMBs' independence. Abolishing constitutionally entrenched EMBs would require, in some national constitutions such as those of Kenya and Nigeria, super majorities, and in Kenya, a referendum.

However, even in some countries where EMBs are written into the constitution, the executive and legislature have sometimes amended the original electoral law to whittle down or frustrate the EMBs. Nigeria's Electoral Act 2010 as amended, for example, has provisions diminishing the oversight and supervisory role of INEC over party nomination—an apparent violation of the 1999 Constitution.

Electoral laws remain an issue of major controversy in many African countries. They are rarely inclusive, and many expert respondents regarded them as favouring the ruling party and seldom providing a basis for managing diversity. Only 14 of the 40 surveyed countries did at least half the respondents consider the electoral law to be mostly or fully adequate for managing diversity, suggesting some dissatisfaction among the people (figure 4.1).

### Autonomy

The autonomy of EMBs is endangered from several angles, and many EMBs suffer from serious deficits.

> **Electoral laws remain an issue of major controversy in many African countries**

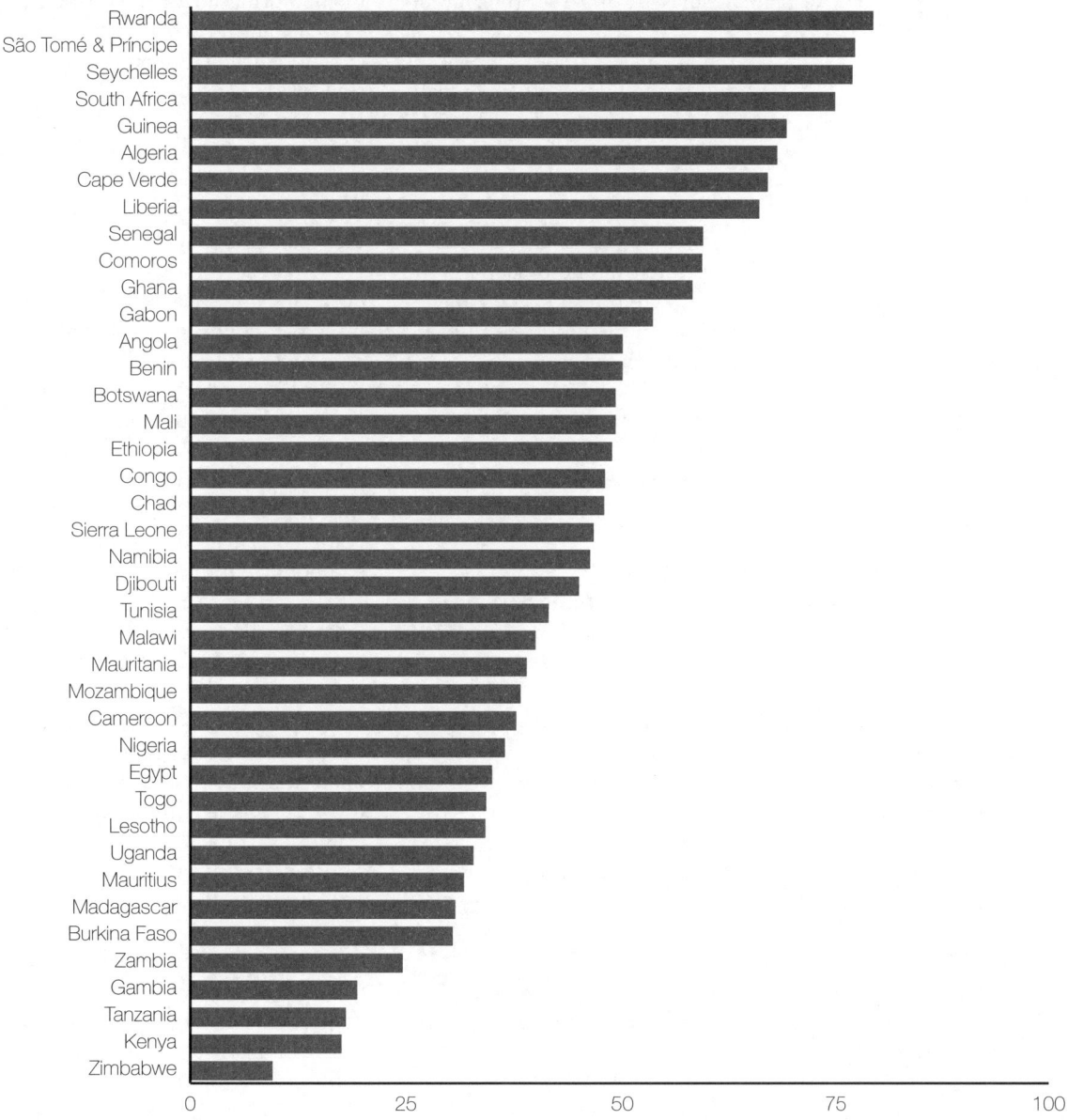

**Figure 4.1 Adequacy of the electoral law for managing diversity at elections—mostly or fully**

Share of experts surveyed agreeing with the statement, by country (%)

*Source:* AGR III Expert Opinion Survey 2012.

*Appointing and removing electoral commissioners*

The procedure differs from country to country, though two main approaches are apparent (box 4.3).

Four elements are important: the procedure should be codified in law or the constitution, and must be clear; it must not be the sole prerogative of any individual—president or otherwise—as this is prone to abuse; it must be open, transparent, inclusive, consultative and based largely on merit; and it must specify and guarantee tenure of office and procedure for removal.

Public debate and even controversy have focused on this procedure in many countries. In Nigeria for example, the Electoral Review Committee led by Justice Mohammed Lawal Uwais in its report of December 2008 proposed that the National Judicial Council play a role in appointing members of INEC. In Senegal, the debate focused on expanding the number of institutions of the Autonomous National Electoral Commission to break the monopoly held by the president in the nomination process. And in Sierra Leone, the power of the president to dismiss members of the National Electoral Commission has been challenged as it might undermine the independence of the commission (Kambale 2011). Also in Sierra Leone, the opposition Sierra Leone People's Party, still feeling "cheated" of victory in the 2007 presidential runoff election, opposed the nominated chairperson to the National Electoral Commission for a second term in June 2010.

These public feelings show through in the Expert Opinion Survey: in only 10 of the 40 countries did more than half the respondents consider the procedure to be mostly or always open, transparent and credible (figure 4.2). This finding has serious implications for the integrity of elections in Africa (see *Promoting electoral integrity*, below).

Respondents were no doubt aware of several examples where electoral commissioners had been removed in questionable circumstances. In December 2011, for instance, the President of Malawi unilaterally issued an order "to close the [Malawi Electoral Commission] immediately, on the grounds of mismanaging 1.4 billion kwacha"

---

**Box 4.3 Two approaches to appointing and removing electoral commissioners**

The politically based approach includes the following:

- the president exercises the sole prerogative in appointing and removing commissioners;
- commissioners are appointed by the president, but nominees are vetted and approved by parliament; and
- the composition of the electoral commission is a completely partisan process, in which political parties nominate senior commission officials. Such composition often reflects the balance of power among the political parties.

The technically driven method includes:

- an independent body initially selects the commissioners and recommends a few to the political authorities (parliament and/or president) to make the final decision; and
- the positions are treated as competitive public service positions, openly advertised, competed for, and filled on the basis of set criteria including merit and integrity.

These two approaches may overlap on appointing commissioners.

---

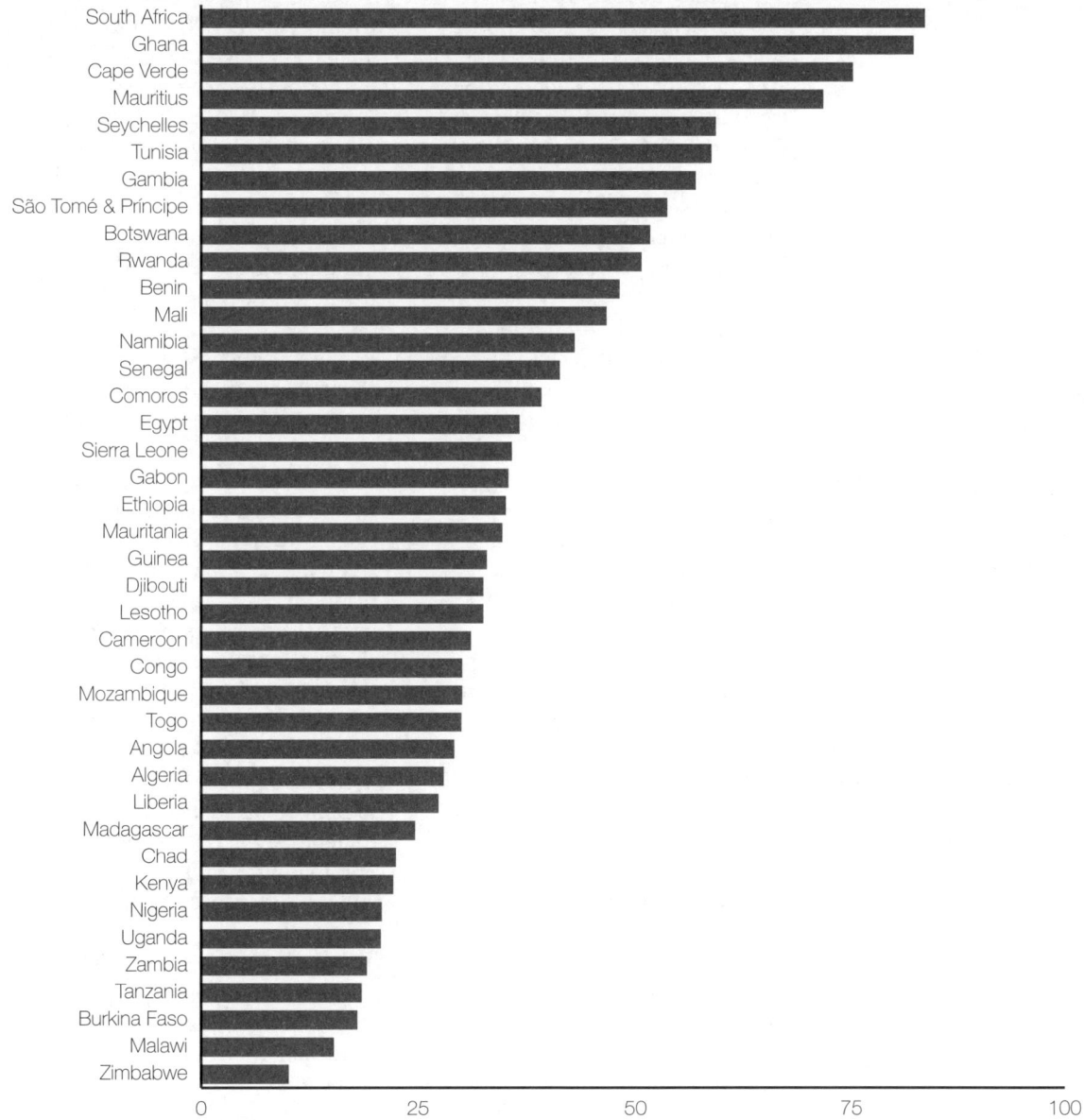

**Figure 4.2 The procedure for appointing and removing the electoral commission is open, transparent and credible—mostly or always**

Share of experts surveyed agreeing with the statement, by country (%)

*Source:* AGR III Expert Opinion Survey 2012.

before the constitutional expiry of the tenure of its members (AGR III Malawi Country Report 2012, 47). During the 1996 presidential elections, the president of Niger dismissed members of the National Independent Electoral Commission. And in 2009, the president of Senegal virtually forced the chairperson of the Autonomous National Electoral Commission, Moustapha Touré, to resign, contravening his security of tenure under the law. Touré was quoted as saying:

> The president of the Republic asked me to come in for an audience, which took place on 5 November 2009 at the presidential palace. When I arrived at his office, he clearly explained to me that he no longer had confidence in me. He repeated several times: "You are against me; you are fighting against my party. Since you no longer have my confidence," he added, "I am asking for restitution of the mandate I entrusted in you in the days before you lost my confidence" (Fall 2011, 188).

In Sierra Leone, the president removed two members of the National Electoral Commission in the wake of a crisis over the results of the 2007 presidential runoff elections, without following constitutionally provided due process. Additionally, some senior administrative staff members, whose "loyalty" was in doubt, were allegedly deployed or "demoted" to other positions within the electoral commission's secretariat. In protest, they resigned their

appointments. This was a repeat of the president's unconstitutional removal of commission officials in 1992.

Members of EMBs removed without due process tend to regard recourse to the courts to enforce their right as "medicine after death". Their perception that the judiciary is under the control of the presidency, combined with that office's overbearing power and the usually long course of litigation, sometimes discourages them from seeking judicial redress.

A more insidious way to undermine the independence of EMBs is the power of reappointment vested in the executive by most constitutions or laws establishing EMBs. It seems that the spirit of such a provision is that of reappointment to ensure continuity, unless there is "cause" not to reappoint. Yet the power of the executive (the president) to reappoint in this case is also in effect a power of removal "without cause". This can be waived to reward compliant members of electoral commissions by nominating them for reappointment, to punish uncooperative ones or to destabilize the commission by not nominating them for reappointment and making new appointments.

These new appointments usually destabilize commission operations, a factor highlighted by the late chairman of Nigeria's INEC, Abel Guobadia:

> The commission in September 2003, with 10 new members, was a different commission from the earlier commission . . .

'Electoral management board top officials need to be appointed and dismissed by an independent body

There was a loss of momentum as a result of the large turnover of the membership. Valuable time was lost in allowing the new members who now constituted the majority to settle down and learn on the job. . . . A permanent body with as large a membership as the commission ought not to . . . have such a large membership turnover at any point in time. The commission should always have a sizeable number of members who are abreast with current activities and development within the commission (Guobadia 2009, 128).

What these examples underline is that a residual issue arising from the constitutional provisions to strengthen the independence of EMBs is that of ensuring the security of tenure of their members. The overriding problem is that when appointment is made on loyalty to the appointing authority—often the executive—this could be revoked unless the appointee maintains his or her loyalty.

So, EMB top officials need to be appointed and dismissed by an independent body in an open and transparent process in order for them to be insulated from interference by the executive in their duties. A more powerful check on the executive might be to extend the Ghanaian model, which grants security of tenure to the chairperson and deputies of the EMB until their retirement, and to all members of EMBs (as is generally the case with High Court and Supreme Court judges in

many African countries, apart from removal for official misconduct).

Finally, EMBs should be granted much more flexibility than the civil service in accounting and procurement procedures, because of the sensitive nature and security implications of elections. However, this must not compromise financial accountability and due process.

### Financial autonomy

The level and security of EMB funding is another key issue. Although most EMBs and electoral processes are supposed to be funded by the state, such funding is often inadequate and delayed, forcing many EMBs to turn to development partners.[7] For these partners, such assistance constitutes part of their democracy- and governance-support activities on the continent. For example, since 1996 the donor community in Sierra Leone has contributed about 75% of the budget for the National Electoral Commission—about 85% for the 2008 local government elections (National Electoral Commission of Sierra Leone 2008, 18).

Most AGR III country reports expressed concerns about this financial dependence (chapter 6), because it can compromise ownership of the electoral process, distort planning in the electoral cycle, compromise the integrity of elections and, politically, undermine national sovereignty. In Nigeria, where the election budget is largely funded by the federal government, INEC has had disagreements with donors over their attempts to influence how their technical support should be used.

> ❛ *Electoral management boards should be granted more flexibility in accounting and procurement procedures*

Increasingly, African countries are learning to bear a large part of their EMB budgets. Tanzania's funding, including that for the electoral commission, rose from 57% of the total election cost in 1995 to 86% in 2000 and then to 95% in 2005. Namibia fully funds its EMB. And to strengthen INEC's financial independence in Nigeria, recent constitutional and electoral reforms have provided for that body's funding to be a first-line charge on the country's consolidated revenue fund, although it remains unclear how much INEC would still be subject to standard civil service administrative and financial procedures.

Still, recruitment, staffing and human capacity are major constraints for most EMBs, which often resort to short-term staff for electoral duties (box 4.4).

## Performance

The above issues of autonomy affect opinions: in only 17 of the 40 countries did more than half the expert respondents consider their EMB to be independent and fairly or fully competent (figure 4.3). Underlying reasons that render them independent and effective are in box 4.5.

The overall performance of EMBs is uneven in Africa. In Cape Verde, Ghana, Mauritius and South Africa, they are credited with organizing free, fair and credible elections, unlike the Democratic Republic of the Congo, Kenya, Nigeria, Uganda and Zimbabwe, where controversy and litigation have dogged the performance of electoral commissions. Only in 11 countries did more than half the experts rate it good or very good (figure 4.4). Similarly, only in 12 (figure 4.5) and 14 (figure 4.6) countries did more than half the experts rate their national and local elections, respectively, mostly or always free, fair and generally transparent.

In short, the performance of most EMBs in Africa is not too encouraging—but with a few bright spots (box 4.6)—and needs to pick up substantially for them to earn credibility and public confidence.

## Promoting electoral integrity

Electoral integrity is ultimately about protecting free and fair elections (box 4.7). A major issue of policy discourse is on how to strengthen the integrity of election administration and management.

Concerns about ensuring and protecting electoral integrity persist in Africa because flawed elections have featured prominently on the

---

### Box 4.4  Heavy staff demand around elections

The staff strength of Nigeria's Independent National Electoral Commission in 2009 was about 12,000, of whom not more than 9,000–10,000 could be deployed for election or voter registration, yet both these activities require some 36,000–48,000 temporary staff.

In Sierra Leone, the National Electoral Commission recruited 35,175 short-term polling staff for the 2008 local government elections (Jinadu 2011b).

Rwanda's National Electoral Commission for the September 2008 legislative elections created 15,429 polling stations at 2,103 polling centres. It recruited and trained 64,233 people, in addition to 61,492 volunteer staff at the stations, 2,103 to coordinate the centres and 638 staff to deal with election matters in districts and provinces (European Union Election Observation Mission 2008)

## Figure 4.3 The electoral commission is independent and fairly or fully competent

Share of experts surveyed, by country (%)

- It is independent and fairly or fully competent
- It is not independent but fairly competent
- It is not independent and not competent or rarely competent

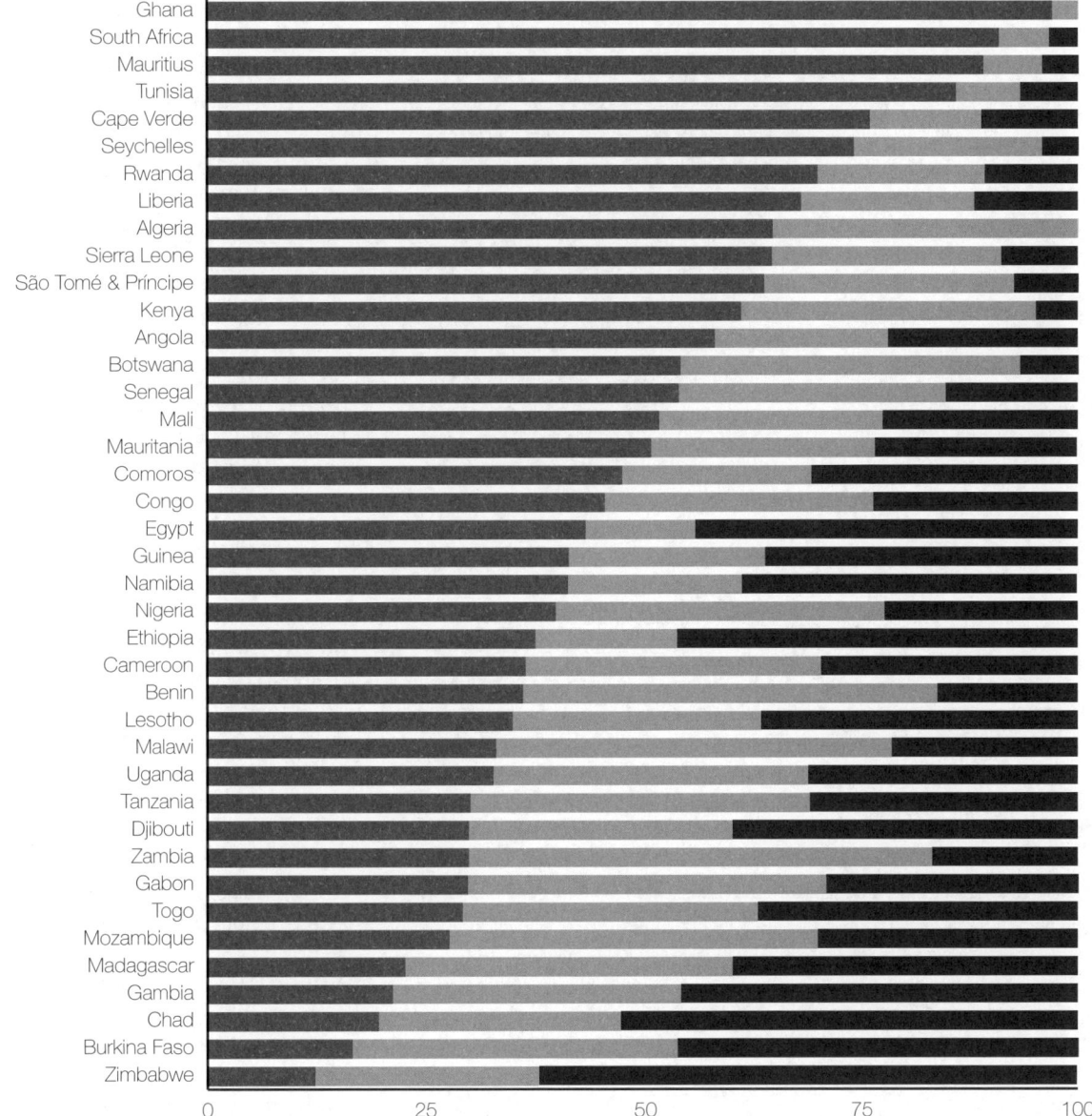

Source: AGR III Expert Opinion Survey 2012.

continent, even before independence. But citizens' perceptions of
electoral integrity have improved
appreciably in various countries since
the 1980s, largely owing to reform
measures to strengthen EMBs, the
electorate's aggressive protection of
their votes, intense voter education,
active networks of pro-democracy
civil society organizations and the
calibre of EMB leadership. Ghana
stands out: referring to key electoral
transparency measures introduced
since the flawed presidential polls of
1992, the AGR III Ghana Country
Report 2012 (111) observed:

> These reforms ensured that
> the subsequent elections have
> been progressively free and
> fairer, with the third and fifth
> ones in 2000 and 2008 pro-
> ducing peaceful electoral turn-
> overs and democratic alterna-
> tion of power. Large majorities
> of the experts surveyed consid-
> ered national and local elec-
> tions (81% and 74%, respec-
> tively) to be free, fair and
> generally transparent. Simi-
> larly, participants in the focus
> group discussions opined that
> elections in Ghana are gener-
> ally fair and credible oppor-
> tunities for all stakeholders in
> the process to contest as well
> as vote in periodic elections.

The AGR III Malawi Coun-
try Report 2012 (84) also showed
a favourable perception of progress towards electoral integrity, in
observing that "when asked about
integrity of national elections, 31%
of the respondents said the elections
were sometimes free and fair, 29%

**Figure 4.4 Performance of electoral commissions**

Share of experts surveyed, by country (%)

- Good or very good
- Fair
- Poor or very poor

*Source:* AGR III Expert Opinion Survey 2012.

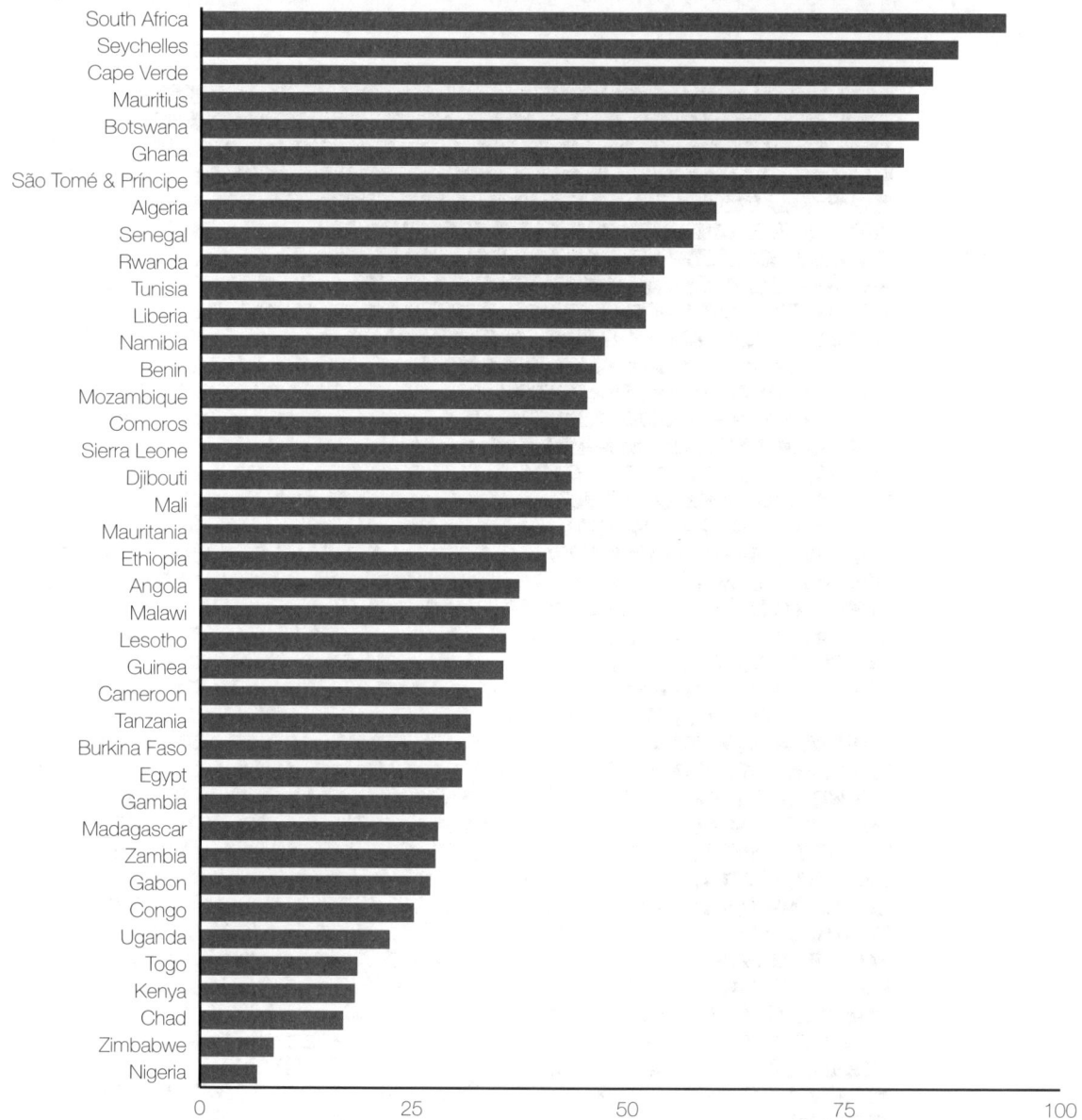

**Figure 4.5 National elections are free, fair and generally transparent—mostly or always**

Share of experts surveyed agreeing with the statement, by country (%)

*Source:* AGR III Expert Opinion Survey 2012.

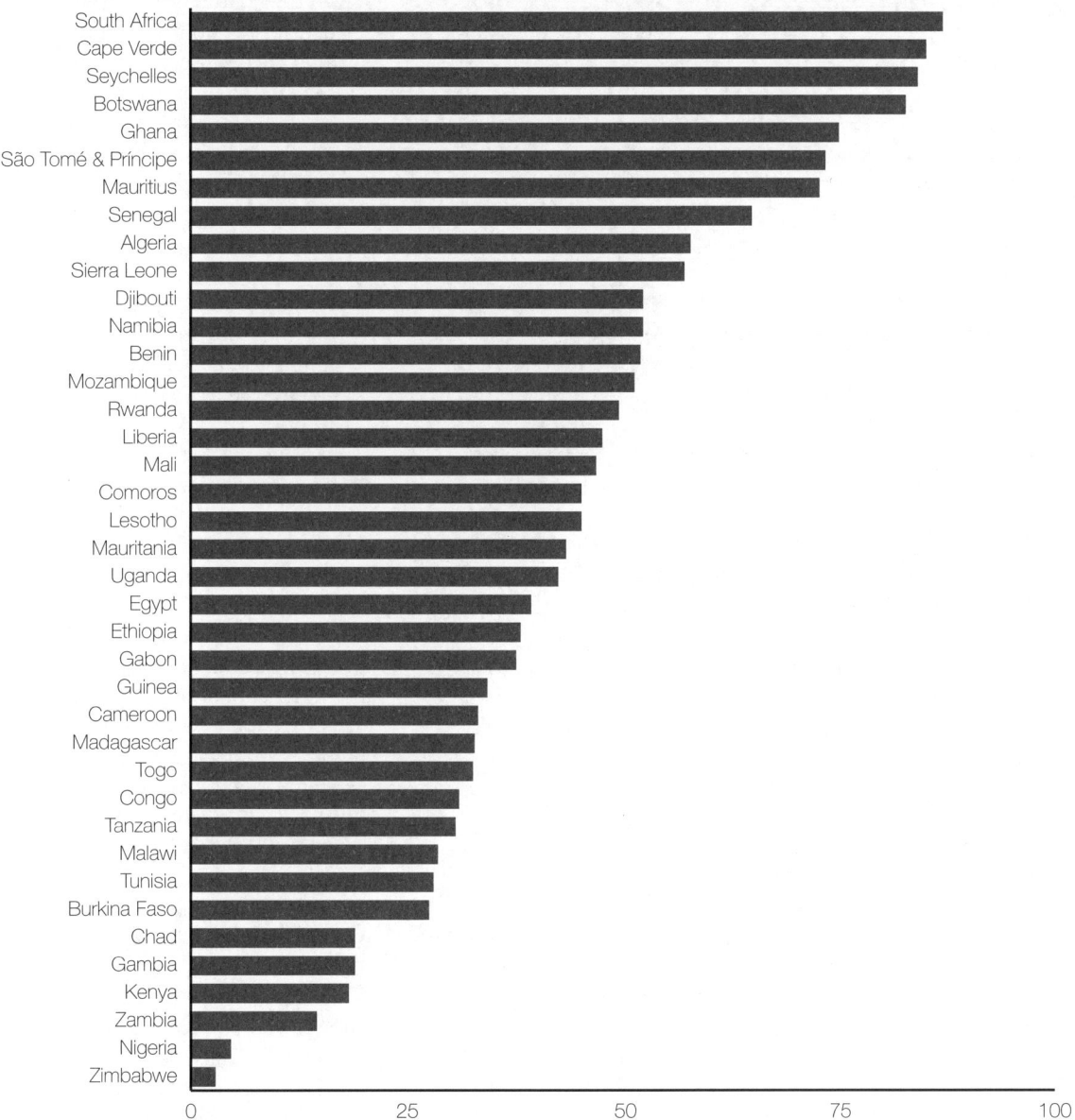

**Figure 4.6 Local elections are free, fair and generally transparent—mostly or always**

Share of experts surveyed agreeing with the statement, by country (%)

*Note:* Angola does not conduct local elections.

*Source:* AGR III Expert Opinion Survey 2012.

threatened by the practice of incumbent political elites during presidential elections or on the countdown to presidential elections, to want to alter the political system with the aim of aborting the succession and hence perpetuate its stay in power, or expanding the political space to allow it room for negotiation with the emerging successor group. This practice is a result of the symbiosis in Kenyan politics between the process of accumulation and political succession (AGR III Kenya Country Report 2012, 93).

Electoral integrity is crucial in volatile and hotly contested elections, particularly in multi-ethnic states, making the role of African EMBs in building general confidence even more important. If EMBs fail to act in a professional, non-partisan manner independent of government, the elections will lose credibility, risking pre- and post-election violence, as seen in Zanzibar (2000), Nigeria (2007, 2011), Kenya (2007), Zimbabwe (2008) and Côte d'Ivoire (2010).

## Oversight of political parties

Most EMBs have few means of enforcing their rules and decisions, and of exercising their oversight powers over party electoral activities, including party financing. "In Benin, the [Autonomous National Electoral Commission] can only report electoral irregularities to the judicial system since it has no power of sanction" (Kambale 2011, 8). In Sierra

said they were mostly free and fair, while 7% said they were always free and fair".[8]

However, serious doubts remain about electoral integrity and its implications for democratic management of diversity in several countries, typified by the following:

The integrity of elections in Kenya has always been

Leone, although the National Electoral Commission has issued regulations to declare invalid any result with more than 100% turnout, disgruntled political parties have challenged its ability to apply this rule. There is also a question whether such regulations have to be enacted into law (Kambale 2011). Unless they are endowed with sufficient powers of sanction, EMBs risk being toothless.

The main issues of oversight of party-political activities are ensuring compliance by parties with internal democracy in their internal nomination processes for party offices and elective public political offices; submitting the audit of their finances in a timely manner, as required by law; enforcing compliance with electioneering campaign regulations; and creating a political environment conducive to reducing violent inter- and intra-party conflicts and violence, through adopting an agreed code of conduct.

Some EMBs have set up working relations with political parties through platforms for inter-party dialogue, such as Sierra Leone's National Code of Conduct Monitoring Committee—which has helped introduce major reforms, including transparent ballot boxes and counting and declaring election results on the spot at polling stations—and Ghana's Inter-Party Advisory Committee.

Similar initiatives involving collaboration between EMBs and political parties (and sometimes civil society organizations) have been introduced in Lesotho and South Africa

> ## Box 4.7 Electoral integrity
>
> We define an election with integrity as any election that is based on the democratic principles of universal suffrage and political equality as reflected in international standards and agreements, and is professional, impartial and transparent in its preparation and administration throughout the electoral cycle.
>
> Elections with integrity are important to human rights and democratic principles. Elections give life to rights enshrined in the Universal Declaration of Human Rights and the International Covenant on Civil and Political Rights, including freedom of opinion and expression, freedom of peaceful assembly and association, the right to take part in the government of one's country through freely elected representatives, the right of equal access to public service in one's country and the recognition that the authority of government derives from the will of the people, expressed in "genuine periodic elections that shall be by universal and equal suffrage and shall be held by secret ballot".
>
> For elections to uphold human rights and democratic principles, they must be conducted with integrity. When elections lack integrity, electoral officials are not accountable to the public, and political candidates and voters are denied equal opportunity to participate in and influence the political process. Citizens lose confidence in democratic processes when elections are not inclusive, transparent and accountable. When elections have integrity, they bolster democracy, respect fundamental rights and produce elected officials who are more likely to represent their citizens' interests.
>
> *Source:* Global Commission on Elections, Democracy and Security 2012.

(box 4.8) as well as Burundi, the Democratic Republic of the Congo, Kenya, Malawi, Tanzania and Zambia. Many of these initiatives draw on or complement existing informal platforms for inter-party dialogue.

The Zambian Centre for Inter-Party Dialogue, for example, provides a platform for political parties to forge cross-party consensus on national issues. In Rwanda, the Constitution (Article 56) provides that "The political will consistently recognizes the Rwanda Consultative Forum . . . to enable political parties to discuss

Lesotho and South Africa have institutionalized party liaison committees, which serve as vehicles for consultation and cooperation between the electoral management board (EMB) and the political parties on electoral matters with the aim of delivering free and fair elections.

These committees have been established nationally, provincially and locally. Each registered political party has the right to appoint two representatives to each committee. The committees meet frequently, and their administration is entrusted with the EMB.

They have helped identify and resolve electoral disputes, and their deliberations are regarded mostly by the people as open and honest. The committees take a consultative and constructive approach and seek to reach consensus among the political parties and their candidates. In South Africa, the tribunals appointed by the Electoral Court generally endorse the conclusions of the committees.

*Source:* Orozco-Henríquez 2010.

the major political issues of national interest, consolidate national unity [and offer] advisory opinion on national politics, serving as mediators in cases of conflict within a political party, at the request of the latter" (AGR III Rwanda Country Report 2012).

Some countries have moved towards alternative dispute resolution mechanisms. They take the form of non-formal mechanisms to back up conventional approaches in Ghana and South Africa, for instance. They adopt indigenous dispute resolution practices to election disputes, emphasizing conciliation rather than litigation, thus saving time and money.

EMBs have to negotiate a slippery political terrain when encouraging

inter-party dialogue, lest they not only become embroiled in inter-party disputes and intra-party factionalism, but also risk accusations of bias. In Ghana, inter-party dialogue has been relatively successful, largely because the parties have a sense of ownership. The Inter-Party Advisory Committee works well, securing parties' agreement to a code of conduct facilitated by the National Electoral Commission, in conjunction with the National Commission for Civic Education and the Institute of Economic Affairs, a non-governmental organization (Hounkpe and Fall 2011).

But elsewhere, international donors have sometimes had to broker inter-party dialogue and parties' codes of conduct, as in Sierra Leone in 2009 when the Executive Representative of the Secretary-General of the United Nations in Sierra Leone played a central role in securing agreement to a joint communiqué by the two major political parties, the All Peoples' Congress and the Sierra Leone People's Party (Jinadu 2011b).

## Conclusions and recommendations

Africa has seen the ebb and flow of electoral administration and management since the 1990s, but some EMBs—notably in Benin, Botswana, Ghana, Mauritius, Sierra Leone and South Africa—have performed reasonably well. They have had real input in enhancing general confidence in their countries' electoral administration and management. Other countries whose EMBs have progressed include Cape Verde, Liberia and Namibia.

Nigeria's INEC was allowed to run the 2011 elections much better than in 2003 and 2007. The federal political leadership kept its distance from it, and INEC's leadership and overall competence were stronger.

Where an election yields a close vote between parties—particularly presidential candidates as in Sierra Leone (2007), Kenya (2007), Ghana (2008, 2012), Zimbabwe (2008), Côte d'Ivoire (2010) and Senegal (2012)—the situation may well get out of hand, turning into ethnic, ethno-regional or religious conflict. The EMBs themselves may be attacked, as in Nigeria (2007), Kenya (2007), Zimbabwe (2008) and Côte d'Ivoire (2010).

EMBs' challenges therefore remain daunting, especially with diversity where their role becomes even more sensitive. It is the task of African EMBs to engineer broad-based coalitions for strengthening electoral administration and management, and for engendering electoral integrity, as momentous investments in democratic consolidation and sustainable development in Africa. This is the overall enduring challenge for the EMBs.

### Sensitivity to diversity
African EMBs need to be particularly sensitive to the needs and challenges of various categories of voters as part of their diversity management role and voter education. They need to continue building bridges of understanding and collaboration across the treacherous and thin divide between maintaining their autonomy and engaging various

stakeholders in state and society as partners in working towards credible electoral administration and management. Without such sensitivity, they will find it difficult to be tactful, impartial or credible. EMBs cannot afford an image of favouritism or dismissiveness towards certain ethnic groups, regions and minorities. They should be professional in their dealings with all groups and parties, rich and poor, the advantaged and disadvantaged.

### Diversity in composition
Efforts should be taken to ensure that EMB membership reflects the composition of wider society, including women, minorities, ethnic groups, religious groups, regions and all political shades. The criteria and process of appointing or selecting members need to be transparent at every stage.

### Political and financial autonomy
The political class and ruling party generally seek to influence an EMB by, for instance, "pulling financial strings" especially during election year. The provisions setting up an EMB should therefore not only guarantee financial autonomy (for example, as an annual subvention from the national budget) but also EMB members' security of tenure, to protect their independence.

Many country reports expressed the need for an independent nonpartisan body to be responsible for appointing and removing EMB commissioners.[9] Relatedly, others called for the positions of commissioners to be advertised and competed for nationally.[10]

> **Electoral boards should be professional in their dealings with all groups and parties, rich and poor, the advantaged and disadvantaged**

### Electoral integrity

Electoral integrity is central to the mission of EMBs, and unless they are seen to have it, their role and reputation crumble. Election integrity is a set of standards based on democratic principles, measures and mechanisms for protecting free and fair elections, but unless these standards are enforced, they remain merely good intentions.

EMBs in Africa need to raise the bar, and codes of conduct are useful. Some studies have gone further and recommended that EMBs organize a global certification process to evaluate and grade EMBs on their professionalism, independence and competence, including a voluntary declaration of principles and code of conduct (Global Commission on Elections, Democracy and Security 2012).

### Constitutional grounding

Autonomy, integrity and professionalism are so fundamental to EMB operations that they should be spelt out and protected by constitutional provisions, reinforcing the current trend. Such provisions should guarantee the permanence of the EMB, giving to it a legal personality in perpetuity. They should also grant the EMB an independent and professional bureaucracy that serves as its secretariat. Further, election-related laws, including amendments to the EMB's mandate and functions, should require special consensus-building measures.

### Collaboration with other institutions

EMBs need to work with other stakeholders, including political parties, civil society organizations and state agencies like ministries and the police. They should strive to create a framework for mutually cooperative links based on professionalism and impartiality, enabling them to iron out any disputes during the electoral process, thus strengthening electoral administration and management as investments for consolidating democracy in Africa.

# Annex 4.1 Structure and composition of EMBs: Southern Africa, July 2010

| Country or area | Structure |
|---|---|
| Angola | **National Electoral Commission**<br>11 members, 4-year term, renewable once<br>• 2 nominated by president<br>• 3 nominated by ruling party<br>• 3 nominated by opposition parties in National Assembly<br>• 1 Justice of the Supreme Court<br>• 1 representative of Ministry of Territorial Administration<br>• 1 elected by National Council of Social Communication<br>• National Electoral Commission president elected from these by the National Assembly |
| Botswana | **Independent Electoral Commission**<br>7 members with 10-year term<br>Nominated at an all-party conference and appointed by the Judicial Service Commission |
| Dem. Rep. Congo | **Independent Electoral Commission**<br>Not yet constituted, governing organic law yet to be passed |
| Lesotho | **Independent Electoral Commission**<br>3 members, 6-year term, renewable once<br>Appointed by the King on advice of the State Council; chairperson must be a judge |
| Malawi | **Malawi Electoral Commission**<br>7 members, 4-year term renewable<br>• Chairperson is a judge nominated by the Judicial Service Commission<br>• 6 appointed by the president in consultation with leaders of political parties in the National Assembly |
| Madagascar | **National Independent Electoral Commission**<br>19 members, 12 with voting rights<br>• 10 nominated by civil society bodies<br>• 2 representatives of administration, 1 each from the Ministry of the Interior and the Ministry of Decentralization<br>• 7 non-voting representatives from political parties: 3 governing, 3 opposition and 1 other |
| Mauritius | **Electoral Supervisory Commission**<br>Supervisory body, 7 members, 5-year term<br>Appointed by president on advice of prime minister after consultation with leader of the opposition |
| Mozambique | **National Electoral Commission**<br>13 members, 5-year term<br>• 5 members designated by parties/coalitions in Assembly of the Republic<br>• 8 members are chosen by 5 from nominees by civil society bodies<br>• president is elected by 13 from among the 8 civil society representatives |
| Namibia | **Electoral Commission of Namibia**<br>5 members, 5-year term<br>Appointed by president from shortlist compiled by Selection Committee (a nominee of the Chief Justice, a nominee of the Law Society and a nominee of the Ombudsman); chairperson must be a judge |
| Seychelles | **Electoral Commissioner**<br>7-year term, renewable<br>Appointed by the president from candidates proposed by the Constitutional Appointments Authority |

| Country or area | Structure |
|---|---|
| South Africa | *Independent Electoral Commission*<br>5 members, 7-year term, renewable<br>Appointed by president on recommendation of National Assembly, following nominations by a National Assembly inter-party committee. One commissioner must be a judge |
| Swaziland | *Elections and Boundaries Commission*<br>5 members, 12-year term, non-renewable<br>• Chairperson and deputy-chairperson appointed by the King on advice of Judicial Service Commission<br>• 3 members appointed by King on consultation with ministers responsible for elections and local government |
| Tanzania | *National Election Commission*<br>7 members, 4-year term<br>Appointed by president, according to complex legislative requirements. Chairperson and vice-chairperson have to be judges of the High Court or the Court of Appeal |
| Zambia | *Electoral Commission of Zambia*<br>5 members, 7-year term, renewable<br>Appointed by president, subject to ratification by the National Assembly |
| Zanzibar | *Zanzibar Electoral Commission*<br>7 members, 5-year term<br>Appointed by president, according to complex legislative requirements |
| Zimbabwe | *Zimbabwe Electoral Commission*<br>7 members, 5-year term, renewable once<br>• Chairperson must be a judge and is appointed by president after consultation with the Judicial Service Commission<br>• 6 members (at least 3 women) appointed by president from 9 nominees supplied by Parliamentary Committee on Standing Rules and Orders |

*Source:* "Electoral Management Bodies: Composition," Electoral Institute for Sustainability of Democracy in Africa, updated June 2010, www.eisa.org.za/WEP/comemb1.htm.

## Notes

1. Also known as electoral commissions.

2. See proceedings of the international workshop on Electoral Management Bodies as Institutions of Governance, Statement with conclusions, Mexico City, 26–29 May 1999.

3. This has been the case in countries as varied as Algeria, Burundi, Chad, Congo, Côte d'Ivoire, the Democratic Republic of the Congo, Eritrea, Ethiopia, Guinea-Bissau, Kenya, Liberia, Mali, Mauritania, Morocco, Niger, Nigeria, Rwanda, Senegal, Sierra Leone, Somalia, South Africa, Sudan, Uganda and Zimbabwe (Nzongola-Ntalaja 1987; Harbom 2004; Douma 2003).

4. To cite some examples: in Senegal, the Ministry of Interior, supervised by the Autonomous National Electoral Commission, and to some extent the National Council for the Regulation of Broadcasting, which is in charge of ballot counting, performs the core electoral functions. In Cape Verde, three bodies—the National Electoral Commission, the Directorate General for Electoral Process Support (in the Ministry of Internal Administration) and the electoral registration committees—share the functions. In the Democratic Republic of the Congo, national elections have been under the supervision of two successive bodies since the early 1990s: the National Elections Organizing Committee and its successor, the National Electoral Commission. Electoral preparations are under the responsibility of the Ministry of Interior, while organization and oversight of elections are vested in the National Electoral Commission.

5. Such as Botswana, Ghana, Kenya, Lesotho, Malawi, Nigeria, Sierra Leone, South Africa, Zambia and Zimbabwe.

6. Such as Angola, Benin, Cameroon, Cape Verde, Côte d'Ivoire, Gabon, Mali, Mozambique, Niger and Senegal.

7. Major contributors through the Joint Donor Basket Fund are the European Union, Department for International Development, Canadian International Development Agency and United Nations Development Programme. Others include the United States Agency for International Development, International Republican Institute, International Federation of Electoral Systems and National Democratic Institute.

8. But the AGR III Malawi Country Report 2012 also stated that the response "reflects that the respondents treated the classification with caution, often [choosing] the middle point and not the extremes of the scale. . . . A further exploration of this question in qualitative interviews revealed that national elections are generally viewed to be free but not necessarily fair as the electoral process is marred by a lot of irregularities, hence compromising the integrity".

9. Including Ethiopia, Ghana, Malawi, Rwanda, Sierra Leone, South Africa, Tanzania and Zimbabwe.

10. Including Cape Verde, Ethiopia, Ghana, Rwanda and Zimbabwe.

## References

Ake, Claude. 1976. "Explanatory Notes on the Political Economy of Africa." *Journal of Modern African Studies* 14 (1): 1–23.

———. 2001. *Democracy and Development in Africa.* Ibadan, Nigeria: Spectrum Books.

Douma, P. S. 2003. *The Origins of Contemporary Conflict: A Comparison of Violence in Three World Regions.* The Hague: Netherlands Institute of International Relations Clingendael.

European Union Election Observation Mission. 2008. "Rwanda, 2008: Final Report on the Legislative Elections, 15–18 September 2008." European External Action Service, Brussels.

Fall, Ismaila Madior. 2011. "Senegal." In *Election Management Bodies in West Africa: A Comparative Study of the Contribution of Electoral Commissions to the Strengthening of Democracy*, Ismaila Madior Fall, Mathias Hounkpe, Adele L. Jinadu and Pascal Kambale, 162–208. Dakar: Open Society Foundations.

Global Commission on Elections, Democracy and Security. 2012. *Deepening Democracy: A Strategy for Improving the Integrity of Elections Worldwide.* Geneva: Kofi Annan Foundation.

Guobadia, Abel I. 2009. *Reflections of a Nigerian Electoral Umpire.* Benin City, Nigeria: Mindex Publishing Company Limited.

Harbom, Lotta, ed. 2004. *States in Armed Conflict 2003.* Uppsala: University of Uppsala, Department of Peace and Conflict Research.

Harris, Peter, and Ben Reilly, eds. 1998. *Democracy and Deep-Rooted Conflict: Options for Negotiators.* Stockholm: International Institute for Democracy and Electoral Assistance.

Hayward M. Fred. 1987. "Introduction." In *Elections in Independent Africa*, ed. Fred M. Hayward, 1–23. Boulder, CO: Westview Press.

Hayward, Fred M., and S. N. Grovogui. 1987. "Persistence and Change in Senegalese Electoral Processes." In *Elections in Independent Africa*, ed. Fred M. Hayward, 239–70. Boulder, CO: Westview Press.

Holleaux, André. 1956. "Les elections aux assemblées des territoires d'outre-mer." *Revue juridique et politique de l'Union française* 10 (1): 1–54.

Hounkpe, Mathias, and Ismaila Madior Fall. 2011. *Electoral Commissions in West Africa: A Comparative Study.* Abuja: Friedrich-Ebert-Stiftung.

Jinadu, Adele L. 1997. "Matters Arising: African Elections and the Problem of Electoral Administration." *African Journal of Political Science, Special Issue: Elections in Africa* 2 (1): 1–11.

———. 2010. "Managing Elections: The Winner-Takes-All Rule, Democracy and Development." Ghana Speaks Lecture Series 2. Institute of Democratic Governance, Accra.

———. 2011a. "Nigeria." In *Election Management Bodies in West Africa: A Comparative Study of the Contribution of Electoral Commissions to the Strengthening of Democracy*, ed. Ismaila Fall, Mathias Hounkpe, Adele L. Jinadu and Pascal Kambale, 108–61. Dakar: Open Society Foundations.

———. 2011b. "Sierra Leone." In *Election Management Bodies in West Africa: A Comparative Study of the Contribution of Electoral Commissions to the Strengthening of Democracy*, ed. Ismaila Fall, Mathias Hounkpe, Adele L. Jinadu and Pascal Kambale, 209–44. Dakar: Open Society Foundations.

Kambale, Pascal. 2011. "Overview: The Contribution of Electoral Management Bodies to Credible Elections in West Africa." In *Election Management Bodies in West Africa: A Comparative Study of the Contribution of Electoral Commissions to the Strengthening of*

*Democracy*, ed. Ismaila Fall, Mathias Hounkpe, Adele L. Jinadu, and Pascal Kambale, 1–11. Dakar: Open Society Foundations.

Lopez-Pintor, Rafael. 2000. *Electoral Management Bodies as Institutions of Governance*. New York: United Nations Development Programme, Bureau for Development Policy.

Mozaffar, Shaheen. 2002. "Patterns of Electoral Governance in Africa's Emerging Democracies." *International Political Science Review* 23 (85): 85–101.

Mozaffar, Shaheen, and Andreas Schedler. 2002. "The Comparative Study of Electoral Governance—Introduction." *International Political Science Review* 25 (1): 5–27.

National Electoral Commission of Sierra Leone. 2008. *Annual Report 2008*. Freetown.

Nicholas, H. G. 1956. "The French Election of 1956: Electoral Law and Machinery." *Political Studies* 4 (2): 139–50.

Nzongola-Ntalaja, Georges, ed. 1987. *Revolution and Counter-Revolution in Africa: Essays in Contemporary Politics*. London: Zed Books.

Orozco-Henríquez, Jesús. 2010. *Electoral Justice: The International Idea Handbook*. Stockholm: International Institute for Democracy and Electoral Assistance.

Smith, T. E. 1960. *Elections in Developing Countries: A Study of Electoral Procedures Used in Tropical Africa, Southeast Asia and the British Caribbean*. London: Macmillan.

**M**ost African elections have improved, reshaping the stereotype that they are perverse and conflict based. Only about 20% of elections held in Africa between 1990 and 2008 involved significant levels of violence (Goldsmith 2010; Straus 2012). Yet outbreaks of conflict remain worrying, and take on a high profile. Since 2007, conflict-ridden elections in Côte d'Ivoire, the Democratic Republic of the Congo, Guinea, Kenya, Nigeria and Zimbabwe show the distance that Africa still needs to cover in improving its elections. Conflicts undermine the legitimacy of elections and their outcomes, and devalue the democratic process.

Nevertheless, the strides that Africa has made in making elections more competitive in the past 25 years have been very encouraging. It was not long ago that a one-party system was ascendant in most countries, and authoritarianism generally the order of the day. In some countries, voting was supervised through the queuing system: instead of casting a secret ballot, voters were required to queue behind their candidate. Further, most media were under the monopoly control of the incumbent party and regime, making it hard for diverse party agendas and candidates to generate support during election campaigns. Most governments have embraced the multi-party system and organized regular elections over the past quarter century, when elections have proliferated impressively.

This chapter's key messages are that the proportional representation electoral system is less prone to acrimonious and violent elections than other systems; countries with previous civil wars or other prolonged conflicts tend to be more prone to electoral conflict; political parties are potential agencies of electoral conflict, both within a party and between them; people regard many state security agencies as partisan in elections; many countries still have weak conflict management frameworks and strategies (though there are some outstanding examples of good practices); and structural socio-economic factors, including friction over access to resources, exacerbate electoral conflicts.

## Electoral competition

The essence of electoral competition is that political parties compete for power through the public vote, and are expected to comply with the rules of the electoral game. So, political parties enter into complex relations with each other, competing to overtake each other or forming alliances. Through negotiations and debates, political parties engage each other. These are crucial ingredients of competitive democratic politics. As part of the structure of the governing political institutions, parties are capable of being beacons of political stability—or major contributors to violent conflict.

Political parties serve as mediating institutions that facilitate and channel people's political activities. Determining whether partisan competition is desirable or conflict ridden is in the domain of party systems, mainly because such systems—how many parties, how large and diverse and how autonomous—make a critical difference in organizing a democratic society (Magarian 2003).

While party competition for votes could be regulated by, for instance, electoral law or election reforms, the exact number of political parties that will be represented in the legislature will not be known until the elections are contested, votes counted and winners declared. The number of political parties that contest is very important for determining the extent to which the elections are competitive, because it reflects the socio-political, ethnic and regional contexts—hence the need for analysts to distinguish among different types of party system (see also table 1.2).

### One party

Historically, one-party systems were associated with post-colonial nationalism and state consolidation. Thus they enjoyed a monopoly of power using political or constitutional means, in effect functioning as permanent governments. They had no institutionalized mechanisms for peaceful transfer of power through competitive elections short of a military coup, revolution or popular agitation. The fusion of the party–state apparatus also implied entrenched party–state relations, with the one-party system enjoying the financial and administrative support of the state.

Most of Africa's civil wars and conflicts during the late 1980s and 1990s are attributable to popular struggles against hegemonic one-party states or states in which party–state relations had become a hindrance to plurality and power sharing.

### Dominant party

Dominant-party systems at times show similar characteristics to one-party systems. Several parties compete for power in elections, but this system is dominated by a single major party that ascends to power through non-democratic means and thus enjoys long periods in power. Of 16 dominant-party systems in Africa in the early 2000s, 8 had either experienced conflict or active armed opposition (Salih 2003).

### Two parties

Two-party systems are duopolistic in that two major parties have roughly equal prospects of winning elections and controlling government. In its classic form, it can be identified by three criteria: only two parties enjoy sufficient electoral and legislative strength to have a realistic prospect of winning elections; the larger party can rule alone with the remaining political parties providing the opposition; and power alternates between these two parties. Both are electable, the opposition serving not only as a shadow government, but also as a government in the wings (Ozler 2008).

This system is associated in African countries less with ideological polarization and more with ethnic affiliation and competition. Despite its association with adversarial politics, violent conflicts have prevailed in only one country (Sierra Leone) of six two-party countries.[1]

> **Most of Africa's civil wars and conflicts during the late 1980s and 1990s are attributable to popular struggles against hegemonic one-party states**

### Multiple parties

A multi-party system is characterized by competition among more than two parties, reducing the chances of single-party government and increasing the likelihood of coalitions. It is hard to define multi-party systems by number of parties or party supporters' social background. Conflict could also be one consequence of party democratization whereby internal squabbles for party leadership engender conflict.

Of 15 countries with multi-party systems, 9 have experienced some form of violent conflict before or after the transition to democracy.[2]

Polarized pluralism is characteristic of multi-party systems in countries where more marked social, ethnic or other severe cleavages separate major parties or where ethnically based political parties lose faith in the electoral process and opt for other means (such as military or electoral violence) to ensure the representation of their ethnic groups in parliament and thus then form the government, either alone or in coalition (Hague et al. 1998; Heywood 2002).

## Electoral systems and violent conflict

The difference between countries where elections take place peacefully and otherwise is, in essence, the depth to which they have institutionalized and consolidated democracy, and internalized democratic values.

An election is a mechanism for calling politicians to account and forcing them out of office when they fail to introduce policies that serve the public good or improve the quality life for citizens. It should be non-violent. And it is not an event—it is a process that influences how democratic processes and party politics unfold, determining what party will govern and the type of government (majority, minority, coalition).

Yet incumbent governments are under tremendous pressure to hold on to power by all means. The pressure emanates from their support base, because of its fear and uncertainty of what would happen if a new government were to win power and to secure access to the resources that come with winning state power. Elections therefore become highly charged, approached with a deadly serious and aggressive mentality designed to defeat political opponents and thus capture state power.

Electoral systems—elections in particular—weigh citizens' preferences and should be considered instruments for conflict management. They can of course contribute to violence, but are not the main factor for it. Most election-related violence subsides once election results are published, and winners and losers declared, as in Burundi, the Democratic Republic of the Congo and Togo. It is only when structural issues are unresolved by election time that conflicts may persist, as in Angola, Liberia, Mozambique (in the immediate post-liberation period) and Sierra Leone.

Does the type of electoral system have an association with violence?[3] Among the 19 countries covered

> **Electoral systems should be considered instruments for conflict management**

in table 5.1, the first past the post (FPTP) electoral system was the most conflict ridden. But despite the association, the system alone cannot explain why conflict is more likely with FPTP. Still, the proportional representation system is less conflictual and makes for inclusiveness in representation—a point backed up by the majority of expert respondents in the African Governance Report (AGR) III Expert Opinion Survey, who felt that electoral stability and diversity management are better promoted through proportional representation.

Thus electoral reforms cannot guarantee preventing violent conflict, as electoral systems are entwined with their manifold contexts. Violent conflicts associated with elections are symptoms of other deeper social problems that cannot be resolved by reforms to the electoral system, either alone or alongside reforms to party regulations.

## Election-related conflicts

Few African states have entirely escaped political conflict, including election-related violence. In 17 of the 40 project countries more than half the respondents agree or strongly agree that violence is a recurring phenomenon in general elections in their countries, with Kenya and Zimbabwe at one extreme and Seychelles and Algeria at the other (figure 5.1).

As suggested by respondents' attitudes, the scale varies widely among countries. For example, after the 2007 Kenyan election, an estimated 1,500 were killed and 600,000 displaced (Leonard et al. 2009; Kagwanja and Southall 2009). About 1,000 people were killed around the time of South Africa's founding elections in 1994. In Zimbabwe, most elections since 2000 have seen violence, with about 200 killed in 2002 and about 300 in 2008 (Commonwealth Secretariat 2002; Zimbabwe Election Support Network 2008). In 2005 in Ethiopia, nearly 200 people were killed during an election (Aalen and Tronvoll 2009). The unofficial death toll in Nigeria was put as high as 200 during the 2007 general election (Zasha et al. 2007; Egwu et al. 2009) and about 800 in post-election violence in 2011—the "Elections Year" (box 5.1). Côte d'Ivoire's disputed

**Table 5.1 Electoral systems and violent conflicts**

| Countries with political or electoral violence | System | Family |
|---|---|---|
| Algeria, Angola, Burundi, Liberia and Sierra Leone | List proportional representation | Proportional representation |
| Chad, Côte d'Ivoire, Egypt, Morocco and Tunisia | Party block vote/list proportional representation and first past the post | Mixed |
| Eritrea, Ethiopia, Nigeria, Sudan and Zimbabwe | First past the post | Plurality/majority |
| Central African Republic, Democratic Republic of the Congo, Guinea and Togo | Two-round system | |

Source: IDEA 2006; Hamdok and Salih 2007.

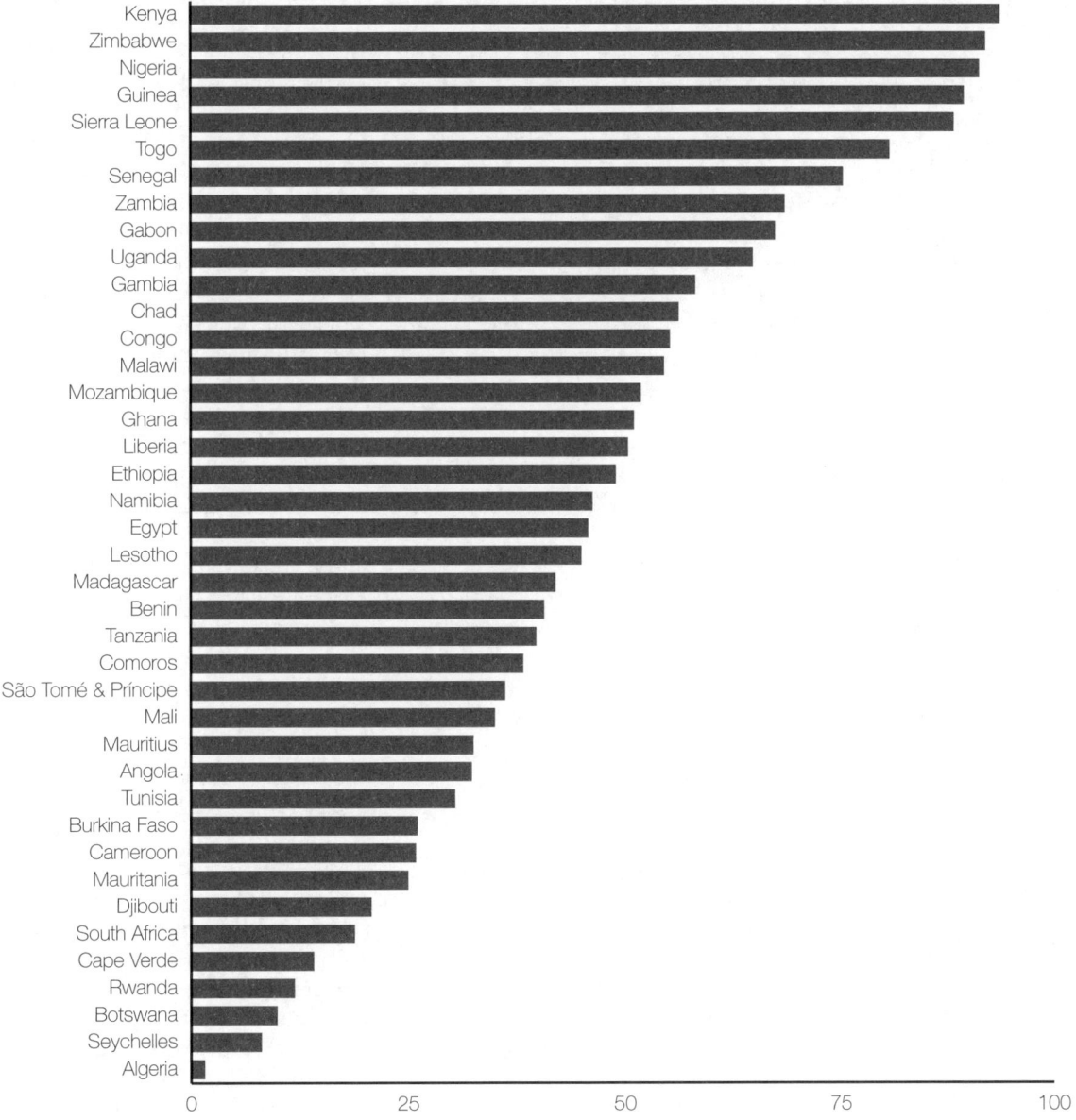

**Figure 5.1 Electoral violence is a recurring phenomenon at general elections—agree or strongly agree**

Share of experts surveyed agreeing with the statement, by country (%)

*Source:* AGR III Expert Opinion Survey 2012.

causes relate to deep-rooted socio-economic concerns related to diversity, or perceived unfairness or discrimination by certain structures in the electoral system. These causes are amplified where levels of diversity along ethnic, racial, religious or regional lines are high.

Conflict usually breaks out because of failure to resolve political and economic discrimination, as competition for resources, including power, intensifies along these lines during elections (boxes 5.2 and 5.3). In the worst case, this failure deepens society's fault-lines, leading to civil war (box 5.4).

The misery of such wars does not end with the postwar political settlement: Côte d'Ivoire, the Democratic Republic of the Congo, Nigeria and Zimbabwe have all experienced election-related violence, signs that earlier wounds had not completely healed, or that the settlements were not well managed.

Worse, controversy in Angola over the outcome of the September 1992 presidential election ignited a resumption of the civil war, which was fought for another 10 years. The outcome had been 49.6% for the incumbent Eduardo dos Santos and 40% for Jonas Savimbi. After disagreement on the outcome, a run-off was not held. Savimbi pulled out his UNITA forces from the national army and fighting resumed, causing thousands of casualties until his death in 2002.

Post-conflict states are prone to election-related violence where

election in 2010 saw about 3,000 killed, with many more displaced (Campbell 2011; Sane 2011).

The causes of election-related violence lie partly in short-term or "trigger" factors and partly in deeply rooted structural factors. Short-term causes relate to conjunctural issues pertaining to disputes about unfairness, disadvantage or misunderstandings about processes, mechanisms or decisions in an election. Long-term social and economic conditions have not improved significantly. In Liberia, for example, a significant portion of those at focus group discussions felt that violence was still a major feature of political campaigning (AGR III Liberia Country Report 2012). Historically rooted inequalities or grievances can also fan separatist demands, as in Eastern Africa, for separate states such as Eritrea, Somaliland and South Sudan. Where there is a large premium on resources like oil as in the Niger delta, violence is employed to press demands for wider redistribution of revenues.

In Kenya, competition for access to land was a major factor in conflicts during the 2002 and 2007 elections (Kanyinga 2009). The Rift Valley was the epicentre of violence in elections in 1992 and 1997, and the heartland of violence in 2007–2008. The Rift Valley is important because:

> It is multi-ethnic with several ethnic groups settled in the province. Numerically, significant groups include the Kalenjin, Masai, Kikuyu and Luhya. [And] the region has the largest share of total national votes and parliamentary constituencies, making it attractive because of the share of total national votes and constituencies that parties can obtain from ethnic blocs in the area. The use of the Westminster style, first past the post electoral system makes this particularly alluring (Kanyinga 2009, 326).

## Box 5.2 Freedom marred by violence, South Africa 1994

In 1994, South Africa experienced election-related violence that claimed more than 1,000 lives (Booysen 2009). It was the culmination of a decade of widespread political violence in KwaZulu-Natal province, where an estimated 20,000 people had lost their lives (Taylor 2002).

The roots lay in the contest for the province between the groups linked to the African National Congress and the Inkatha Freedom Party. While the former drew its support from a wider national base, the latter under Chief Gatsha Buthelezi drew from the ethno-regional base of the Zulus, one of the most populous sections of South African society.

Owing to the suspected hand of apartheid security forces, the contest for territory was especially sharp before 1994. Ethno-regional tensions were fanned, exacerbating the conflict between the two parties. The legacy of that contest was the violence of 1994.

Election-related violence has, though, fallen steeply in later elections, reflecting steps to prevent and manage conflict (see *Managing electoral conflict—other approaches*).

## Box 5.3 Electoral violence and the indigenous–settler divide in Nigeria

The November 2008 violence in Jos was some of the worst ever seen in the country: 200 (official) or 634 (other sources) killed. What was particularly frightening was that the violence had been increasing around elections since April 1994.

At its core was the battle for "ownership" of the city between the indigenous people of the Jos environs and the Hausa-Fulani community who had settled in the city.

It was a battle beyond the material gains of who became local government chairman or councillors. It was the symbolic meaning of ethnic origin of those elected, since that is directly linked to the issue of ownership. Religious identity was also implicated in the Jos crisis—while most Hausa-Fulani are Muslim, most indigenous groups are Christian.

*Source:* Egwu 2010.

Further, most of the former "white highlands" are in the Rift Valley, where groups compete to secure land rights.

Land-based conflicts were also prominent in Zimbabwe's elections in 2000 and 2002. Although the racial factor was a major element in land politics, the incumbent government manipulated the conflict to displace black farmworkers and intimidate them from voting for the opposition (Hammar et al. 2003; Sachikonye 2003).

More than half the experts surveyed in 10 countries agree or strongly agree that violence is a major feature of political campaigns in their country. In only four countries did fewer than 10% of respondents consider violence such a feature (figure 5.2).[4]

# Party democracy and conflict

*Internal party democracy*
Internal party democracy can benefit parties by strengthening partisan attachments, mobilizing members and supporters for participation in party activities, providing mechanisms for internal dispute settlement and nurturing a popular image for the party. It can also enhance the participatory and representational quality of democracy in the general polity (Bojinova 2007).

Applied to Africa, such democracy is in short supply for the following reasons:

- Political party functions— other than as bodies for contesting elections to control government—are poorly understood by the African public.

- Most parties are associated with the "big man" phenomenon in which parties become their fiefdoms.

- Most parties have no systematic registration of membership or fee collection, and so depend on a few interest groups, mostly educated elite supported by traditional leaders and chiefs, particularly during elections.

- The previous point also hinders party supporters' ability to hold the leadership accountable for finance and for selection of candidates at party primaries. When the party depends

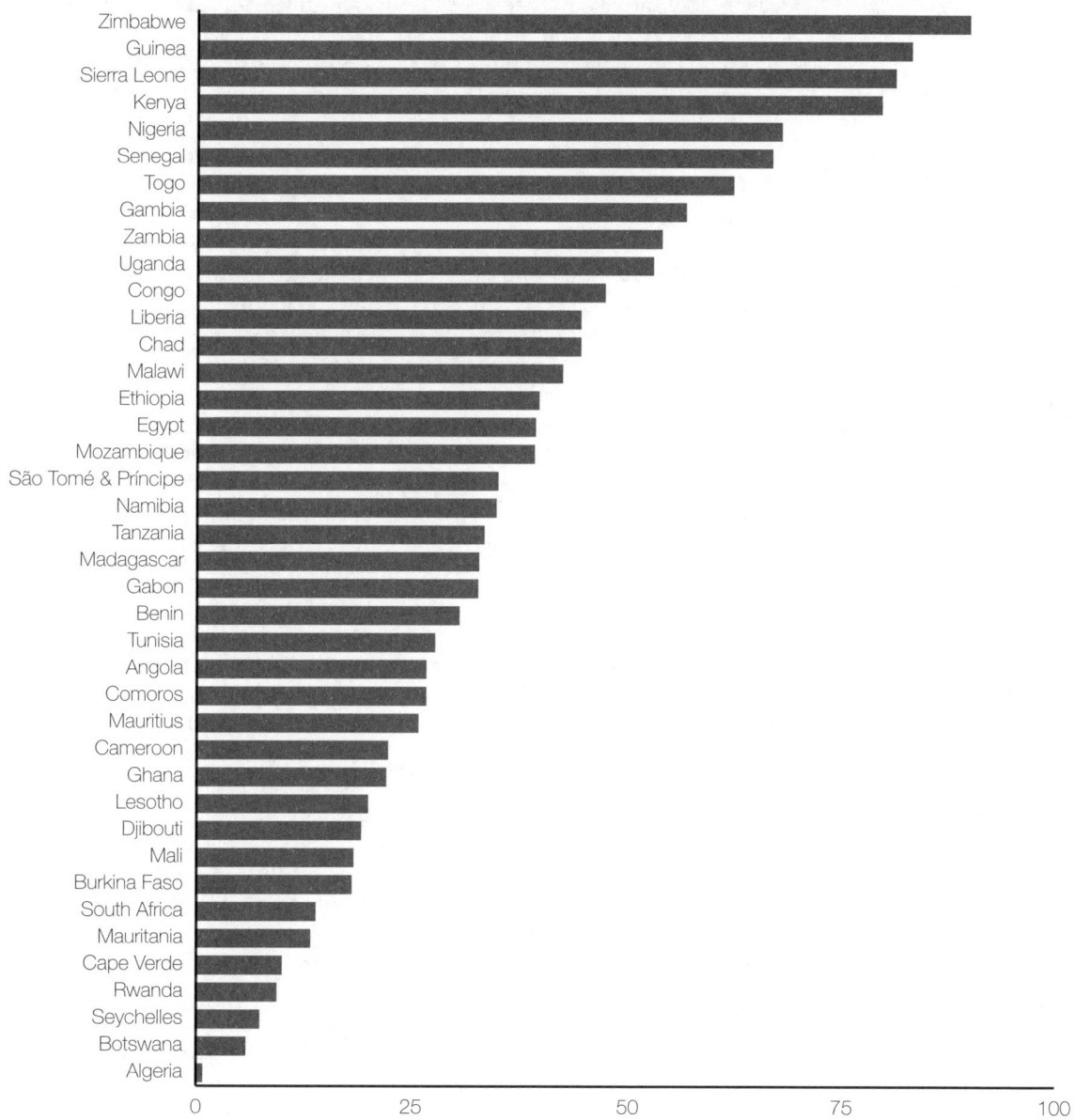

**Figure 5.2 Violence is a major feature of political campaigns—agree or strongly agree**

Share of experts surveyed agreeing with the statement, by country (%)

Zimbabwe
Guinea
Sierra Leone
Kenya
Nigeria
Senegal
Togo
Gambia
Zambia
Uganda
Congo
Liberia
Chad
Malawi
Ethiopia
Egypt
Mozambique
São Tomé & Príncipe
Namibia
Tanzania
Madagascar
Gabon
Benin
Tunisia
Angola
Comoros
Mauritius
Cameroon
Ghana
Lesotho
Djibouti
Mali
Burkina Faso
South Africa
Mauritania
Cape Verde
Rwanda
Seychelles
Botswana
Algeria

0  25  50  75  100

*Source:* AGR III Expert Opinion Survey 2012.

on a tycoon as a financier, party democracy shrinks greatly.

The lack of internal party democracy shows that the dominant interest group can manipulate intra-party democracy. It thus makes party leaders all the more important when they discuss both major issues that concern their party and the broader concerns of citizens and the state.

Internal disputes often spill over to party members and create division that either contributes to the split of the party and a new offshoot or weakens the party's resolve to address public issues. The more a political party is consumed by its own internal squabbles, the more unable its leaders are to govern or pay attention to managing it or to muster the goodwill of its membership.

As with public elections, party primaries can be highly contested affairs, particularly when they are the gateway to state power and wealth. Election irregularities, including rigging, are not uncommon, and other procedures are flouted. Competing candidates may mobilize groups, often among youth, to campaign for them, including through intimidation, bribery and violence (Tijjani 2003). Patrons and "godfathers" play a central role in party primary election contests, pitting their immense resources behind a candidate in the hope of exerting control once they win (chapter 6).

In Nigeria, in the build-up to the 2007 general elections, two governorship candidates were assassinated in what seemed internal party conflict during the party primaries (Adejumobi and Kehinde 2007). Zimbabwe, too, saw pre-election intra-party violence in both the Zimbabwe African National Union–Patriotic Front and the Movement for Democratic Change.

Such violence is symbolic of low levels of tolerance and democratic culture in parties more generally. Few countries ensure that primaries are beyond manipulation, and impunity is widespread. And intra-party violence feeds into the inter-party form, producing a lethal combination.

### Inter-party violence

Democratic stability is threatened when ethno-political cleavages reflect "the configuration of deeply divided societies in which two or more internally cohesive, sharply polarized, and spatially mixed groups are implacably arrayed against each other" (Mozaffar et al. 2003, 380–81), although there is no causal relationship between ethnic diversity and democratic instability.

Party systems, instead of treating ethnicity as a resource, sometimes foster ethnic exclusion. According to Horowitz (2003, 118–19), pooling electoral systems that:

> require candidates to achieve a regional distribution of votes in addition to a national plurality may foster conciliatory behaviour if territory is a proxy of ethnicity because groups are regionally concentrated. However, systems that do not provide incentives for vote

> *Patrons and godfathers play a central role in party primary election contests*

pooling and reaching out to other ethnic groups may make post-election reconciliation difficult, if not impossible.

Some scholars have put their faith in centripetalism, through political systems that promote inter-ethnic accommodation, multi-ethnic political parties and centre-based politics. A representative argument is:

> Divisive, zero-sum outcomes are not inevitable characteristics of politics in divided societies, but often a reaction to institutional rules of the game under which democratic competition of electoral processes takes place. Changes to these institutional rules, for example, by the introduction of electoral systems that facilitate cross-communal communication, bargaining and interdependence between rival politicians and the groups they represent can have a major impact on the promotion of moderate politics and thus prospects for democracy in divided societies (Reilly 2001, 2).

In ethnically divided countries, democracy tends to suffer, and under the usual types of electoral system, ethnic parties are likely to form, which can exacerbate the ethnic conflict (Chapman 2004). However, it is possible to design electoral systems that encourage moderate pan-ethnic parties responsive to all ethnic groups and able to get these groups' votes, as in Botswana, Ghana and Senegal.

The effects of election-related violence are not confined to contesting parties. When such violence spreads, it engulfs communities, as during the post-election period in Kenya in 2007–2008 and Côte d'Ivoire in 2010 (annex 5.1). Displacement causes major disruption to economic and social lives of communities. A great deal of trauma and post-stress disorder is generated, especially among victims, including many women and children (more than 1 million in Côte d'Ivoire in 2010–2011). Thus the multiple consequences of election-related violence are felt far beyond the parties and actors directly involved.

### State security agencies, militias and youth gangs

Ruling political parties can influence election campaigns and intimidate political opponents through state security agencies, party militias and youth groups.

State agencies

The police, army and intelligence forces make a real difference in promoting—or negating—free and fair elections. They may fan election conflict and are often prominent in rigging results and engendering disputes and even violence. In theory, they thus tarnish their reputation, becoming partisan bodies that cannot be trusted to run elections. When this happens, election-related conflicts can spread and explode. Such political bias within the security forces is evidenced in the failure to apprehend and prosecute offenders, resulting in a culture of impunity (Egwu 2010).

'*Party systems, instead of treating ethnicity as a resource, sometimes foster ethnic exclusion*

Although Egwu's observation covers just Nigeria's experience, it has clear relevance to other countries such as Côte d'Ivoire, the Democratic Republic of the Congo, Kenya and Zimbabwe. It is tempting for incumbent regimes to use state agencies such as the police to tilt the electoral process in their favour. In other instances, the military is also opportunistically used to buttress a regime that would have lost the election, as Côte d'Ivoire under former President Gbagbo suggested.

In the AGR III Expert Opinion Survey, in fewer than half the countries (19) did more than half the expert respondents consider their security agencies mostly or always fair and non-partisan in the electoral process (figure 5.3). But some countries' security forces have shown real professionalism (box 5.5).

Militias

Some militia groups of political parties camouflage themselves as youth wings; others are overtly militant with political affiliations. In Zimbabwe's elections in 2002 and 2008, sections of war veterans and state security groups were linked to the Zimbabwe African National Union–Patriotic Front, and fanned violence against the opposition parties (Zimbabwe Election Support Network 2002; Commonwealth Secretariat 2002). In the 2008 run-off, state-backed forces raised the level of violence, which ultimately dissuaded the Movement for Democratic Change leader, Morgan Tsvangirai, from standing (Zimbabwe Election Support Network 2008; Solidarity Peace Trust 2008;

EISA 2008). The compromise was a "Government of National Unity" in September 2008, brokered by Thabo Mbeki, with the Southern African Development Community (SADC) and African Union (AU) as guarantors.

Kenya provides an example where ethnic-based militias and private armies mushroomed, eroding the state's monopoly of violence.[5] They were part of the post-election violence of 2007–2008 (AGR III Kenya Country Report 2012), each fighting for their ethnic group's cause. Similarly in Nigeria, that particular state monopoly is challenged by ethnic militias, "area boys" and vigilante groups. Political actors sometimes take control of these groups, as in the Rivers, Anambra and Katsina states (AGR III Nigeria Country Report 2012). Militia groups are part of the political landscape in that country—arms in political parties' negotiations for power (Adejumobi and Kehinde 2007).

State-linked militia in Côte d'Ivoire were linked to post-election violence in 2010 and early 2011.

Youth gangs

In states that experience election-related violence regularly, some of the principal actors are young people. Although they are not usually the initiators of the strategy, they play a major role in the violence itself at the behest of party leaders. In much pre- and post-election violence, youths are recruited and unleashed as "foot soldiers" by party leaders or patrons. Predominantly young males, they are weaned on

Share of experts surveyed, by country (%)

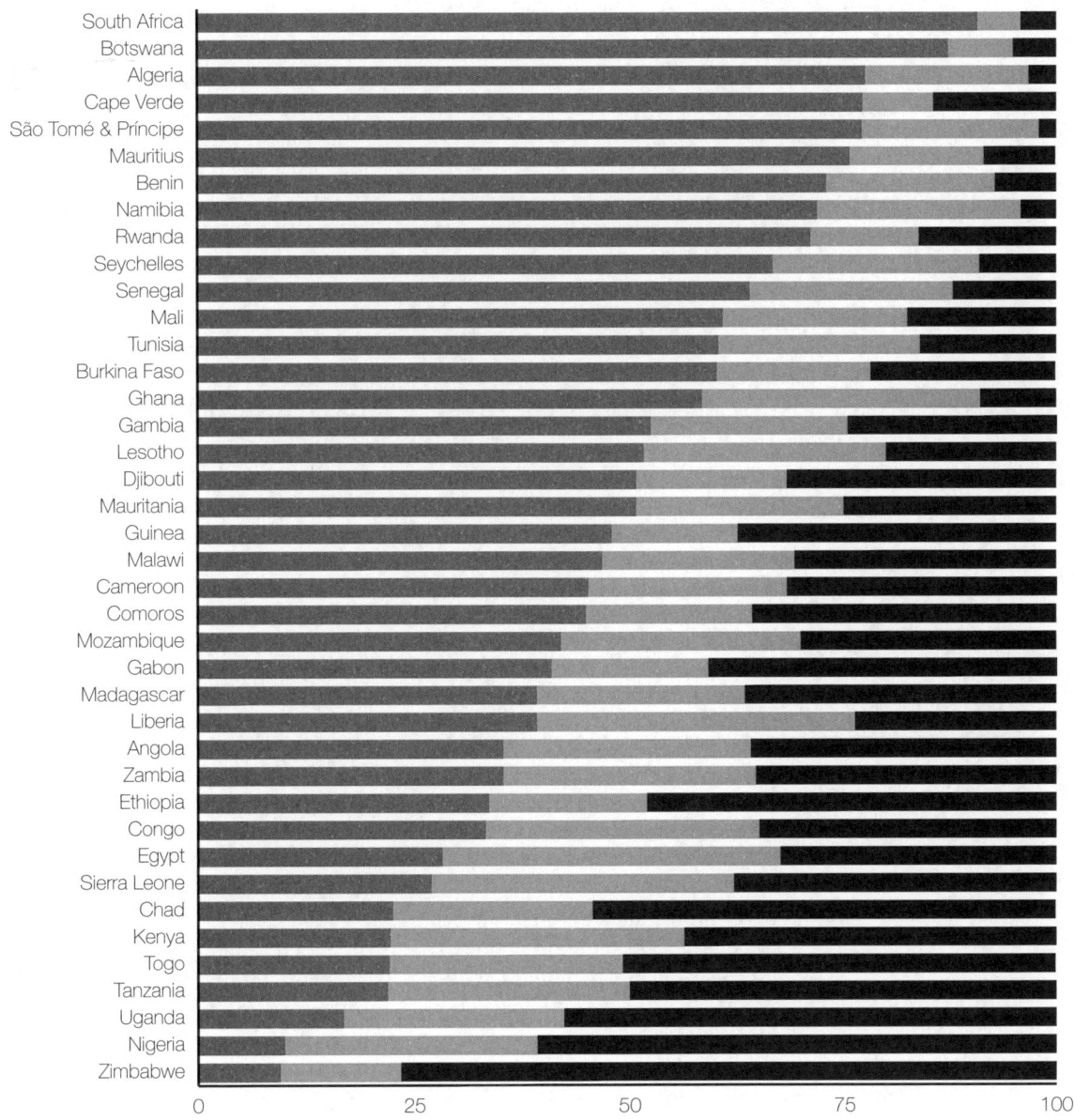

- ■ Mostly or always
- ■ Sometimes
- ■ Not at all or rarely

*Source:* AGR III Expert Opinion Survey 2012.

party propaganda and hate speech before they are set upon opponents (of the same or a different party).

High unemployment and poverty turn youth into fertile ground for participants in violence. Cash, alcohol, food and promises for work and positions in party and government are baits. There is little or

no ideological training to act with restraint, which explains the chilling and mindless violence against opponents in Burundi, Côte d'Ivoire, the Democratic Republic of the Congo, Kenya, Nigeria, Sierra Leone and Zimbabwe (box 5.6).

## Role of media in election conflicts

The role of the media is strategic: it has the power and influence to inflame the situation or to lower the political temperature through impartial reporting. In some instances of violence, the media fan the embers of hate and revenge, as seen in the Rwandan genocide and Kenyan post-election violence. Elsewhere, as in Zimbabwe's post-election violence, some sections of the media play a disinformation and partisan campaign to shore up the incumbent party.

During electoral conflict in particular, the media are expected to behave more responsibly and not deliberately inflame matters. In Rwanda, for example, a legal provision states that no party or candidate should threaten or commit violence on another or candidate, or invite anyone to do this or otherwise impede the freedom to campaign (AGR III Rwanda Country Report 2012).

The media should also form independent and diverse views while at the same time avoiding comments that exacerbate conflict, and ensure that their information is correct and timely so as to mitigate the possibility of misinformation in the electoral process (AGR III Kenya Country Report 2012). In Kenya, the media handled around two-thirds of the information on political and electoral issues. During the 2007 general election, vernacular radio stations especially had a large impact on the outcome, and were linked to inciting election-related violence. In Sierra Leone, party-owned radios were accused of degenerating into "hate and propaganda mongering" (AGR III Sierra Leone Country Report 2012, 130). Owned at the time by the ruling and main opposition party, they were subsequently closed.

In Zimbabwe, the biased reporting on political and electoral processes by the state broadcaster has generated calls for it to turn into a genuinely public broadcaster that would cover elections on a "fair and balanced" basis (AGR III Zimbabwe Country Report 2012). The Zimbabwe Electoral Commission was enjoined to use its authority under the Electoral Act to ensure the broadcaster did not use hate speech during the campaign.

Electoral codes and media regulations need to contain provisions that guard against party and state media being inflammatory during electoral conflict.

## Managing electoral conflict—state mechanisms

Conflicts or disputes can arise at any stage of the electoral process (box 5.7). The critical point is how to prevent, manage and then resolve them, preventing them from festering, as that deepens mistrust between parties and candidates. Leonard (2010, 49) makes this

---

### Box 5.6  Youth and political violence in Sierra Leone

At the root of the decade-long civil war lay a class of marginalized young people, especially from rural areas, lacking education and jobs. Sierra Leone has a very high population of unemployed youth who are susceptible to recruitment. Because of their involvement in the conflict, their situation—especially the under- or unemployed—is a major concern for policy makers: there are more than 30,000 youth ex-combatants, sometimes used in violence.

Youth are becoming an ever-growing army of unemployed, socially alienated and a perennial threat to security, as seen in the political tensions before the 2012 elections.

*Source:* AGR III Sierra Leone Country Report 2012.

---

point, noting that the most important of the violence-mitigating features needed to make elections free and fair in Africa include:

> an independent electoral management body, . . . prompt and substantially fair judicial resolution of election disputes, effective and non-partisan oversight of the security of the electoral process (non-partisan police and an uninvolved army), and the assurance that losing parties will not be permanently disadvantaged.

This calls for mechanisms to speedily resolve the conflicts when they arise (as in Tunisia, box 5.8). Such mechanisms should include representatives of parties and contestants in the shape of committees that have authority to investigate causes of conflicts and prescribe solutions to them. In South Africa, for example, the mechanisms include conflict management panellists, law enforcement structures (such as joint operation committees), party liaison committees and the courts (Moepya 2010).

The most sensitive conflicts relate to ballot handling, and counting and announcing results. When there is little trust in how electoral management boards (EMBs) handle these stages, disputes flare up and can quickly become violent. Delays in announcing election results often raise the political temperature and fuel suspicion of ballot tampering.

Conflicts and especially violence at the counting and results-announcement stage harm the integrity of the process, and once it has been damaged, it is extremely hard to restore confidence in the process in the face of electoral disputes and violence. It is therefore vital to watch out for potential triggers of conflict.

These include suspicions about the handling of ballots, including their movement to and from counting centres, their collation and the timing of the results announcement. This phase of the electoral process in Africa—balloting and declaring results—can take two to four days, sometimes more, and is a period of very high tension. Handling this phase in a professional, transparent and even-handed manner would greatly reduce that tension and potential for conflict.

An electoral process cannot, however, always avoid genuine mistakes. There should be a built-in mechanism to enable a transparent process of recounting ballots or organizing a rerun in the affected constituency or district. Such was the case in Ghana's 2008 election, which was widely judged to have been free and fair (Kelly 2009). Even in that case, the election results showed that ethnic rivalries had not disappeared but, thankfully, "the key Akan–Ewe divide only manifests itself in electoral rather than violent rivalry, and regime changes enable this to be contained with each ethnic group having an opportunity to benefit from periods of being in government" (Kelly 2009, 446).

### Adjudicating disputes

The more efficient and effective an electoral system is, the fewer the electoral disputes requiring adjudication by courts or other bodies. Still, few elections are so perfect that they do not generate disputes. They can occur between parliamentary candidates, competing parties and rival presidential candidates. The United States in 2000 attracted the eyes of the world with the dispute between George Bush and Al Gore, the Republican and Democratic candidates. Africa more recently has seen heated disputes in Ethiopia (2005), Kenya (2007), Nigeria (2007), Zimbabwe (2008), Côte d'Ivoire (2010), Guinea (2010) and the Democratic Republic of the Congo (2011).

Most electoral disputes in Africa arise from the following malpractices: violations of electoral law or party electoral regulations; administrative inefficiency; procedural flaws; and corruption in the electoral process.[6]

While disputes are not preventable, what is crucial is whether mechanisms are in place to resolve them peacefully and satisfactorily (see chapter 4). The EMB, for example, needs to have certain principles for handling disputes, and its procedures should be known to everyone, rule based and predictable (AGR III Kenya Country Report 2012).

### Constitutional and legal basis of dispute adjudication

African constitutions and electoral law typically provide for adjudication mechanisms to resolve pre- and post-election disputes. The importance of such provisions is that the mechanisms would help reduce or eliminate the incidence of such disputes and prevent them from erupting into violence. In other words, without such provisions and mechanisms alongside other democratic diversity-management provisions and mechanisms, African elections will become mechanisms not for conflict prevention or resolution, but for conflict precipitation and aggravation.

Where there are provisions for adjudication, it is common for the EMBs and the courts to share the powers. While pre-election disputes are generally handled through internal party-adjudication mechanisms or the normal law courts (or both), post-election disputes in a number of countries such as Nigeria and Sierra Leone are handled in special courts (or election tribunals). Both types usually come under provisions for reviewing their decisions—by the EMBs, for review by the courts; by courts, for review by higher courts.

A general principle for reviewing decisions in electoral disputes adjudicated by EMBs is that aggrieved candidates and parties must have recourse to the courts because EMBs, embedded as they often are in the political "thicket", should not be judge or jury in their own case.

> ❦ **African constitutions and electoral law typically provide for adjudication mechanisms to resolve pre-and post-election disputes**

In Ethiopia, Electoral Law Proclamation No. 53 grants the National Electoral Board powers to "investigate, cancel election results, order re-election or order injunction of the act and bring perpetrators before the court of law where it has received information about violation of law in the election process". In South Africa, Electoral Commission Act No. 15 of 1996 empowers the Independent Electoral Commission to adjudicate election-related disputes arising from the organization, administration and conduct of elections, if they are of an administrative nature, and to resolve issues that are a subject of objection or appeal to it by conciliation. The law also provides for appeal against the decisions of the electoral commission on disputes to the Electoral Court, which acts as the final court of appeal on such matters and which has the same status as the Supreme Court.

In Nigeria, in cases decided by the Supreme Court, the jurisprudence of election dispute adjudication has shifted from a position of noninterference in what was described as "a domestic affair" of political parties regarding their nomination processes for elective public office to one of accepting and adjudicating election-related party disputes brought by aggrieved party members.

The credibility of the election courts is not always high. In 2007 after Kenya's disputed presidential election, one of the contenders declined to apply for an election petition over ineffective judicial procedures. Their impartiality is also sometimes contested. For example in Sierra Leone, corruption was believed to undermine the independence of judges (AGR III Sierra Leone Country Report 2012).

Delays are also an issue. Election petitions have all too commonly dragged out in court, hurting public confidence and government legitimacy. Tardiness by the Supreme Court to rule on a case between the National Electoral Commission and the main opposition party in Sierra Leone over cancellation of 477 polling stations produced tension between the Chief Electoral Commissioner and the opposition for more than four years. Delays in dealing with 2007's electoral complaints created a legitimacy crisis for government in opposition strongholds in the Southern and Eastern regions (AGR III Sierra Leone Country Report 2012).

Responding to delays, Ghana has instituted a mechanism to provide timely electoral dispute resolution. In 2008, the Chief Justice of Ghana issued a policy directive to designated judges and courts to hear election disputes and petitions as well as electoral offences that would be brought before them (AGR III Ghana Country Report 2012). Election disputes and petitions would be heard by supervising High Court judges and designated judges in the regions. In Mauritius, election-related disputes are usually monitored at the judicial level, where results of elections can be challenged through election petitions (AGR III Mauritius Country Report 2012).

Malawi too has risen to the challenge (box 5.9).

Unflattering perceptions of dispute management
The general picture from the Expert Opinion Survey is that election disputes are not well managed (figure 5.4). Only in eight countries did at least half the respondents agree or strongly agree that election disputes are well managed to the satisfaction of the political parties. In 15 countries more than half the respondents disagreed or strongly disagreed. These findings point to a serious vacuum in institutional mechanisms for handling election disputes.

States should therefore devise appropriate mechanisms—election courts or tribunals. The mechanism must be rooted within the judicial system, and work closely with the EMB.

High costs
As processing election disputes and petitions is expensive, only parties and candidates with deep pockets "need apply". Those with limited resources will struggle, so a legal assistance fund to assist them to file and sustain their petitions may be needed, for example. This would help dispute mechanisms cater to the diversity of players in the electoral process.

**Experiences in managing electoral conflicts**
In Southern Africa, mechanisms of mediation, arbitration and conciliation are being increasingly used in conflict prevention and management. Their merit lies in their

---

**Box 5.9  Malawi's reform of adjudication**

Because of weak deadlines to deal with election-related cases, most cases before the high court in Malawi drag on way beyond the election period and most of them turn purely academic.

Noting that justice delayed is justice denied, the Chief Justice issued a Practice Direction (No. 2) in February 2009 abridging the time periods for the cases to be dealt with. The document stipulates steps and time-frames for proceedings to be respected by the High Court and Supreme Court of Appeal as well as the parties involved to avoid unnecessary delays. It provides for 24 days between the time an application is made and the time the High Court should rule. These steps were needed: Malawians are generally dissatisfied with how electoral disputes are managed (see figure 5.4).

*Source:* AGR III Malawi Country Report 2012.

---

cost-effectiveness, accessibility and swiftness during the electoral process. Mauritius, Namibia and South Africa usually take their disputes to election tribunals and courts (Kadima 2009), although the Democratic Republic of the Congo (and South Africa) uses other mechanisms, too.

Conflict management panels are appropriate, especially where even courts are not seen as impartial, and in rural areas where courts are scarce. The creation of multi-party liaison committees in some countries has enabled EMBs to consult stakeholders regularly and address issues as they arise. In South Africa, party liaison committees have been a major force in reducing electoral deaths by defusing electoral disputes (box 5.10).

A recent attempt in Sierra Leone to address inter-party strife is a 2012 amendment to the Political Parties

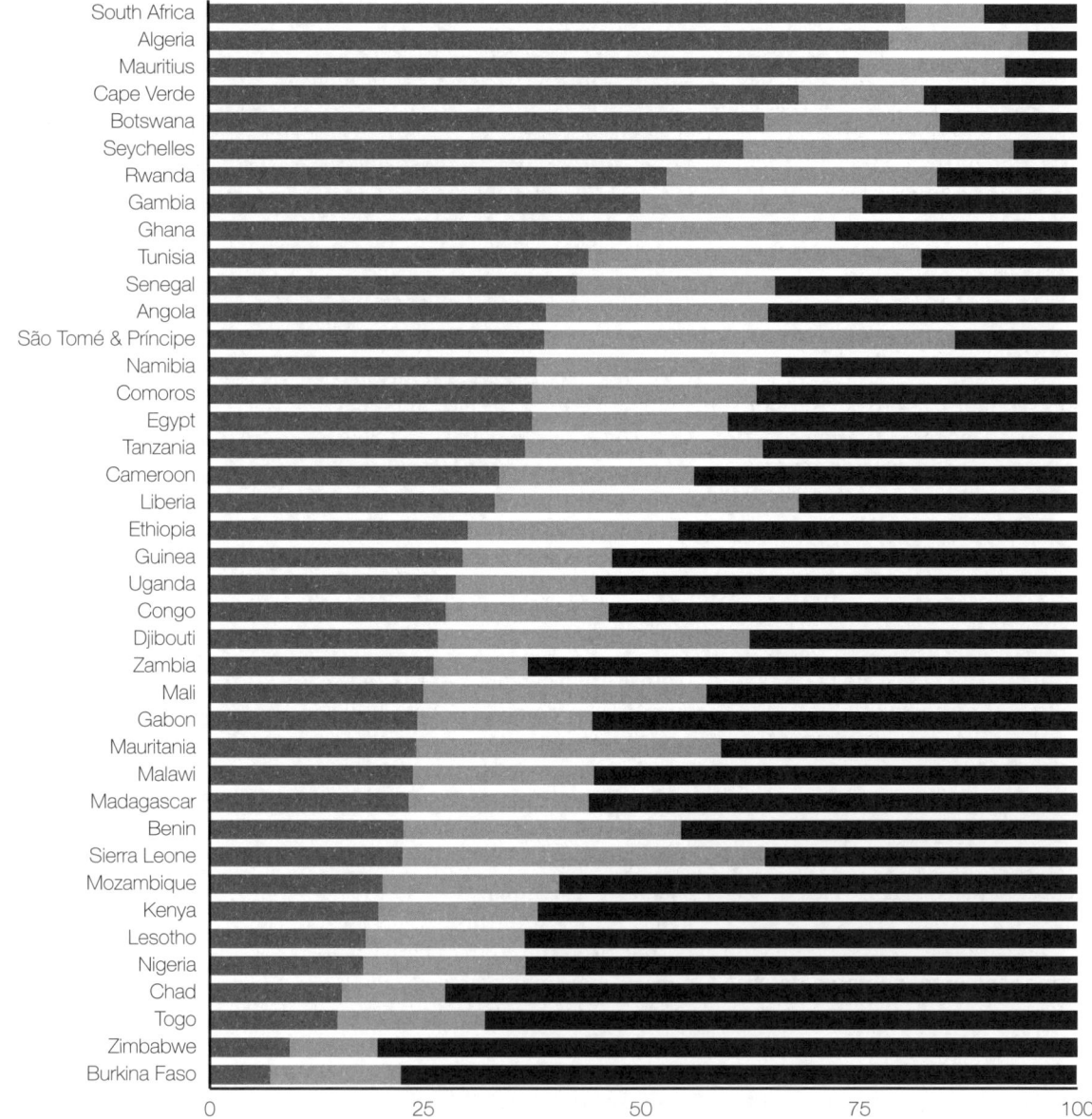

**Figure 5.4 Election disputes are usually well managed to the satisfaction of the political parties**

Share of experts surveyed, by country (%)

■ Agree or strongly agree
▨ Neither agree nor disagree
■ Strongly disagree or disagree

South Africa
Algeria
Mauritius
Cape Verde
Botswana
Seychelles
Rwanda
Gambia
Ghana
Tunisia
Senegal
Angola
São Tomé & Príncipe
Namibia
Comoros
Egypt
Tanzania
Cameroon
Liberia
Ethiopia
Guinea
Uganda
Congo
Djibouti
Zambia
Mali
Gabon
Mauritania
Malawi
Madagascar
Benin
Sierra Leone
Mozambique
Kenya
Lesotho
Nigeria
Chad
Togo
Zimbabwe
Burkina Faso

0    25    50    75    100

*Source:* AGR III Expert Opinion Survey 2012.

Registration Commission, which seeks to strengthen the commission's regulatory powers over political parties. The amendment has been described as "remarkable in that it is the first of its kind in the region and provides extensive oversight powers on political party activities" (Fortier 2012).

## Managing electoral conflict—other approaches

The discourse on conflict management and resolution needs further development. For one thing, good practices are too rarely disseminated—not all election conflicts turn violent and displace people. For another, electoral policy makers need to learn from and build on those experiences that have not only successfully defused electoral conflicts but have established electoral systems that minimize grievances grounded in diversity and unfairness. Some good practices—from civil society and international and regional organizations—that have helped to prevent or resolve election-related conflicts are now highlighted.

### Civil society initiatives

South Africa. Election deaths fell from more than 1,000 in 1994 to zero in the 2004 and 2009 elections. This sterling achievement stems largely from pre-emptive work by civil society organizations (CSOs) and the Independent Electoral Commission, as well as party liaison committees. Tackling political intolerance, the KwaZulu-Natal Democracy and Elections Forum—a network of 17 CSOs—was formed in

> ### Box 5.10  Party liaison committees in South Africa
>
> Created in 1998 with membership drawn from two representatives of each registered party, the party liaison committees serve as a vehicle for consultation and cooperation between the Independent Electoral Commission and political parties on electoral matters.
>
> They have played a direct and crucial role in ensuring that the immediate and direct contestants in an election regularly consult each other and the commission on any matter that may harm the credibility, freeness and fairness of any legislative election. These committees keep up their activities, unlike other conflict resolution mechanisms, throughout the electoral cycle.
>
> One example: to avoid the issue of boundary disputes, the commission consults party liaison committees in all spheres of government, on the time-frames and principles for each cycle of delimiting voting districts, and the approval system to be followed.
>
> *Source:* Moepya 2010.

1998 to ensure a provincial electoral environment that would accommodate free and peaceful participation (Mottiar 2010). Five subcommittees were set up on democracy and voter education, violence monitoring, mediation and conflict resolution, election observation, and legal compliance and litigation (box 5.11).

The CSOs succeeded in defusing political violence in the most volatile province in South Africa. Election-related violence across the country also fell heavily over the 15 years after 1994. These CSO initiatives were complemented by the Electoral Act (1998), which contains a binding Code of Conduct for parties and candidates, and by an Electoral Court (Booysen 2009).

The Electoral Institute for Sustainable Development in Africa (EISA) model helped assuage election-related conflict through community-based mediation panels. Named after the regional EISA, which conceived and propagated it, the model emerged out of the institute's practical experiences in assisting countries. Starting in South Africa, it has been replicated in Lesotho and Zambia. Some traditional chiefs, security forces and even the judiciary have joined the effort (Kadima 2009).

Democratic Republic of the Congo. EISA helped to set up panels with the EMB, political parties and CSOs. Grass-roots initiatives were used to prevent and manage conflicts (Kadima and Tshiyoyo 2009). The mediators played a crucial role in defusing and managing conflicts that emerged among the grass roots, especially in North and South Kivu and Maniema, where the potential for violence was high (Kadima and Tshiyoyo 2009).

Nigeria. The National Campaign on Reduction of Electoral Violence was introduced in 2007 as a systematic approach to tracking election violence and making information available in the form of an early warning system to stakeholders, police and state authorities, and creating channels for responding to violence as it developed (Egwu 2010).

### Election-related mediation by international and regional organizations

Mediation in election disputes by international and regional organizations has grown recently, including that by the United Nations (UN), AU, Economic Community of West African States (ECOWAS) and SADC. It proved critical in Guinea, Kenya and Zimbabwe. These efforts should be made sustainable to provide a sufficient basis for those countries to wean themselves off such assistance in the medium to long term.

The challenge now is to set up an early warning system through which these organizations can intervene to pre-empt conflict in the first place. Their protocols on governance and elections should therefore be ratified so that they can begin to get involved more closely in managing conflict (AU 2007; SADC 2004).

Already, the AU's innovative Continental Early Warning System is an attempt to forestall diversity-related conflicts, especially related to elections (box 5.12). It needs further strengthening. The same applies to the commitment of the AU to EMBs when they require such support. Elections should be transformed into conflict management tools rather than conflict and instability triggers (AU Panel of the Wise 2010).

An even larger issue is tackling the very structure—of diversity and inequality—that incubates election conflict. As seen, its conditions are historically rooted, and only concerted political action by national governments, parties and CSOs will suffice. The root problems must be eradicated—it is not enough to deal with their manifestations during election time.

African countries have already developed regional and subregional mechanisms. At the pan-African level, the AU's African Charter on Democracy, Governance and Elections stipulates that state parties to the Charter shall (AU 2007):

- establish and strengthen independent and impartial national electoral bodies responsible for the management of elections;

- establish and strengthen national mechanisms that redress election-related disputes in a timely manner;

- ensure fair and equitable access by contesting parties and candidates to state controlled media during elections; and

- ensure that there is a binding code of conduct governing

### Box 5.12  The Continental Early Warning System

Article 12 of the Protocol Relating to the establishment of the Peace and Security Council of the African Union (AU) provides for the establishment of the Continental Early Warning System (CEWS) whose primary purpose is the "provision of timely advice on potential conflicts and threats to peace and security to enable the development of appropriate response strategies to prevent or resolve conflicts in Africa".

The CEWS consists of two parts:
- an observation and monitoring centre known as "the situation room" at the Conflict Management Directorate of the AU, and responsible for data collection and analysis on the basis of an appropriate early warning indicators module; and
- observation and monitoring units of the regional mechanisms to be linked directly through appropriate means of communications to the situation room, and to collect and process data at their level and transmit them to the situation room.

Since 2006, efforts have been made to get the CEWS up and running, although much more needs to be done to ensure that it effectively deals with election-related conflicts.

*Source:* AU Panel of the Wise 2010, 46–47.

legally recognized political stakeholders, government and other political actors before, during and after elections. The code shall include a commitment by political stakeholders to accept the results of the election or challenge them through exclusively legal channels.

The AU and subregional organizations such as ECOWAS and SADC have mounted election observation missions in almost all elections where countries allow them. Further, Article 19 of the ECOWAS Conflict Prevention Framework stipulates the grouping's responsibility towards conflict prevention, that is, early warning, mediation, conciliation, preventive disarmament and preventive deployment, such as the ECOWAS mediating arm and its Standby Force (ECOWAS 2008).

At the subregional level, ECOWAS has also set a solid track record in bringing to bear its Conflict Prevention Framework (which should be read alongside "The Supplementary Protocol on Democracy and Good Governance"; ECOWAS 2001).

- Article 38 advocates for the strict adherence to constitutional norms in electoral practices that reject unconstitutional accession to or maintenance of power, and sets the parameters for the conduct of peaceful and credible elections that are free, fair and transparent. The Protocol further tasks ECOWAS to assist member states in electoral matters.

- Article 53 outlines mechanisms for ensuring the efficacy of the Democracy and Governance Protocol by outlining activities such that ECOWAS shall facilitate the provision of assistance to member states and local constituencies in the preparations for credible elections, including technical and financial support for the conduct of census, voter education, enactment of credible electoral codes, compilation of voters' registers and training of electoral officials, monitors and observers.

- Article 53 also urges member states to encourage the establishment of permanent

platforms that bring together electoral management boards, political parties, security services, the media and civil society for the exchange of views, formulation of electoral codes of conduct and modalities for the peaceful resolution of election-related disagreements.

ECOWAS has used intervention (Sierra Leone and Liberia), mediation and reconciliation approaches (Gambia, Guinea and Togo), as well as the threat of force (Burkina Faso, Côte d'Ivoire and Mali) in some West African countries where national mechanisms had failed.

The East African Community (EAC) and SADC have also established mechanisms in their member states. The SADC Principles and Guidelines Governing Democratic Elections have been tested twice (Matlosa 2005). Although SADC's efforts have not managed to gain more than a government of national unity in Zimbabwe, it did remove Madagascar's president, who staged a coup in March 2009. In that instance, SADC not only refused to recognize the usurpers but also suspended the country from all SADC institutions (Møller 2009).[7]

Coalitions of SADC countries have intervened—with UN or SADC mandates—to restore democracy in countries under political stress. In response to the joint Rwandan and Ugandan military intervention in the Democratic Republic of the Congo in 1998, Angola, Namibia and Zimbabwe sent forces to protect the regime of Laurent Kabila, which

> ' *The African Union's innovative Continental Early Warning System is an attempt to forestall diversity-related conflicts*

might be seen as collective defence in the sense of the UN Charter's article 51. Even though the mission initially had no formal SADC mandate, it was later endorsed, after the fact. Earlier in 1998, South Africa and Botswana launched an intervention in Lesotho, officially to prevent a military coup, which likewise received an SADC mandate of sorts (Møller 2009).

The EAC is developing its election observation guidelines and the long-awaited EAC Protocol on Good Governance. However, the sub-regional community has put to good use the AU Declaration on the Principles Governing Democratic Elections in Africa, the UN Declaration on Human Rights and the International Covenant on Civil and Political Rights. It is under these guidelines that the EAC launched several election observation missions to Kenya in 2007 and Burundi in 2010.

These actions by the AU illustrate the strong role it is playing in mediation—though some conflicts still need urgent defusing work.

## Conclusions and recommendations

This chapter tentatively draws the following conclusions:

- Party systems and electoral systems are invariably linked to propensity for conflict, with proportional representation associated with less acrimonious and violent elections than other systems.

- Most political parties have a deficit in intra-party democracy,

which is sometimes manifested in clashes between contenders' supporters. More ominous, however, is inter-party conflict during election campaigns and over disputed election outcomes.

- Party liaison committees have been potent in defusing disputes during elections.

- Successful mediation by international and regional organizations has increased. Although positive in Kenya and Zimbabwe, the challenge remains to remove the root causes of these conflicts, as well as their conjunctural triggers.

- Dispute-settlement mechanisms are still not properly institutionalized in most countries—too little is done, too late.

- The tools for preventing violence should be woven into each stage of the electoral cycle.

EISA (2010) sums up some lessons from Africa's election crises (box 5.13), which, along with the above conclusions, set the stage for the following recommendations.

### A holistic approach

In situations of diversity, as in much of Africa, elections should not be viewed as a quick fix to challenges of access to power, development and peace and stability. The conditions should be suitable and appropriate, and it inadvisable to rush an election before enough preparation has been carried out. The legal, constitutional and electoral framework

> *Successful mediation by international and regional organizations has increased*

should be clear, transparent and strictly followed by contestants, as disputes among them about the framework and time-frame do not augur well.

### Elections as a conflict management tool

Free, fair and peaceful elections contribute towards resolving competition for power and succession. They give citizens an opportunity to choose between different ideologies and programmes at local, regional and national levels. The best parties, candidates and programmes should win. Elections should be transformed into conflict management tools rather than triggers for conflict and instability (AU Panel of the Wise 2010), and thus structures should be set up to ensure that electoral disputes are handled amicably and early so that they do not escalate into violence.

### Early warning system on elections

Those charged with election administration should set up an early warning system that identifies areas prone to election-related conflict, so that contesting parties, the EMB, state security agencies and CSOs work together to defuse disputes. Their work may well be front-loaded to the early stages of the electoral cycle before grievances develop further. Information from national and regional research bodies, the African Peer Review Mechanism and the media should form the basis of the collective knowledge on these hot spots (AU Panel of the Wise 2010).

### Electoral codes of conduct and party liaison committees

In addition to formal electoral regulations, also important are electoral codes of conduct endorsed by contesting parties, the EMB and state authorities involved in elections.

These codes place an obligation, particularly on contesting parties and candidates, to desist from activities such as hate speech and violence. Penalties for infringing such codes should be specified and enforced.

Party liaison committees can play a valuable role during election campaigns by providing a channel for airing grievances and misunderstandings during campaigns. Constant communication between committee members, the EMB and state agencies such as the police can help to defuse tension.

### Professional and non-partisan role of state security agencies

Some state security agencies move beyond their professional and non-partisan boundaries during elections. This amounts to an abuse of power, which skews the electoral playing field and can generate considerable violence. Many agencies can act with impunity, dissolving respect for them. It is absolutely imperative that state agencies remain non-partisan and professional, and those that do not should be judged in the appropriate courts.

### Policies towards youth

Some of the worst election violence has been committed by gangs of unemployed youths, recruited by unscrupulous politicians. Strategies to address election-related violence should therefore include ways to gainfully occupy or rehabilitate youth so that they do not fall prey to such approaches. Programmes should also be launched for them to be exposed to civic education so as to dissuade them from violence.

### Mediating role of regional organizations

Countries should be encouraged to ratify protocols that relate to elections and democratic governance. Africa's regional and subregional initiatives on democracy and good governance, and dispute management of elections, should be harmonized and coordinated to maintain pan-African policy coherence. AU (2007) provides a laudable policy framework, which should be put into practice and implemented by the subregional integration organizations in an active rather than reactive manner.

### Election observation and monitoring

Contesting parties may be deterred from electoral abuse if they know that they are being watched and their activities documented. There should therefore be unrestricted scope of their observation and monitoring during elections by groups that meet the criteria in the electoral law.

### Research

Africa's research base on elections and related violence, dispute management, EMBs and the increasing role of regional and subregional organizations is far too small. Research centres and institutions need support to analyse the processes of democratic governance, including the role of political parties, EMBs and elections.

Research should be conducted to reconsider the factors influencing the relationship among party systems, electoral systems and diversity, and should examine the

> *Africa's regional and subregional initiatives on democracy and good governance should be harmonized and coordinated to maintain pan-African policy coherence*

circumstances in which diversity is a factor of stability rather than violence and instability.

The linkages between electoral systems and conflict should also be researched further, to find out the extent to which a particular electoral system reduces prospects of conflict. (For instance, how much more capable of defusing election-related conflict is the proportional representation system?)

### Policy dialogue

Legal and administrative dispute-management instruments are plentiful, but a chasm yawns between principle and practice. Some of them are too imperfect to stymie the more sophisticated malpractices. A review of them is therefore needed.

There is an urgent need to redress the intra- and inter-party democratic deficit and to establish credible mechanisms for managing internal party disputes. Owing to common factors that propel inter- and intra-party disputes, it is important that these two processes are treated as an integral part of promotion efforts for internal democracy. Platforms for party-to-party dialogue are needed for responding to national, non-partisan issues.

### Training

Programmes are needed to develop the capacity of election administration staff.

# Annex 5.1 Inter-party violence in six African countries

### Burundi (2010)

In April 2009, the Party of the Liberation of the Hutu People abandoned armed struggle and formed a political party. Pierre Nkurunziza, former leader of the Hutu rebel group, National Council for the Defence of Democracy–Forces for the Defence of Democracy, became president in August 2005 after the group swept local and parliamentary elections—a coalition of 17 opposition groups.

In line with the new constitution, the government consists of a 60/40 Hutu–Tutsi ratio. Yet in May 2010 the situation began deteriorating when 13 opposition parties rejected the results of Burundi's landmark district elections, claiming massive fraud. Twelve of them formed a coalition, the Alliance of Democrats for Change, in early June and announced a boycott of the presidential elections of 28 June 2010. The elections were further marred by political violence that escalated with the start of the presidential campaign on 12 June.

### Côte d'Ivoire (2010)

In April 2008, political party leaders signed a landmark code of conduct in a high-profile ceremony attended by UN Secretary General Ban Ki-moon. On 12 February 2010, President Gbagbo dissolved both the government and the Independent Electoral Commission, in which he accused the head of the commission, Robert Mambé, of adding names to the electoral register to boost the opposition vote.

A presidential election was held in two rounds. The first was held on 31 October 2010, and a second, in which President Laurent Gbagbo faced opposition leader Alassane Ouattara, was held on 28 November 2010. Former president Gbagbo refused to step down after African and Western countries declared that his rival, Alassane Ouattara, won the election. Gbagbo, backed by the army and youth militias, hung onto power, while Ouattara set up a rival power centre from a local hotel, protected by UN troops and soldiers from a former northern rebel group. The stalemate was ended with the capture of Gbagbo in April 2011.

### Guinea (2010)

In elections of 27 June 2010, Cellou Diallo, Prime Minister and candidate of the Union of Democratic Forces of Guinea, obtained 44% of the votes, setting up a run-off with the veteran opposition politician and leader of the Rally of the Guinean People, Alpha Condé, who emerged as the runner-up of the contest with 18% of the votes. Following the first round of voting, Condé lodged a complaint with the courts, accusing officials of the electoral commission of defrauding his candidacy of 600,000 votes. The courts upheld Condé's accusations and sentenced the head of the Independent Electoral Commission of Guinea and another top official to one year in jail. The conviction sparked a week of violence between supporters of the two remaining contestants for the presidency.

### Kenya (2007–2008)

The 27 December 2007 elections pitted President Mwai Kibaki and his Party of National Unity against Raila Odinga, leader of the Orange Democratic Movement, and Kalonzo Musyoka, head of the Orange Democratic Movement–Kenya. The Electoral Commission of Kenya announced Kibaki the winner, with 4,584,721 votes against Odinga's 4,352,993 votes. In the parliamentary elections that took place at the same time as the presidential elections, Kibaki's party won 43 of 210 parliamentary seats, Odinga's party won 99, and small parties won the other seats. In the local government elections, Kibaki's party won 437 of 2,484 seats while Odinga's party won 1,037 seats. Fighting between supporters of Mwai Kibaki and the Party of National Unity—mainly members of the Kikuyu tribe—and supporters of Raila Odinga's Orange Democratic Movement Party—mainly members of the Luo and the Kalenjin tribes—occurred in Nairobi, the Rift Valley and Kisumu.

### Malawi (2009)

About 30 armed police officers stormed Njaba Freedom Park to stop the first Mgwirizano Coalition rally after the Blantyre City Assembly had issued an eleventh-hour ban on the rally because President Muluzi was holding another rally in Bangwe Township, about 8 kilometres away. In a separate incident, National Democratic Alliance leader Brown Mpinganjira and members of his entourage escaped unhurt when about 20 Young Democrats armed with stones and machetes allegedly deployed by the United Democratic Front Director of Youth pelted stones at their vehicles while a service was in progress. In all these incidents, there were confrontations between the various youth militias.

### Zimbabwe (2008)

Violence continued after the election as talks between Zimbabwe African National Union–Patriotic Front and the Movement for Democratic Change failed to stem their tide. For example, three opposition activists were killed since the talks began. In Buhera South, more than 17 Movement for Democratic Change activists were badly beaten by militia around 17 July. Widespread political rather than limited electoral violence has been the hallmark of Zimbabwean politics over the last decade.

*Source:* ECOWAS 2010; EAC 2010; Human Rights Watch 2010; Justice 2010; Zimbabwe Human Rights NGOs Forum 2008; Omotosho 2008.

## Notes

1. Benin, Cape Verde, Ghana, Nigeria, Sierra Leone and Seychelles. The 2011 elections indicate that Nigeria is drifting towards a dominant-party system through the capacity of the governing People's Democratic Party to manipulate elections.

2. Algeria, Burundi, Central African Republic, Egypt, Liberia, Mali, Morocco, Niger and Tunisia. Although Egypt and Tunisia are classified as multi-party democracies, their electoral systems were designed such that the authoritarian National Democratic Party in Egypt and the Constitutional Party in Tunisia remained unchallenged and governed unopposed. Both parties were dissolved after the revolutions in 2011.

3. A subtle concept of violence would factor in psychological dimensions, including intimidating, harming or blackmailing political opponents around elections with a view to influencing the electoral process (Albert 2007; Ochoche 1997).

4. Algeria, Botswana, Seychelles and, encouragingly, Rwanda.

5. By 2007, militia groups were countrywide, including Mungiki, Jeshi la Embakasi, Baghdad Boys, Amachuma, Sungu Sungu and Jeshi la Mzee.

6. Corruption in the electoral process includes abuse of power of incumbency to gain allegedly unfair political advantage and to distort the electoral process; ballot design; ballot stuffing; ballot snatching; candidate substitution; contested declaration of election results; disappearance/abduction of polling officials; election financing; electioneering campaigns; electoral violence; establishment of illegal polling stations/units; harassment by police and security agents; inadequacy of polling stations/units; nature of the franchise; nomination processes; polling procedures; and residency requirements for voters and candidates (Leonard 2010).

7. See also Matlosa and Zounmenou (2011).

## References

Aalen, Lovise, and Kjetil Tronvoll. 2009. "The End of Democracy? Curtailing Political and Civil Rights in Ethiopia." *Review of African Political Economy* 36 (120): 193–207.

Adejumobi, Said, and Michael Kehinde. 2007. "Building Democracy without Democrats? Political Parties and Threats of Democratic Reversal in Nigeria." *Journal of African Elections* 6 (2): 95–114.

Albert, Isaac O. 2007. "Reconceptualising Electoral Violence in Nigeria." In *Perspectives on the 2003 Elections in Nigeria*, ed. Isaac O. Albert, Derrick Marco, and Victoria A. O. Adetula. Abuja: Stirling-Holding Publishers.

AU (African Union). 2007. "African Charter on Democracy, Governance and Election." Adopted by the Eighth Ordinary Session of the Assembly of the African Union, 30 January 2007, Addis Ababa.

———. 2012. "Note on the Elections Year and Elections Observation in Africa." Addis Ababa.

AU Panel of the Wise. 2010. *Election-related Disputes and Political Violence: Strengthening the Role of the AU in Preventing, Managing and Resolving Conflict*. New York: International Peace Institute.

Bekoe, Dorina. 2010. "Trends in Electoral Violence in Sub-Saharan Africa." Peace Brief 13, United States Institute of Peace, Washington, DC.

Bojinova, Denitza. 2007. "Internal Party Democracy in the European Old and New Democracies: Causes and Consequences." Paper presented at the annual meeting of the Southern Political Science Association, 3 January 2007, New Orleans. www.allacademic.com/meta/p143496_index.html, accessed 20 December 2010.

Booysen, Susan. 2009. "The Political Environment of Election 2009: Democracy Contestation." In *Election Update South Africa: February–July 2009*, 8–12. Johannesburg: Electoral Institute for Sustainable Development in Africa.

Campbell, Horace. 2011. "Gbagbo and the Ivorian Test: Moving Beyond Anti-imperialist Rhetoric." *Pambuzuka News*, 13 January, issue 512.

Chapman, David. 2004. "The Role of the Electoral System in the Resolution of Ethnic Conflict." Published in the Compendium of the Workshop on Analysing Conflict and its Resolution, Institute of Mathematics and its Applications, 28–30 June 2004, Oxford, UK.

Commonwealth Secretariat. 2002. *The Zimbabwe Presidential Election, 9–11 March 2002: The Report of the Commonwealth Observer Group*. London.

EAC (East African Community). 2010. *Preliminary Report of the EAC Election Observation Mission for the Legislative Elections in the Republic of Burundi*. Arusha, Tanzania: African Press Organization.

ECOWAS (Economic Community of West African States). 2001. "The Supplementary Protocol on Democracy and Good Governance." Abuja, 21 December 2001.

———. 2008. "The ECOWAS Conflict Prevention Framework." Regulation MSC/Reg.1/01/08. Abuja.

———. 2010. "Observer Mission for the Second Round of the 2010 Presidential Election in Guinea." Abuja, 8 November.

Egwu, Sam. 2010. "Elections and Violence in Nigeria." In *When Elephants Fight: Preventing and Resolving Election-related Conflicts in Africa*, ed. Khabele Matlosa, Gilbert M. Khadiagala, and Victor Shale. Johannesburg: Electoral Institute for Sustainable Development in Africa.

Egwu, Sam, David Leonard, and Khabele Matlosa. 2009. "Nigerian Elections since 1999: What Does Democracy Mean?" *Journal of African Elections* 8 (1): 108–44.

EISA (Electoral Institute for Sustainable Development in Africa). 2008. *The Zimbabwe Harmonized Elections of 29 March 2008*. EISA Election Observation Report 28. Johannesburg.

———. 2010. *When Elections Become a Curse: Redressing Electoral Violence in Africa*. EISA Policy Brief 1. Johannesburg.

Fischer, Jeff. 2002. "Electoral Conflict and Violence: A Strategy for Study and Prevention." IFES White Paper 2002-01, International Federation of Electoral Systems, New York.

Fortier, A. 2012. *Sierra Leone: Making the Votes Count*. Dakar: Open Society Initiative for West Africa.

Goldsmith, Arthur A. 2010. "Mixed Regimes and Political Violence in Africa." *Journal of Modern African Studies* 48 (3): 413–33.

Hague, Rod, Martin Harrop, and Shaun Breslin. 1998. *Comparative Government and Politics: An Introduction*. Basingstoke, UK: Macmillan.

Hamdok, Abdalla, and M. A. Salih. 2007. "A Preface to an Inclusive African Electoral Reform Agenda." *Journal of African Elections* 6 (1): 118–33.

Hammar, Amanda, Brian Raftopoulos, and Stig Jensen, eds. 2003. *Zimbabwe's Unfinished Business: Rethinking Land, State and Nation in the Context of Crisis*. Harare: Weaver Press.

Heywood, Andrew. 2002. *Politics: An Introduction*, second edition. New York: Palgrave Macmillan.

Horowitz, Donald L. 2003. "Electoral Systems: A Premier for Decision Making." *Journal of Democracy* 14 (4): 115–27.

Human Rights Watch. 2010. "Burundi: Crackdown on Rights Following Elections." News Release, 23 November 2010. www.hrw.org/en/news/2010/11/23/burundi-crackdown-rights-following-elections.

IDEA (International Institute for Democracy and Electoral Assistance). 2006. *Electoral Management Design: The International IDEA Handbook*. Stockholm. www.idea.int/publications/emd/upload/EMD_inlay_final.pdf.

Justice, William Ouko. 2010. *Final Report of the Task Force on Judicial Reforms*. Nairobi: Government Printers.

Kadima, Dennis. 2009. "Overview." In *Compendium of Elections in Southern Africa 1989–2009: 20 Years of Multiparty Democracy*, ed. Dennis Kadima and Susan Booysen. Johannesburg: Electoral Institute for Sustainable Development in Africa.

Kadima, Dennis, and Dieudonné Tshiyoyo. 2009. "Democratic Republic of Congo." *Compendium of Elections in Southern Africa 1989–2009: 20 Years of Multiparty Democracy*, ed. Dennis Kadima and Susan Booysen. Johannesburg: Electoral Institute for Sustainable Development in Africa.

Kagwanja, Peter, and Roger Southall. 2009. "Introduction: Kenya—A Democracy in Retreat?" *Journal of Contemporary African Affairs* 27 (3): 259–77.

Kanyinga, Karuti. 2009. "The Legacy of the White Highlands: Land Rights, Ethnicity and the Post–2007 Election Violence in Kenya." *Journal of Contemporary African Affairs* 27 (3): 325–44.

Kelly, Bob. 2009. "The Ghanaian Election of 2008." *Review of African Political Economy* 36 (121): 441–59.

Leonard, David K. 2010. "Elections and Conflict Resolution in Africa." In *When Elephants Fight: Preventing and Resolving Election-related Conflicts in Africa*, ed. Khabele Matlosa, Gilbert M. Khadiagala, and Victor Shale. Johannesburg: Electoral Institute for Sustainable Development in Africa.

Leonard, David K., Felix O. Ouwor, and Katherine George. 2009. "The Political and Institutional Context of the 2007 Kenyan Elections and Reforms Needed for the Future." *Journal of African Elections* 8 (1): 71–107.

Magarian, Gregory P. 2003. "Regulating Political Parties under a 'Public Rights' First Amendment." *William and Mary Law Review* 4 (5): 1939–2061.

Matlosa, Khabele. 2005. "Managing Democracy: A Review of the SADC Principles and Guidelines Governing Democratic Elections." In *People, States and Regions: Building a Collaborative Security Regime in Southern Africa*, ed. Anne Hammerstad 153–76. Johannesburg: South African Institute of International Affairs.

Matlosa, Khabele, and Dossou D. Zounmenou. 2011. "Identity, Diversity and Electoral Violence: Dilemmas of Democratic Transformation in Africa." *African Review* 3 (2): 141–59.

Moepya, Mosotho. 2010. "The Role of Multi-party Liaison Committees in

Preventing and Managing Conflicts in South Africa." In *When Elephants Fight: Preventing and Resolving Election-related Conflicts in Africa*, ed. Khabele Matlosa, Gilbert M. Khadiagala, and Victor Shale. Johannesburg: Electoral Institute for Sustainable Development in Africa.

Møller, Bjørn. 2009. "Africa's Subregional Organizations: Seamless Web or Patchwork?" Crisis States Research Centre Working Papers Series 2, Crisis States Research Centre, London School of Economics and Political Science.

Mottiar, Shauna. 2010. "The Role of Civil Society in Elections: The KwaZulu-Natal Democracy and Elections Forum—Reducing Conflict Dynamics and Promoting Peace." *Journal of African Elections* 9 (1): 110–27.

Mozaffar, Shaheen, James Scarlitt, and Glen Galaich. 2003. "Electoral Institutions, Ethnopolitical Cleavages, and Party Systems in Africa's Emerging Democracies." *American Political Science Review* 97 (3): 379–90.

Ochoche, Sunday. 1997. "Electoral Violence and National Security in Nigeria." *Journal of the Centre for Peace Research and Conflict Research* 1 (1).

Omotosho, Mashood. 2008. "Electoral Violence and Conflict in Nigeria: The 2007 Elections and the Challenges of Democratisation." Paper presented at the 27th Annual Nigerian Political Science Association Conference, Benue State University, 16–19 November 2008, Makurdi, Nigeria.

Ozler, Serife. "The Relationship between Political Party System and Social Movements: A Test of the Political Opportunity Structure." Paper presented at the annual meeting of the Western Political Science Association, 20 March 2008, San Diego, CA.

Reilly, Benjamin. 2001. *Democracy in Divided Societies: Electoral Engineering for Conflict Management*. Cambridge, UK: Cambridge University Press.

Sachikonye, Lloyd M. 2003. *The Situation of Commercial Farm Workers after Land Reform in Zimbabwe*. Harare: Farm Community Trust of Zimbabwe.

SADC (Southern Africa Development Community). 2004. "SADC Principles and Guidelines Governing Democratic Elections." Adopted by the SADC Summit, August 2004, Mauritius.

Salih, M. A. 2003. *African Political Parties*. London: Pluto.

Sane, Pierre. 2011. "Côte d'Ivoire Elections: Chronicle of a Failure Foretold." *Pambuzuka News*, 6 January, issue 511.

Solidarity Peace Trust. 2008. "Desperately Seeking Sanity: What Prospects for a New Beginning in Zimbabwe?" Durban.

Straus, Scott. 2012. "Wars Do End! Changing Patterns of Political Violence in Sub-Saharan Africa." *African Affairs* 111 (443): 179–201.

Taylor, Rupert. 2002. "Justice Denied: Political Violence in KwaZulu-Natal after 1994." *Violence and Transition* 6 (September).

Tijjani, Kyari. 2003. "Strategies for Controlling Political Violence and Regulating Campaigns." In *Strategies for Curbing Election-related Violence in Nigeria's North-West Zone*, ed. Attahiru Jega, Haruna Wakili, and Muhammad A. Umar. Kano, Nigeria: Centre for Democratic Research and Training.

Zasha, James, Abdul R. Mustapha, and Ruth Meyer. 2007. "A Lesson Learnt:

Exercise Following the 2007 Elections in Nigeria." United Nations Development Programme Basket Fund, Abuja.

Zimbabwe Election Support Network. 2002. *The Zimbabwe Presidential Election, March 2002*. Harare.

———. 2008. *Report on the Zimbabwe 29 March 2008 Harmonized Elections and 27 June Presidential Run-off*. Harare.

Zimbabwe Human Rights NGOs Forum. 2008. "Political Violence Report: A Report by the Zimbabwe Human Rights NGO Forum." Harare.

# 6

## The Economics of Elections

Elections are expensive, and becoming more so in Africa because of rapid population growth and civil conflicts. Resources, especially money, are therefore critical to electoral competition in both the established and emerging democracies (Nassmacher 2009; Samuels 2001; Austin and Tjernstrom 2003). As the US politician Jesse Unruh observed, money is the "mother's milk of politics" (Nassmacher 2003, 5). Money is a double-edged sword, however, and can also distort the electoral process (Igwe 2011), such that successful, sustainable democracy demands particular attention to political finance (Nassmacher 2003).

The skewed distribution of resources—financial, human, logistical—affects political parties and candidates. Ruling parties (and indirectly their candidates) usually have more resources than the opposition owing to their access to state resources, undermining the opposition's ability to compete. Female, youth and poorer candidates, even within the ruling party, tend to receive fewer resources than other candidates—and it is worse still for those from opposition parties. These disparities deny many citizens the opportunity to compete for power.

Elections require resources, disbursed on time, every four or five years, as well as security and peace. Some activities, such as those of electoral management boards (EMBs) like demarcation or delimitation, voter registration and civic education, require regular input. Some African states, especially after conflict, are finding this hard, thus their recourse to external support.

Several key messages stand out. Resources are critical to electoral outcomes, but are not the sole determinant in reflecting the will of the people. Strong political finance regulatory regimes and powerful EMBs are other factors. Yet very few countries have such regimes, giving ruling parties a marked advantage, as they often use both legal and extra-legal means to access electoral resources, especially as few EMBs have much financial autonomy. Equally, public funding for parties is usually very limited, affecting their viability and visibility, and turning some of them to illicit practices for campaign funding. Elections themselves are at times funded externally, from donors in the West (a flow that must be gradually curtailed to ensure self-determination and democratic consolidation) as well as the diaspora and regional organizations (which are gradually assuming important roles in providing electoral assistance).

## Election resources and political competition

The new era of competitive politics that really started in the third wave of democratization in the 1990s (see chapter 5)—increasing the number and regularity of elections indispensable for a regime's legitimacy—has raised election-funding costs. These costs must be met by the state directly or indirectly, by parties and by candidates, and in the main have risen hugely, making elections an activity now affordable largely to wealthy candidates and well-endowed parties.

Since the inception of the third wave, many African states have conducted regular multi-party presidential, legislative, regional and local elections, bidding farewell to authoritarianism and its non-competitive single-party elections. In 2012, for example, elections were held in Algeria, Angola, Burkina Faso, the Congo, Egypt, Gambia, Ghana, Lesotho, Senegal and Sierra Leone, and postponed in Guinea-Bissau and Mali. The range of spending for presidential and legislative elections varied from about $7.5 million in Sierra Leone in 2007, $8 million in Burundi in 2010 and $24 million in Ghana in 2008 to $139 million in Sudan in 2010 and $647 million in Nigeria in 2011.

The backdrop to election funding has been changing, attracting new players such as business elites, foreign companies and donors (ranging from governments and aid agencies to fraternal parties) and the African diaspora, now a major source of funding for both parties and elections. Yet old habits die hard. Incumbents still draw on substantial, taxpayer-funded state resources

to finance or buttress their campaigns, in which voter outreach—for all candidates—is usually the main election expense (box 6.1).

Political parties in the African states that hold multi-party elections show disparities in election resources. The major dimension is between the ruling and opposition parties. Levitsky and Way (2010, 57) observed that:

> These disparities rarely emerge naturally; rather they are usually rooted in illicit or autocratic behaviour, including partisan appropriation of state resources, systematic packing of state institutions and state-run media, politicized distribution of state resources, concessions, and licenses.

Election resources are critical to levelling the electoral playing field in the game leading to the electoral outcome (box 6.2). Most respondents in the Expert Opinion Survey for African Governance Report (AGR) III shared the view that heavily resourced parties and candidates are usually advantaged. In only 4 of the 40 countries did at least half the respondents believe that parties had equal access to electoral resources, mostly or always (figure 6.1).

Opposition political parties have adopted various means to close the election resource gap. One is electoral alliance or coalition, which allows for resource pooling. Another is merger, based on the idea that, to improve their election resources, opposition parties need to reduce their number, especially smaller ones, by ceding individual party sovereignty to new and larger parties that would command a larger resource base. The gap has also been narrowed when disgruntled members of local ruling classes decamp from the ruling party and join the opposition.

Various external sources, including some governments in Africa, as well as governments, private groups and individuals in several established democracies, have helped opposition parties by assisting them with money, logistics and paraphernalia such as T-shirts and caps. The assistance is clandestinely provided, especially from governments in some of the democracies, so as not to cause conflict with the African government or undermine the legitimacy of the opposition (Saffu 2003).

## Election spending and effect on GDP

In the period before elections, governments are tempted to splash spending in a thinly disguised buy-off to attract potential voters, which can involve new roads, clinics, dams and houses. This is a form of patronage aimed at courting voters, and can harm the economy well beyond election year itself.

Such politicized election spending is seen in a wide range of countries, from authoritarian regimes to those consolidating their democracies. Countries that have spent heavily before elections include Angola (1992), Botswana (2009), Côte d'Ivoire (2010), Ethiopia (2005), Kenya (1992) and (2007), Malawi (2010), Namibia (2009), Nigeria (1999),

> ### Box 6.2 Electoral outcomes
>
> Do political parties and candidates with the most resources win elections in Africa? Usually yes—but victory is not automatic, as seen in presidential elections in Zambia (1991), Malawi (1994), Ghana (2000), Senegal (2000 and 2012) and Kenya (2002).
>
> Other factors are at work: the electorate could be so disenchanted with the ruling party that this outweighs the advantages of resources, as could a stand by the electoral management board in ensuring that the election results are honoured.
>
> Enforcement of political finance regulations is another factor, as it minimizes the use of money to distort electoral competition, and possibly the outcome, helping to see off money as the decisive advantage.

South Africa (2009), Sudan (2011) and Zimbabwe (2000 and 2002; World Bank data, various years). This list is far from exhaustive. In some of these countries, such actions contributed to wide government budget deficits as well as a decline in economic growth during the election year or shortly after the election.

Some ruling parties spend heavily on rural development projects during the election year. Before 2008, *harambee* (self-help) projects were converted into election campaign platforms and became conduits for vote buying, determining regional voting patterns in Kenya (AGR III Kenya Country Report 2012). One report estimated that the former ruling KANU party spent about $60 million on vote buying in 1992; some funds were stolen from the National Social Security Fund (AGR III Kenya Country Report 2012). Consequences included the collapse of "political banks" such as the Trade Bank and Euro Bank following dubious money-siphoning transactions

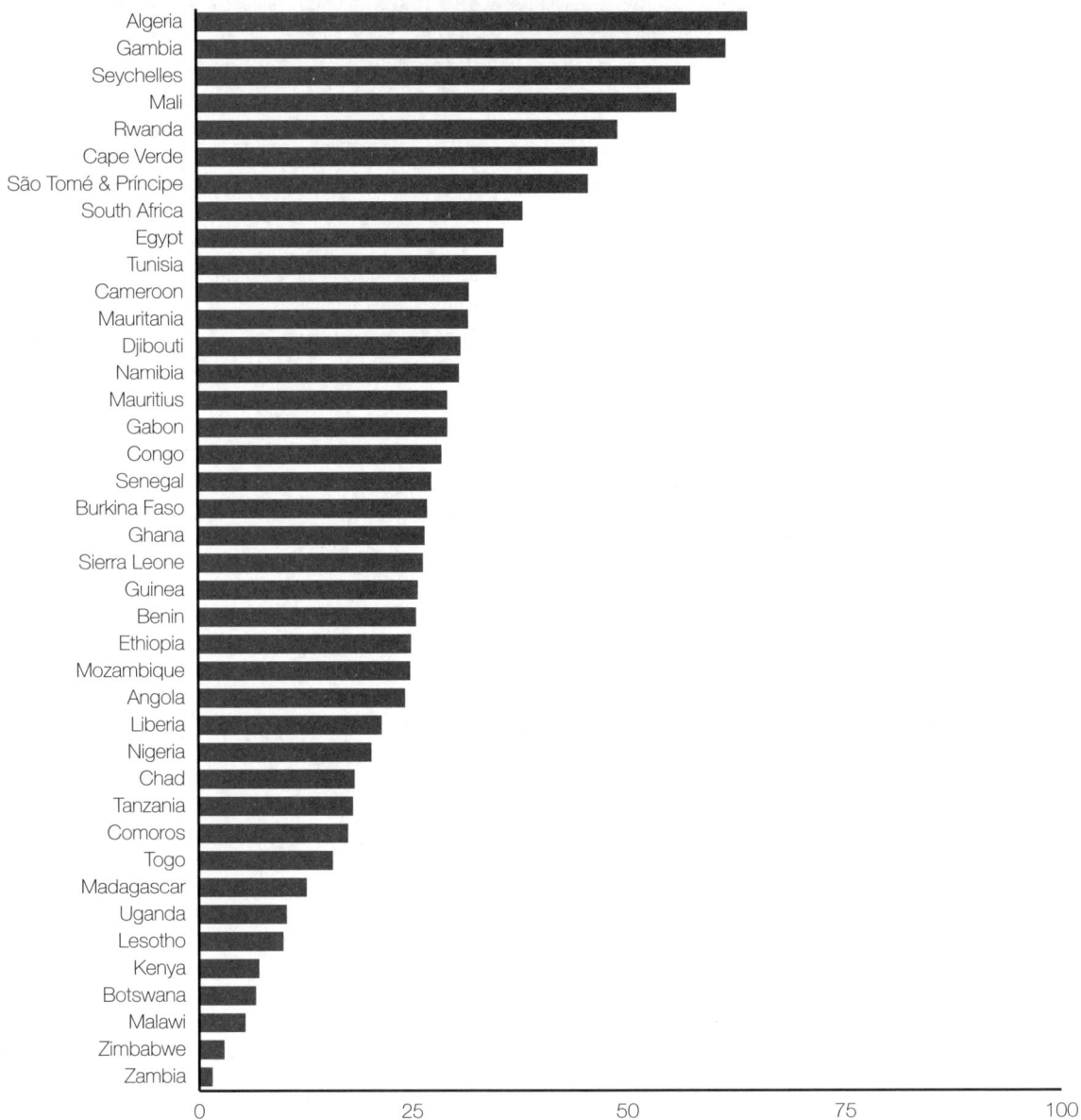

**Figure 6.1 Political parties have equal access to electoral resources—mostly or always**

Share of experts surveyed agreeing with the statement, by country (%)

*Source:* AGR III Expert Opinion Survey 2012.

with several parastatals, costing the government huge sums of money.

The large release of funds into the economy in the form of campaign financing generally increases money in circulation in the economy, fuelling inflationary pressures and other economic distortions.[1] More widely, the uncertainties that often accompany election periods tend to discourage the private sector and businesses, inducing them to slow or delay their investments. Foreign direct investment in productive sectors also slows (except for the extractive enclave industries).

## Funding electoral institutions and parties

*Electoral management boards*
Adequate funding is critical for EMBs to effectively "umpire" contestations for power through the electoral process (see chapter 4), in two main areas—operational expenses and election-related spending—but the amount varies hugely among countries.

Operational expenses
Operational expenses cover a broad gamut, including salaries, logistics and supplies. The main expenses borne by EMBs usually relate to voter registration, boundary delimitation, the voting operation, counting and transmission of results. Dispute adjudication, voter education and voter information are others.

Voter registration is time-consuming and expensive, especially if not integrated as a routine in the registration of vital statistics but repeated every electoral cycle. In Nigeria, for example, one estimate put the budget of about 85 billion naira ($575 million) for the country's 2010 voter registration exercise, or about 1,300 naira ($8.60) per registered voter, the world's highest per capita, even though similar full-scale registration exercises had been carried out in 1987, 2002 and 2007 (Jinadu 2011).

Countries' voter-registration systems also vary: some are manual, others computerized,[2] and both types pose challenges for reliability of the electoral roll. The common problem is the lack of a civil register for generating credible demographic statistics. In some countries, this stems from logistical difficulties posed by the country's topography, especially in mountainous and riverine areas, resulting in poor coverage of the national territory by registration and polling stations, and the lack of a consistent and uniform system for voter registration (Kambale 2011).

Other costs include funding of political parties (where legislated), salaries and emoluments of electoral commissioners and their staff, and other administrative and capital expenses.

A major challenge is the huge cost of electoral administration and management, when set against the massive structural problem of underdevelopment and the enduring economic crisis of the typical African state, especially in view of competing budgetary demands for declining, sometimes scarce, public revenue and resources among ministries departments and agencies.

*Adequate funding is critical for electoral management boards to effectively umpire contestations for power through the electoral process*

This makes efficient administrative machinery of EMBs indispensable to free and fair elections.

### Election-related spending

Four countries exemplify spending trends. Benin is one of the new democracies where hugely increased election costs are a concern and bring fears for future funding if nothing is done. The budget of the electoral commission has shot up, in presidential elections from 1.7 billion CFA francs ($3.6 million) in 1996 to 12 billion CFA francs ($26 million) in 2006, and in legislative elections from 1.1 billion CFA francs ($2.4 million) in 1995 to 6.7 billion CFA francs ($14 million) in 2003 (Hounkpe 2011).

In Cape Verde, each of the three key bodies involved in election management is funded separately. The normal operating budget of the Directorate-General for Electoral Process Support is around $850,000 (in local currency). In an election year, its budget covering normal operations and the conduct of elections is nearly $1.2 million. Before the 2007 electoral law, this budget included budgets of the Electoral Registration Committee. In a non-election year, the regular operating budget of the National Electoral Commission is around €250,000 ($340,000) and in election years more than €2.5 million ($3.4 million). For the 2008 local elections, it was around €4 million ($5.4 million) of which at least half was to support political parties (Fall 2011).

Ghana's annual budget for its Electoral Commission has had four headings since 2007: staff salaries and remuneration cost $8 million; administrative expenses, $4 million; other expenses, $4 million; and capital budget, $6 million. Elections used to cost $24 million on average, but in 2008 the commission budgeted $50 million, as it had to update technology for voter registration, renew the car fleet and increase election officials' stipends (Hounkpe 2011).

In its 2011 annual budget, Nigeria's government allocated $299 million to the Independent National Electoral Commission to underwrite its expenses. Of this, $106.3 million was allotted to personnel costs (mainly salaries), $146.5 million to overheads and $46.9 million to capital projects.

### Funding disparities among countries

African states allocate vastly differing amounts to their EMBs in annual budgets to cover operating costs (outside elections), ranging from less than $0.1 million (Mauritius in 2010) and $1.3 million (Sierra Leone in 2009) to $135 million (South Africa in 2010). Population is important of course. The government of Nigeria, Africa's most populous country, spent $647 million on presidential, legislative, state and local government elections in 2011 (including the nearly $300 million to the Independent National Electoral Commission), while the government of Comoros the year before spent only $2.1 million.

Costs per voter also vary widely (box 6.3), suggesting that a regime's commitment to free and fair

> **African states allocate vastly differing amounts to their electoral management boards in annual budget**

elections is another major determinant, as is the EMB's relationship with the country's executive, parliament and ruling party, particularly in states lacking this commitment.

### Successes and struggles in funding institutions and elections

Countries with a reasonably good record of supporting their EMBs include Namibia, South Africa and Cape Verde.

Despite its relatively small economy and population, Namibia has fully funded its election process and institutions since independence in 1990, receiving neither foreign funding nor external assistance for conducting elections (AGR III Namibia Country Report 2012). The Namibia Country Report observed that the Electoral Commission of Namibia was generally well resourced, with transparent budget allocation and expenditure.

South Africa's Independent Electoral Commission not only funds elections but also finances political parties. It has funding from the national budget, for which it is accountable to parliament (AGR III South Africa Country Report 2012). It has witnessed a steady decline in the overall cost of election administration, largely owing to efficiency gains.

Cape Verde's National Electoral Commission is financed exclusively by state funds (AGR III Cape Verde Country Report 2012). Its budget grew by 32% in 2008–2010.

Some states have found it harder to fund their elections. Sierra Leone,

---

**Box 6.3 Per voter election costs**

The data on election costs in Africa are sparse and rarely up to date, making comparisons hard. What can be gleaned, though, suggests that cost variations reflect the democratic environment—stable, transitional, authoritarian or post-conflict (ACE Electoral Knowledge Network 2011).

Elections in countries with a longer multi-party democratic history are consistently less expensive per voter than where they are a new undertaking—a trend that cuts across regions and economic development, as suggested by the following: Angola $22 per voter, Botswana $2.7, the Democratic Republic of the Congo $2.5, Ghana $0.7, Lesotho $15, Liberia $6.1, Malawi $2.1, Mauritius $11, Mozambique $6.4, Namibia $1.8, Nigeria $8.0, Seychelles $5.8, Senegal $1.2, South Africa $7.3, Tanzania $7.6 and Uganda $3.1. (These figures are purely illustrative since they range from 1992 for Angola to 2011 for Nigeria.)

*Source:* ACE Electoral Knowledge Network 2011; AGR III Nigeria Country Report 2012.

---

for instance, has needed external support to fund elections since 1996. International donors, including the Economic Community of West African States (ECOWAS), European Union, United Nations and US government made large financial contributions. "Without [the international community's] support, it would have been almost impossible for the [electoral commission] to conduct genuine elections since 1996" (AGR III Sierra Leone Country Report 2012, 110). The cost of elections is expected to decline there, especially if a biometric system is introduced, if civic education is mounted (to minimize violence and tension) and if the cost of election security is cut.

In other instances, EMBs experience challenges of limited financial autonomy and delayed disbursement of funds for the election process from registering voters to printing ballots, marring the transparency of elections (box 6.4).

Some have used the high cost of electoral administration and management to inveigle against democratic competitive party and electoral politics, seen in a milder form as outrage at these costs. But as others have pointed out, these expenses are best viewed as unavoidable investments in democracy, development and security. Still, there is also general agreement among expert respondents that much more vigorous enforcement of limits on party activities and finances by African EMBs and similar agencies would help hold down rising electioneering costs.

### Political parties

General operations
The transition from authoritarianism to democracy and the consolidation of that democracy in Africa depend partly on the ability of parties—especially those in opposition—to fund their operations outside elections (Ettinghausen 2006). The funding of parties' general operations (their non-campaign spending) is thus crucial for them to

prepare for the ballot box, as parties also need to function between elections. They may need, for example, to maintain their national, regional or local headquarters (or keep paying rent on them), and meet the costs of personnel, logistics, travel, equipment and public relations.

These activities are pivotal to establishing or extending parties' presence, which is linked to a party's capacity to compete electorally at all levels. Ruling and major opposition parties that have national reach generally fare better in elections than parties with only a local presence.

Most political parties fund their general operations from four major clusters: the state (in about half of African countries—table 6.1), internal party sources, diaspora partisans (that is, active or party members in the diaspora), and political parties and organizations in industrialized countries. (The last two less common funding sources are discussed below under *External funding and assistance*.)

Parties have to meet certain criteria to qualify for state funding. Some 30% of countries give equal amounts to registered parties, some 30% provide funding based on the number of seats that a party has in parliament and about 27% use the criterion of the proportion of votes received in the last election. New political parties in Chad, for example, receive a subsidy of $10,000 from the government to cover costs. Helpful perhaps, but it could encourage parties to set up purely to get the subsidy—and then become moribund.

### Box 6.4  Challenges of election funding in Africa

States sometimes hold off providing their share of election funding (Mutume 2005), which adversely affects the election timetable in planning for activities like voter registration and education. This may result in adjusting the election calendar or executing those election-related activities poorly. Changing the election schedule or poorly organized pre-election activities usually raises voters' anxieties and sometimes generates political tensions, which if not well managed may distort or undermine the entire electoral process.

## Table 6.1 State funding for parties, 2011

| Countries that provide funding for parties' general operations | Countries that provide funding for election campaigns[a] | Countries that do not provide either type of funding |
|---|---|---|
| Algeria | Angola | Botswana |
| Burkina Faso | Benin | Central African Republic |
| Benin | Cameroon | Gambia |
| Cameroon | Burkina Faso | Ghana |
| Côte d'Ivoire | Burundi | Guinea |
| Congo | Cape Verde | Guinea-Bissau |
| Dem Rep. Congo | Chad | Liberia |
| Djibouti | Equatorial Guinea | Libya |
| Egypt | Gabon | Mauritania |
| Ethiopia | Lesotho | Senegal |
| Gabon | Mozambique | Sierra Leone |
| Kenya | Rwanda | Swaziland |
| Madagascar | Tunisia | Zambia |
| Malawi | Uganda | |
| Mali | | |
| Morocco | | |
| Namibia | | |
| Niger | | |
| Nigeria | | |
| Rwanda | | |
| São Tomé and Príncipe | | |
| Seychelles | | |
| South Africa | | |
| Tanzania | | |
| Togo | | |
| Uganda | | |
| Zimbabwe | | |

a. Some countries in addition to general operations.

*Source:* IDEA 2012; AGR III Country Reports 2012.

Public funding of parties' operations faces three main problems. First, funding formulas have ambiguities that give the incumbent regime latitude to favour or punish parties when distributing funds (as in Tanzania). Second, eligibility requirements favour established political parties with seats in parliament (Burkina Faso, for example). Third, both total funding and allocation per party are too small, especially for non-established opposition parties, for them to make any real headway.

Internal party sources are multiple. Membership dues are important and come mainly from well-off members.[3] Some members even pay more than their dues (voluntarily or as a wealth levy). Some political parties hold fund-raising events, and some well-established parties generate revenue from their investments, as exemplified by Zimbabwe's ZANU-PF, the ruling party, and the Movement for Democratic Change, the main opposition party. They have extensive webs of business interests from which they derive income (Masunungure 2006).

Ruling parties of course have access to various lucrative sources (for both general operations and campaigning), including the state treasury (Wondwosen 2009; Saffu 2003), and kickbacks and donations from contractors and other businesses, at home or abroad (Levitsky and Way 2010; Saffu 2003). With these huge resources, they can construct or rent offices throughout the country and employ national and local staff. Some have their own radio stations and newspapers. All these activities allow them to maintain a nationwide presence and to be regularly in the public eye, positioning them well for elections through reach and name recognition (alongside the other advantages of incumbency).

The private sector often contributes to the ruling parties (Wondwosen 2009) and opposition parties that they determine have the good chance of winning the next election. One reason is that they expect a later return on their contribution, such as contracts and other privileges, once the election is over.

### Campaigns

Fourteen of 53 states in Africa (see table 6.1, column 2) provided different amounts of public funding for election campaigns to parties

and candidates in 2011. States usually grant payments on various criteria, such as eligibility requirements for which political parties and candidates should receive subsidies; the vexing issue of the timing of the payment of the subsidies; spending restrictions; and reporting obligations (Walecki 2006).

Equatorial Guinea, Mozambique and Tanzania provide public funding to both political parties and presidential candidates: $30,000 per candidate in Equatorial Guinea, and $9,600 each in Tanzania. Benin provides public funding in the form of reimbursement only for the political campaigns of presidential candidates who win at least 10% of the votes, and parliamentary candidates who win a seat. The total allocation for reimbursement is at the incumbent president's discretion.

One issue is that public funding for political parties and candidates is small in per capita and aggregate terms. (Although in Morocco, for example, it is steep. Morocco provided $13.6 million in 1997 to help fund parties' political campaigns in the parliamentary election.) Another problem is that total funding is not always specified. The related problem is then that, as in Benin and Morocco, the decision is left to presidents and prime ministers, who have partisan interests.

Ruling parties tend to have far greater funding than other parties, and some use their control of the state's political machinery to illegally use public resources in their political campaigns. In the 2011 Ugandan

‘ *The disparities in resources between ruling and opposition parties have profound implications for electoral competition and outcomes in Africa*

presidential and parliamentary elections, for example, the conduct of the National Resistance Movement, the ruling party, prompted Dame Billie Miller, the Head of the Commonwealth's Election Observer Team, to lament, "the magnitude of resources [the National Resistance Movement] deployed and huge level of funding challenged the notion of a level playing field" (Sebunya 2011).

Some of the major opposition parties also have huge resources—the Action Congress of Nigeria and the New Patriotic Party (Ghana) even rival the ruling parties—giving them national presence and reach and thus a competitive position during elections. But most opposition parties have few resources. Some have permanent national headquarters but fewer do in the regions, and they find running their own media or gaining access to them problematic. Their marginal existence makes it hard for them to prepare for elections.

Undoubtedly, the disparities in resources between ruling and opposition parties have profound implications for electoral competition and outcomes in Africa. Using what Greene (2007) calls "hyper-incumbent advantage" (box 6.5)—as in their control of vast amounts of election resources—ruling parties can dispense largesse to voters, distribute campaign paraphernalia *en masse*, conduct huge media campaigns and establish a presence in virtually every corner of the country to reach nearly all voters.

Conversely, inadequate resources inhibit opposition parties from

> ### Box 6.5  Grass-roots view on incumbent advantage in Uganda
>
> A focus group discussion in Mukono reported that "in Uganda, there is no equal distribution of electoral resources" adding that "money, transport [and] security . . . go to those in the system. Therefore, some people cannot compete with those in the system".
>
> The incumbent president moved with a fleet of vehicles, helicopters and a huge number of security staff. He also hired musicians to entertain prospective voters, swaying many fence-sitters as they realized that victory was virtually already secure.
>
> The ruling party used the local village council structures to run its campaigns, so that every village had 30 people to carry out its campaign.
>
> *Source:* AGR III Uganda Country Report 2012.

competing for state offices, especially the presidency (Levitsky and Way 2010), though with exceptions (see box 6.2).

Little is known about parties' campaign resources. Decisions on raising or spending money are usually made by a small group of individuals—often the leaders of the party—and "procedures for recording financial transactions are weak due to negligence, lack of capacity, or purposefully to prevent evidence of illegal activity" (Bryan and Baer 2005, 3), masking parties' lost or wasted funds. And the parties do not expect their candidates to do any better—the information required to meet disclosure laws (where they exist) is simply missing.

### Candidates

Self-funding is the principal method used by candidates (party nominees and independents) to support their campaigns, as other sources of funding are quite limited (Bryan and Baer 2005). Legislative candidates in Nigeria have invested large amounts of their savings to contest elections (box 6.6; Okunade et al. 2009).

During the 2007 Nigerian elections, a gubernatorial candidate spent $3 million in the primary election of the ruling People's Democratic Party (personal discussion with George Kieh in 2010). Despite this, the candidate did not win the party's nomination. In Ghana, several members of parliament revealed during a survey that they spent large amounts of their personal financial resources to fund their campaigns for parliament (Lindberg 2003).

The increasing costs of candidates funding their campaigns have several ramifications. Only individuals willing to invest serious amounts of money can become candidates (Okunade et al. 2009). The related consequence is that with no rigorous expenditure monitoring systems in place throughout Africa, candidates with deep pockets can spend what far exceeds the allowed amount when campaign-spending ceilings are in place (El-Rashidi 2010).

Candidates who are interested in serving the "common good" but are hamstrung by lack of money cannot afford to run for public office either within political parties or as independents. Amid a crisis of leadership on the continent, African states are being deprived of the services of committed individuals, including women.

### Little access to campaign finance for women

Access to electoral finance is a major obstacle to women's election to parliament, presidency or other representative institution partly because women have traditionally been relegated to the private, domestic sphere. Women "thus have neither the personal financial resources nor the moneyed networks to allow them to compete effectively in increasingly expensive electoral politics" (Ballington 2003).

Two attempts to rectify the balance stand out, the first in Malawi during the 2009 election. A group of local non-governmental organization representatives founded a Gender Coordination Network for Women in Politics, which encourages women to take more active roles in politics and elections by providing them with moral, monetary and other material support (AGR III Malawi Country Report 2012). International aid agencies also pumped resources into the project. Concurrently, the Ministry of Women and Child Development launched a national programme to increase the number of female

---

### Box 6.6  Candidate funding in Nigeria

The electoral process in Nigeria has become so expensive that only the rich or those dependent on the rich can run for political office. The absence of effective regulation of the amount of private funding that parties can receive from private sources has made all forms of political mercantilism attractive and possible.

There is a heavy reliance on private funding. Parties generate income through sale of nomination forms, fund-raising dinners, donations from party big wigs, contractors and those who control major sectors of the economy.

*Source:* AGR III Nigeria Country Report 2012.

---

parliamentarians. Called the "50–50 Campaign", it was aimed at achieving equal representation of male and female candidates (AGR III Malawi Country Report 2012). Female candidates won about 22% of the seats in the 2009 election. It was a start.

The second was in Ghana, where the two main parties, the National Democratic Congress and the New Patriotic Party, have sometimes been accused of not doing enough to ensure that enough women are elected to the legislature. Thus they granted a 50% rebate in filing fees to female parliamentary and presidential aspirants. The impact of these concessions has not yet been established, however (AGR III Ghana Country Report 2012).

## Campaign finance and corruption

"Godfatherism", illegal funding, vote buying and kickbacks are four main campaign finance issues common to political parties and their candidates.

### Godfatherism

Godfatherism is a major feature of the electoral landscape in some African states. According to Ibrahim (2003), "Godfathers are generally defined as men who have the power personally to determine both who gets nominated to contest elections and who wins".

They have several assets: wealth or access to wealth that can be used to fund the campaigns of preferred candidates; influence in political parties to the extent that they can determine the nominees; control over patronage networks that are critical to carrying out services for the chosen candidates, including vote rigging; and the financial resources for mobilizing thugs to spread fear and violence, including death.

As Jolly Nyame, the former governor of Terabi State in Nigeria, put it: "Whether you like it or not, as a godfather, you will not be a governor, you will not be a president, but you can *make* a governor, you can *make* a president" (Ibrahim 2003, emphasis added). So, some candidates for public offices in various African states where godfatherism is prominent believe that they cannot entirely rely on voters to win democratic elections (Ibrahim 2003).

Godfatherism subverts democratic elections and broader democratization by using an assortment of unethical, immoral and even criminal methods to fund the campaign of candidates chosen by godfathers, and to foist them on the citizenry at various levels. In return, godfathers receive paybacks from the candidates whom they financed and got elected, such as access to the corridors of power, contracts for themselves, relatives and clients, and access to state resources.[4]

The godfather phenomenon has accentuated politics as the route to acquiring power for privately accumulating wealth by public officials and their supporters (and family), and reflects "the crudeness with which wealth triumphs over the rule of law, and powerful people employ wealth and political power to subvert the sovereign will of the people" (Agbaje and Adejumobi 2006, 40).

### Illegal funding

Undermining the integrity of democratic elections, domestic or external donors funnel illegal funding to some political parties and candidates. Domestically, some individuals and groups, including businesses, provide illegal funding to their preferred political parties and candidates. Externally, some governments provide money.

During the 2011 Ugandan presidential and parliamentary elections, about $2 million was reportedly funnelled from a neighbouring state to the opposition Forum for Democratic Change, which received another $3 million from other external sources (Sebunya 2011). Apparently, that support from the neighbouring state was a tit for tat for the claim that the Ugandan government had funded the campaigns of opposition candidates during that neighbouring country's election (Sebunya 2011). The governments of some of the established democracies and other countries have also used what the ACE Electoral Network (2011) refers to as "secret funds" to support the campaigns of their preferred parties and candidates.

### Vote buying

Vote buying is a two-way electoral transaction between candidates for public office and voters, initiated by either side. Candidates have three main ways to get recipients to vote—or not vote—for a particular candidate (Schaffer 2002).

First, candidates might hope to produce "instrumental compliance"—if successful, the voters as recipients change, or do not change, their electoral behaviour in exchange for tangible rewards. Second, givers might have to generate "normative compliance"—if successful, recipients change, or do not change, their electoral behaviour because the offer convinces them of the goodness or worthiness of the candidate, or because they somehow feel normatively obligated. Third, givers may hope to generate "coercive compliance"—namely, by bullying recipients into changing, or not changing, their electoral behaviour. Recipients fear retribution if they decline the offer or if they do not vote as directed after accepting the offer (Schaffer 2002). Candidates use a range of methods to monitor voters' compliance, although it is unclear if vote buying secures those votes.

Voters may initiate the transaction with candidates in two major ways. Based on "rational choice" calculations, they ask several candidates for a pay-off for their votes, and vote for the highest bidder. The other approach is framed by rent-seeking logic: realizing that few politicians cater to their needs as citizens after they are elected, voters initiate transactions with as many candidates or parties as possible, in a bid collect as much rent as possible from them, irrespective of the size of the pay-offs.

As an anonymous voter in São Tomé and Príncipe explained "We [the voters] do *like* vote buying. It is *essential*. That is the only way we have to see anything good coming from the politicians. Anyway, I can vote for whoever I want" (Vincente 2013, emphasis added; box 6.7).

In Nigeria, almost one in five people is personally exposed to vote buying. It enhances partisan loyalty but, perhaps because most citizens condemn campaign manipulation as wrong, their compliance with politicians' wishes is not assured. Defections from threats and agreements is more common than compliance, especially where voters are cross-pressured from both sides of the partisan divide (Bratton 2008).

### Kickbacks

These are a major source of campaign finance for some ruling parties. Because they are necessarily opaque, authenticated evidence is scarce. Kickbacks are negotiated between a ruling party and investors, local or foreign, in exchange for government contracts and substantial campaign donations. Privatization of assets as part of economic reforms may offer wide opportunities for an incumbent party (box 6.8).

## Regulating political finance

Money in political financing is a double-edged sword. It is indispensable for funding party establishments and political campaigns. But, unregulated, it can distort and corrupt the electoral process and ultimately undermine the broader democratization project (Igwe 2011). As Pollock (1932, 32) put it eight decades ago: "Healthy political life is not possible as long as the use of money is unrestrained".

In Africa, political financing is underregulated, or a matter of unregulated self-help (Saffu 2003),

---

### Box 6.7  Banho in São Tomé and Príncipe

With the illegal practice of *banho,* many voters gather around the polling venue, discreetly implying to candidates' or parties' promoters that their finger has not yet been marked by the ineffaceable ink that shows that they have voted—and that they are open to an "inducement". They must get this before voting because few voters believe that the officials, once elected, will fulfil their campaign promises.

*Source:* AGR III São Tomé and Príncipe Country Report 2012.

---

### Box 6.8  Kickbacks and donations to campaigns funds

The difference between the amounts of money available to governing and to opposition parties tends to be far larger in Africa than elsewhere. The difference in fortune cannot be explained in ideology, policies or the social bases of party support.

Instead, the primary explanation lies in the advantages of incumbency. Kickbacks, abuse of office and corruption play a large role in party financing. Only governing parties are in a position to award contracts, grant other favours or divert funds illegally to themselves. African governments exploit the opportunities of office to bankroll their parties without many of the political constraints and restraints that operate in mature democracies.

In Africa, because there is not much alternation in power between competing powers or clear ideological differences, or because the competitive multi-party process has only just begun again, opposition parties tend to attract political entrepreneurs, rather than business owners, if they manage to find any wealthy business backers at all.

The reluctance of ordinary business owners to donate to opposition parties is one legacy of the recent authoritarian past and explains much. Governments still find it difficult to accept that business owners who donate to opposition parties are as entitled to bid for government contracts as anyone else.

*Source:* Saffu 2003.

---

which has three main implications. First, some African states do not have regimes for regulating political finance covering the funding

majority of financial transactions in Africa, including election-related expenditures, are cash would make their task extremely hard, casting out the potential gains of proper regulation (box 6.9).

## External funding and assistance

*Party funding from the diaspora*

Diaspora partisans are major sources of funding. Some political parties (including some ruling parties) have members and chapters abroad that contribute to their operations. This has made these partisans major players in some parties, even up to using their contributions as springboards for party nomination for elected office.

African diaspora groups residing especially in the United States, Canada and Europe constitute a major cluster of party campaign funding, as they are in a better economic position than their compatriots at home. For example, during the 1996 Ghanaian presidential election, some groups of Ghanaians in the United States contributed $100,000 to the presidential campaign of the opposition New Patriotic Party (Wondwosen 2009). Similarly, during the 2005 parliamentary election in Ethiopia, diaspora Ethiopians served as the principal source of campaign funding for opposition parties, especially the main opposition group, the Coalition for Unity and Democracy (Wondwosen 2009).

Diaspora members contribute for several reasons. They may be genuinely interested in being involved in

of party establishments and political campaigns. This gives political parties and candidates freedom to raise money from a raft of sources, including illegal ones.

Second, even if particular political parties have excellent visions for building democratic and developed societies, the constraints imposed by money militate against their ability even to articulate their plan to the electorate, let alone to compete and win.

Third, even in countries like Benin and Liberia with full regulatory regimes, enforcement is a problem, especially the lack of monitoring systems (Saffu 2003). Even if they were in place, that the overwhelming

their home-country politics. Others might have selfish motives, such as government positions or, for entrepreneurs, government contracts (if their party wins the next election).

Legitimate contributions (where a political finance regime permits them), can help to level the inter-party playing field by helping cut the enormous resource advantage of the ruling party (though not all contributions of course go to the opposition).

But illegitimate contributions (that is, contravening political finance regulations) serve to corrupt the electoral process by, for example, supporting vote buying. They may also bolster factionalism in political parties, possibly leading to conflict.

### Election funding from states and organizations in industrialized countries

Some African states expect external donors, especially in their presidential and parliamentary elections, to underwrite some of the cost—such sources are becoming indispensable in African elections. Twenty-one countries, however, have banned candidates from receiving foreign funds for campaigns (table 6.2 and box 6.10).

External funds are often used to help underwrite the costs of electoral activities, including voters' registration and education, and ballot printing. Some funds provide technical assistance in managing elections, including preparing for and running them. This assistance is either given directly by the external donor or by

**Table 6.2 Countries that ban or allow foreign donations to political parties and campaigns**

| Ban | Allow |
|-----|-------|
| Algeria | Benin |
| Angola | Burkina Faso |
| Burundi | Central African Republic |
| Cameroon | Chad |
| Congo | Lesotho |
| Côte d'Ivoire | Malawi |
| Dem. Rep. Congo | Mauritius |
| Egypt | Mozambique |
| Ethiopia | Namibia |
| Gabon | Seychelles |
| Ghana | South Africa |
| Guinea | Swaziland |
| Guinea-Bissau | Tanzania |
| Kenya | Togo |
| Liberia | Zambia |
| Libya | |
| Madagascar | |
| Mauritania | |
| Morocco | |
| Niger | |
| Nigeria | |

*Source:* AGR III Country Reports 2012; IDEA 2012.

a donor-funded body such as the International Federation of Electoral Systems. External donors provided funds for elections in 2007–2010 (table 6.3), with positive and negative effects.

Benefits

In light of the lukewarm attitude that some African states have towards funding their own elections (possibly due to doubts about democracy; box 6.11), as well as

2011), which is important to the elections' integrity. Fifteen countries in the AGR III survey accept foreign donations for party campaigns (see table 6.2).

Various non-government sources in the established democracies as well as international party federations (Liberal International, Socialist International and others) provide funding for African political parties. These include German *Stiftung*s (political foundations), the Westminster Foundation (from UK political parties mainly to Anglophone African states) and the Netherlands Institute for Multiparty Democracy (in South Africa and Mozambique; Mathisen and Svasand 2002).

Disadvantages

Democratic procedures are still fragile, especially in post-conflict states, and the case remains strong for external electoral assistance. Still, it generates concerns (box 6.12). Abderhamane Nang, an election consultant in Mali's 2002 elections, said: "The foreign funding, which we received for running [our elections], undermined our national sovereignty" (Tadegron

the cost, the funds from states and inter-governmental organizations in industrialized countries are critical to free and fair elections (Cyllah 2010). Funds are used on such activities as voter registration, voter education and ballot preparation and production.

Furthermore, since democratic elections are a fairly new phenomenon on the continent, most African states are still developing the necessary technical know-how (Kimenyi

**Table 6.3 Examples of external sources of funding, 2007–2010**

| Country | Year | Donor | $ million |
|---|---|---|---|
| Sierra Leone (P&P) | 2007 | International community | 17.5 |
| Rwanda (P) | 2010 | European Union, United Kingdom and Netherlands | 4.4 |
| Sudan (P&P)[a] | 2010 | European Union | 175.5 |
| Tanzania (P&P) | 2010 | European Union and United Kingdom | 22.1 |
| Uganda (P) | 2011 | International community | 13.5 |

a. Includes a contribution of $55 million from the United Nations Mission in the Sudan.

P&P = presidential and parliamentary; P = presidential.

*Source:* Compiled from www.eisa.com and AGR III Country Reports 2012.

2003), typifying the "loss of sovereignty" argument.

This is linked to a second worry, that donors may use their electoral contribution to interfere directly. In the 2005 Liberian elections, for example, the United States used its contribution to attempt to influence the electoral process, when the US ambassador arrogated to that country the right to vet the presidential and vice-presidential candidates (interview with a presidential candidate, 23 February 2011). As Mwesiga Baregu at St. Augustine University in Tanzania puts it: "By interfering in the social contract space, donor funding has the effect of undermining electoral legitimacy. Donor funding creates a patron–client rather than a citizen–public servant relationship between the citizens and elected leaders" (Muramira 2010).

Another concern is that some external donor states might use their funding to impose their preferred electoral framework on recipient states, usually reflecting the historical experiences of both sides and often when the recipients are transitioning to post-conflict peace building. Some have sought to persuade African states to adopt an electoral template used in other post-conflict states in Asia, Europe or Latin America.

Such funding can hobble Africa's steps to democracy because, when clandestine, it undermines state efforts to regulate political finance, as it is impossible to regulate money given this way. It also usually favours only some opposition political parties and candidates (not necessarily

those the voters support), and makes it hard to forge local ownership over choosing national leaders.

### Electoral assistance from regional and subregional organizations

The African Union and some subregional organizations have given modest funding for elections. ECOWAS, for example, contributed $350,000 to help fund the 2009 presidential election in Guinea-Bissau (Pan African News Agency 2009). It also gave the government of Guinea $500,000 to help conduct the presidential election in 2010 (Jalloh 2008). Although too small to fund the elections fully, they represent important steps towards Africa's self-reliance in conducting elections.

### Moves to self-sufficient election funding

Some states have enough domestic resources to fund the entire electoral

---

### Box 6.11  Are all governments convinced by democracy?

Some government officials on the continent resort to the proverbial "lack of money in Africa" claim as a veneer to mask resistance to democratic elections. This sense of revulsion towards elections, however masked, reflects the broader problem that the authoritarian mind-set remains the bedrock of some states' political cultures even as they sing, as it were, a requiem to the demise of authoritarianism in Africa.

The belief underlying this mind-set is that elections are not a major national priority, but rather a pet project of the established democracies. In other words, some African leaders regard regular free and fair elections as both an irritant and a waste of public resources and not as a public good indispensable to peace, stability and democracy. Hence, they reason, because the established democracies are enamoured of elections, the best an African state can typically do is contribute to the elections' costs, rather than underwrite them fully.

*Source:* UNECA 2011.

## Conclusions and recommendations

This section aims to give pointers for ensuring effective and fair financing of elections in Africa and thus for promoting democracy and development. Success ultimately rests on the willingness of African citizens to become involved in their country's affairs, including the electoral process.

### Making election funding a national priority

It is very important for African states to assume sole responsibility for funding their elections for two reasons. First, it establishes national ownership over the electoral process, including the critical issue of choosing the country's leaders. This would augur well for the broader democratization project.

Second, it would help to obliterate the external prejudice that sees Africa as a region where people are intrinsically incapable of governing themselves, and much more broadly "cannot do anything right". Such self-reliance would also help to end the depiction of the continent as a perpetual crisis zone that requires seemingly unending interventions from external actors.

If democracy is to take firm root throughout Africa, governments should make election funding a national priority. Government officials, political parties, civil society and citizens throughout Africa need to assume primacy as stakeholders, because collectively they have the ultimate responsibility for the well-being of their countries. Thus all these groups need to play pivotal roles in ensuring that their governments

process (including Botswana, Cape Verde, Mauritius, Namibia, Seychelles and South Africa). Others require large external assistance (including São Tomé and Príncipe and Tanzania as well as post-conflict states such as the Democratic Republic of the Congo, Liberia, Mozambique, Rwanda, Sierra Leone and South Sudan). And yet others have improved their capacity to finance the process over the past decade, with the hopeful prospect that they will be self-sufficient in a few years (Ghana, Kenya, Malawi and Uganda).

treat elections as public goods indispensable to democracy, development and durable peace (although international donors, especially the industrial democracies, may be able to help encourage regimes that view elections as a Western imposition).

African states should endeavour to fully fund their own elections. Although external funding helps states transition from war to peace, thereafter these states should assume the sole funding burden.

Donor states should give technical assistance for electoral management before an election, enabling states to select electoral officials for training. Subsequently, these trained election officials could then conduct in-house workshops and seminars for the staff of their EMBs to prepare for later elections.

### Moving to full state support for EMBs and elections

Administrative and operational expenses of EMBs need to be fully funded in African states' annual budgets, and once approved, disbursed promptly. Similarly, the budget for conducting elections should be spent well. The government would need to ensure that the funding process does not provide opportunities for corrupt activities by EMB staff or state officials, and that the budget reflects actual, cost-effective spending.

Since elections are held periodically, a strategic funding plan could be developed that includes setting aside a portion of the state's annual budget to fund elections in the future. For example, if an African state holds its presidential or parliamentary elections every five years, the budget for the election could be formulated. Then based on the total cost, the state would allocate money in the annual budget over a five-year period covering the total cost. The Election Commission of Sierra Leone is an example of good practice on this, having written a budget for presidential and parliamentary elections in 2012 and 2016.

A complementary step would be setting up a "basket fund" for helping to support elections. Managed by the African Union, participating states would make annual contributions (using a formula to be collectively decided). Based on a state's needs, money from the fund would help that state fully support its election costs. Such a continental approach to self-help would be far more acceptable to electorates than continually relying on the established democracies.

### Preventing abuse of public resources in campaigns

Some incumbent parties and leaders pilfer state resources for campaign purposes. The ruling party tends to dominate public media. Other states enlist state security agencies such as the police and intelligence services to support their campaign. All these elements tilt the balance heavily in favour of the incumbent party and leader and away from the opposition.

Laws are therefore needed to level the playing field for contesting parties, and they should be enforced impartially and rigorously to ensure

> ❝ **African states should endeavour to fully fund their own elections**

the credibility of the electoral process. The rules governing access to the media should be fair and transparent—and enforced.

### Adopting public funding of parties and campaigns

Given the gross disparities in resources between and among political parties and candidates, African states not already doing so should consider adopting public funding, using a formula reflecting each state's needs. Each system would need to be equitable.

Public funding is less dangerous than having politicians in search of funds turn to interested money or corrupt practices, but public funding needs to strike a balance between encouraging parties to maintain their grass-roots base (through membership support including dues) and funding from taxpayers (which should not make the parties remote from that base).

### Regulating political finance
African states that do not have political finance regulatory regimes may consider establishing them. This is important because the distortive influence of money on electoral processes needs to be addressed if elections are to have integrity. Those countries that do have such regimes need to improve how they monitor—cash transactions particularly—and enforce the regulations.

Since parties lie at the heart of the party funding challenge, they should be necessarily included in any solution through regulation, because no anti-corruption legislation can be passed without the support of parties holding elected power and controlling parliamentary action (Bryan and Baer 2005). Even when such laws have been passed, the ease with which parties often escape regulation through loopholes suggests that genuine reform can only come about when parties voluntarily adopt reform measures.

### Reducing the cost of elections
Elections are expensive affairs, and this partly explains why some African states accept external funding. Efforts to reduce their cost, such as automation, need to be replicated. South Africa, for example, has seen its election expenses per voter decline in the past three elections.

Countries that have rising costs per voter, such as Nigeria, should seek ways to cut costs, including rigorously enforcing electoral regulations and addressing corruption in the election process itself.

### Developing a consensus for political finance reform
Unless key stakeholders—chiefly the contesting parties and electoral institutions—share a consensus on political finance reform, such reform will not advance, as laws that do not draw on the legitimacy of wide consent are unlikely to be sustainable. Hence stakeholders need to carefully build understanding and support on this matter, including among smaller parties. They should consult a wide range of experts (individual or entities) on proposals for such reform. But new political finance laws should be clear and suited to a country's capacity.

> ' Efforts to reduce the cost of elections in Africa need to be replicated

In short, a "one-shoe-fits-all" approach will achieve little. Each country has an opportunity to develop laws and mechanisms for its own needs, aiming to make its political finance regime transparent, accountable and equitable.

### Building skills in fund-raising and reporting

Beyond public funding, parties need to broaden the base of supporters engaged in fund-raising beyond a small coterie in the leadership. A more professional approach is required, particularly when a party heavily raises funds among the private sector and individual party supporters. Fund-raising skills are required in persuading individuals and corporates to make donations. They are also required in identifying organizations in civil society that have potential for positive response to appeals for donations. Parties should therefore invest in training their cadres in this area. Parties also need to boost their reporting and accounting expertise, for funds from the private and public sectors.

Thus in a culture of disclosure and transparency, parties need staff both to raise funds and account for them. EMBs and donors can help to provide all-party training programmes on such skills.

### Managing election funding and diversity

A core issue of this report is that diversity should be positively managed in the electoral process. As earlier chapters argued that affirmative action for representing some social groups such as women and youth, people with disabilities and minorities is necessary, so there is a need to remove the barriers to their election funding. Campaign finance regulations and electoral system procedures should be reviewed and reoriented to improve opportunities for these groups.

## Notes

1. These funds come from both domestic and external sources: diaspora funds, funds stashed illegally abroad by political actors (among others) and funds from businesses.
2. Ghana, Kenya, Nigeria and Sierra Leone have taken or are considering measures to use digital and biometric equipment as a measure to enhance the reliability of voter registration and as a cost-saving measure in the long run, although steps to do this are controversial.
3. Given the poverty on the continent among most of the rank and file they are usually symbolic.
4. Some godfathers fall out with their—now powerful—client when he seeks to assert himself but they insist on retaining control and recouping their investment (Agbaje and Adejumobi 2006).

## References

ACE Electoral Knowledge Network. 2011. "Electoral Systems." http://aceproject.org/main/english/st, accessed 20 February 2011.

Agbaje, Adigun, and Said Adejumobi. 2006. "Do Votes Count? The Travails of Electoral Politics in Nigeria." *Africa Development* 31 (3): 25–44.

Austin, Reginald, and Maja Tjernstrom, eds. 2003. *Funding of Political Parties and Election Campaigns.* Stockholm:

International Institute for Democracy and Electoral Assistance.

Ballington, Julie. 2003. "Gender Equality in Political Party Funding." In *Funding of Political Parties and Election Campaigns*, ed. Reginald Austin and Maja Tjernstrom. Stockholm: International Institute for Democracy and Electoral Assistance.

Bratton, Michael. 2008. "Vote Buying and Violence in Nigerian Election Campaigns." *Electoral Studies* 27 (4): 621–32.

Bryan, Shari, and Denise Baer, eds. 2005. *Money in Politics*. Washington, DC: National Democratic Institute for International Affairs.

Cyllah, Almami. 2010. "Democracy and Elections in Africa: Recent Trends and the Role of the International Community." Testimony before the U.S. House of Representatives' Subcommittee on Africa and Global Health, 24 March, Washington, DC.

El-Rashidi, Yasmine. 2010. "Hire a Thug and Other Campaign Expenditures." Ahramonline. 15 December.

Ettinghausen, Clare. 2006. *Paying for Politics: The Principles of Funding Political Parties*. Hansard Society Discussion Paper. London: Hansard Society.

Fall, Ismaila. 2011. "Cape Verde." In *Election Management Bodies in West Africa: A Comparative Study of the Contribution of Electoral Commissions to the Strengthening of Democracy*, ed. Ismaila Fall, Mathias Hounkpe, Adele L. Jinadu and Pascal Kambale, 49–75. Dakar: Open Society Foundations.

Fogg, Karen, Patrick Molutsi, and Maja Tjernstrom. 2003. "Conclusion." In *Funding of Political Parties and Election Campaigns*, ed. Reginald Austin and Maja Tjernstrom. Stockholm: International Institute for Democracy and Electoral Assistance.

Greene, Kenneth. 2007. *Why Dominant Parties Lose: Mexico's Democratization in Comparative Perspective*. New York: Cambridge University Press.

Hitimana, Bosco. 2009. "Rwanda: Presidential Election to Cost $10.6 million." allAfrica.com, 19 September.

Hounkpe, Mathias. 2011. "Benin." In *Election Management Bodies in West Africa: A Comparative Study of the Contribution of Electoral Commissions to the Strengthening of Democracy*, ed. Ismaila Fall, Mathias Hounkpe, Adele L. Jinadu and Pascal Kambale, 12–48. Dakar: Open Society Foundations.

IDEA (International Institute for Democracy and Electoral Assistance). 2012. "Political Finance Database." Stockholm.

Ibrahim, Jibrin. 2003. "The Rise of Nigeria's Godfathers." BBC News, 10 November.

Igwe, Uche. 2011. "Nigeria: Political Financing, Incumbency and Free and Fair Elections." *Pambazuka News*, 10 January.

Jalloh, Bhoyy. 2008. "ECOWAS to Contribute U.S.$500,000 to Country's Election." *Concord Times* (Freetown), 7 February.

Jinadu, Adele L. 2011. "Nigeria." In *Election Management Bodies in West Africa: A Comparative Study of the Contribution of Electoral Commissions to the Strengthening of Democracy*, ed. Ismaila Fall, Mathias Hounkpe, Adele L. Jinadu and Pascal Kambale, 108–61. Dakar: Open Society Foundations.

Kambale, Pascal. 2011. "Overview: The Contribution of Electoral Management Bodies to Credible Elections in West Africa." In *Election Management Bodies in West Africa: A Comparative Study of the Contribution of Electoral Commissions to the Strengthening of Democracy*, ed. Ismaila Fall, Mathias Hounkpe, Adele

L. Jinadu, and Pascal Kambale, 1–11. Dakar: Open Society Foundations.

Kimenyi, Mwangi. 2011. "Africa's 2011 Elections." *Foresight Africa*, 3–5 January.

Levitsky, Steven, and Lucan Way. 2010. "Why Democracy Needs A Level Playing Field." *Journal of Democracy* 21 (1): 57–68.

Lindberg, Staffan. 2003. "It's Our Time to 'Chop:' Do Elections in Africa Feed Neo-patrimonialism Rather Than Counteract It?" *Democratization* 10 (2): 121–40.

Masunungure, Eldred. 2006. *Regulation of Political Parties in Zimbabwe: Registration, Finance and Other Support.* Harare: Zimbabwean Elections Support Network.

Mathisen, Harold, and Lars Svasand. 2002. *Funding Political Parties in Emerging African Democracies: What Role for Norway?* Report 2002:6. Bergen, Norway: Chr. Michelson Institute.

Muramira, Gashegu. 2010. "East Africa: EAC Delegates Rap Donors on Election Funding." allAfrica.com, 21 August.

Mutume, Gumisai. 2005. "Beyond the Ballot." *African Renewal* 18 (4): 10.

Nassmacher, Karl-Heinz. 2003. "Introduction: Political Parties Funding and Democracy." In *Funding of Political Parties and Election Campaigns*, ed. Reginald Austin and Maja Tjernstrom. Stockholm: International Institute for Democracy and Electoral Assistance.

———. 2009. *The Funding of Party Competition.* Berlin: Nomos Publishers.

Okunade, Bayo, Olalekan Taiwo, Stephen Lafenwa, and Idowu Johnson. 2009. "Campaign Financing Distorts Nigerian Elections." Briefing Paper, Center for the Study of African Economies, Oxford, UK.

Pan African News Agency. 2009. "ECOWAS Leaders Move to Ensure Successful Elections in Guinea, Guinea-Bissau." Abuja, 22 June.

Pollock, James Ker. 1932. *Money and Politics Abroad.* New York: Alfred Knopf.

Saffu, Yaw. 2003. "The Funding of Political Parties and Election Campaigns in Africa." In *Funding of Political Parties and Election Campaigns*, ed. Reginald Austin and Maja Tjernstrom. Stockholm: International Institute for Democracy and Electoral Assistance.

Samuels, David. 2001. "Money, Elections, and Democracy in Brazil." *Latin American Politics and Society* 43 (2): 27–48.

Schaffer, Frederic Charles. 2002. "What Is Vote-Buying?" Paper presented at the International Conference on "Trading Political Rights: The Comparative Politics of Vote-Buying," Center for International Studies, Massachusetts Institute of Technology, 26–27 August, Cambridge, MA.

Sebunya, Crespo. 2011. "Huge Uganda Election Funding Questioned." Medeshivalley News, 2 March.

Tadegron, Noel Kokou. 2003. "Africa: Foreign Funding for Elections Comes under Attack." Inter Press Service, 1 May.

UNECA (United Nations Economic Commission for Africa). 2011. "Background Paper on the Economics of Elections." Addis Ababa.

Vincente, Pedro. 2013. "Is Vote-buying Effective? Evidence from a Field Experiment in West Africa." January. www.pedrovicente.org/banho.pdf.

Walecki, Marcin. 2006. "Direct Public Funding of Political Parties." 2 June. www.knab.gov.lv/uploads/eng/public_funding_in_latvia.pdf.

Wondwosen, Teshome. 2009. "Political Financing in Africa: Ethiopia as Case Study." *International Journal of Human and Social Sciences* 4 (6): 406–19.

The objectives of electoral, constitutional and political reforms, as a strategy to improve and democratize governance in Africa, are threefold: to manage diversity in ways to mute diversity-related fallout—especially violence—when ethnicity and other identity-based diversity is mobilized; to bring about structural and institutional changes in the architecture of democratic governance; and to reorient anti-democratic political cultures through civic and voter education to advance the prospects and possibilities of democracy.

Encouragingly, many African countries have made long strides in these three interlinked areas of reform since the democratic transition of the 1990s, but unevenly—and a few too slowly to signal a break from authoritarianism.

South Africa's historic constitution in the mid-1990s was followed by those in Kenya and Zimbabwe, as well as by reviews in Nigeria, Tanzania, Zambia and elsewhere to deal with deficits that had contributed to political crisis. In North African countries such as Egypt, Libya and Tunisia, new constitutions became imperative to map out new patterns of distributing power in the aftermath of authoritarianism, making way for a democratic transition. Electoral reforms have necessarily been part of those reforms.

But further constitutional reforms are necessary in some countries to address limitations in their electoral systems. This chapter looks at key areas where further reforms are imperative if the steps towards democracy are to be sustainable. It does this through the prism of the African Governance Report (AGR) III country reports and Expert Opinion Survey.

This chapter finds that, for reforms to be deepened, just as the impetus for democratic transition did not originate only from parties and state institutions (pressures from above), so too will the role of civil society and other sectors remain vital in safeguarding and then broadening reforms (pressures from below; box 7.1). In combination, these elements of reform will determine the quality of overall democratic transformation on the continent.

## Dynamic links among electoral, constitutional and political reforms

State institutions, political parties and society are not static. Africa is undergoing deep economic, social and demographic changes. Diversities are also in flux. Countries therefore need to respond to these changes promptly and appropriately, adapting their electoral systems and, beyond them, to the advances in communication technology.

How the state and parties respond to these wider changes is significant. Neither state institutions nor parties are models of democratic practices and they suffer from deficits in internal democracy. It will thus remain a challenge for parties to interpret the changes and resulting demands in society, and dynamically shape them into constitutional and electoral reforms that will manage diversity.

Yet societies are not homogeneous, and they are a source not only of progressive ideas but also regressive tendencies. The interface between parties and state institutions, on the one hand, and society and its various constituent groups, on the other, is crucial in reforming the electoral system and in managing diversity. The pressures from below should not be ignored in favour of arrangements between elites—the pressures from above.

The following sections show the views of respondents to the AGR III Expert Opinion Survey on aspects of the three areas of reform, including political-party reforms. They also indicate areas for further reform, drawing heavily on the country reports.

## Electoral reforms

Pressures from above and below in a range of African countries have helped generate electoral reform—a central development in the post-colonial history of such countries as Cameroon and Gabon in Central Africa; Kenya, Tanzania and Uganda in East Africa; Algeria, Egypt, Morocco and Tunisia in North Africa; Benin, Cape Verde, Ghana, Liberia, Nigeria and Sierra Leone in West Africa; and Malawi, South Africa, Zambia and Zimbabwe in Southern Africa.

Electoral reforms in Africa have attempted to resolve the deficits of electoral governance through three main strategies (box 7.2 and see chapter 3). First, they have modified electoral systems, particularly first past the post (FPTP). The objective is to bring about electoral diversity by redressing the historical underrepresentation of marginalized groups, such as ethno-regional, linguistic or religious groups; women; and small or weak political parties.

Second, electoral reforms have generally sought to strengthen the independence of EMBs. The objective is to enhance the procedural certainty of the electoral process to ensure the substantive uncertainty of its outcome, and so enhance the general public confidence in, electoral administration and management.

Third, in the post-1990 democratic transitions in Africa, managing diversity took on concrete constitutional and political form in entrenching constitutional provisions that guarantee the rights of marginalized groups to corporate existence and to inclusion in governance institutions and processes. The provisions also recognize group rights to promote group interests and sometimes set up human rights commissions to monitor observance or violations of these rights.

Electoral reform in post-1990 Africa has also been about issues of access to the electoral process and its integrity to accommodate and promote pluralism in public policy. Improving and democratizing the legal framework for managing elections have featured in electoral reforms in several African countries.

Promoting and protecting diversity is therefore a major force for ensuring accountability in public political life. Improving the credibility of electoral governance and management strengthens elections for democratically managing diversity and political succession. Explicitly accommodating diversity through electoral, constitutional and political means also makes up for the inadequacy of liberal democratic theory to recognize minority group rights as requiring constitutional protection and promotion.

That is the theory. How then do the expert respondents view African's on-the-ground progress in electoral reforms?

### Electoral system

The major systems in Africa are FPTP and proportional representation, whose merits are greatly debated (see chapters 3 and 5). More than half the respondents in 36 of the 40 countries favour proportional representation

| Box 7.2 Three strategies of electoral reform |
| --- |

Electoral reform in Africa reveals three overlapping themes.

*Redesigning electoral systems.* Some governments took steps to achieve a more democratic management of diversity by combining elements of first past the post and proportional representation to make party representation in legislatures reflect more accurately the proportion of votes cast, as in Lesotho, or to achieve fair representation and diversity in the legislatures, as in South Africa. They also took steps to require a second round of elections, or run-offs, in presidential elections if the initial electoral outcomes did not meet certain requirements, either of a minimum regional spread of support, as in Nigeria, or if no candidate won 50% or more (an absolute majority), as in Ghana, Senegal and Sierra Leone.

*Strengthening electoral management boards' (EMBs) independence.* Governments diminished the influence of the executive by strengthening the mechanism for appointing and removing EMBs' members and by guaranteeing the bodies' financial independence. (They also entrenched EMBs in the constitution.) See, for example, Ghana, Kenya, Sierra Leone and South Africa (AGR III Country Reports 2012).

As part of these strengthening moves, some countries unbundled EMBs' powers and functions by creating two (or sometimes more) EMBs to undertake major elements of electoral administration and management. Examples are seen in the National Electoral Commission and the Political Parties Registration Commission in Sierra Leone; the National Election Commission and the Registrar of Political Parties in Tanzania; and the National Electoral Commission, the Directorate General for Electoral Process Support (in the Ministry of Internal Administration) and electoral registration committees in Cape Verde.

*Entrenching constitutional or electoral laws.* Sometimes these measures included a Bill of Rights, as in Kenya's and South Africa's constitutions. Other laws provided for regulation and oversight of party activities, including financing, nomination processes and electioneering campaigns by either a national electoral commission (Ghana, Kenya and Nigeria), a political parties regulation commission (Sierra Leone) or a registrar of political parties (Tanzania); and for public finance of political parties (Nigeria).

(figure 7.1). Three of the remaining four (Egypt being the exception) have fairly small populations, perhaps indicating that diversity is not a major issue for them.

## Figure 7.1 Proportional representation promotes electoral stability and diversity management—agree or strongly agree

Share of experts surveyed agreeing with the statement, by country (%)

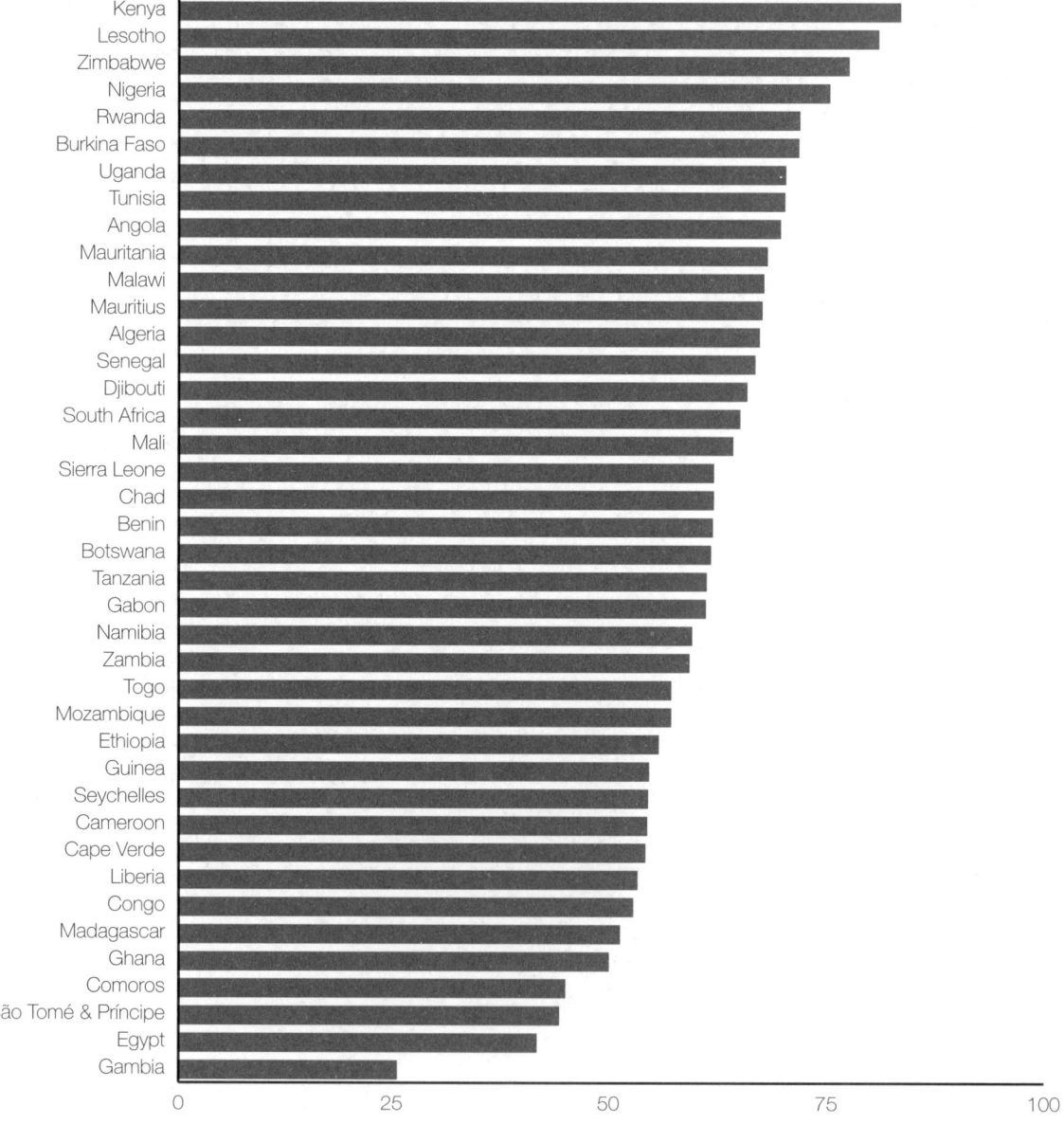

*Source:* AGR III Expert Opinion Survey 2012.

*Procedure for appointing and removing electoral commissioners*
The procedure for appointing and removing electoral commissioners is a major recurring reform issue in electoral management and administration, and an overwhelming majority of expert respondents in nearly all countries believe it should be handled by an independent non-partisan body (figure 7.2).

The jobs of electoral commissioners should be openly advertised and competed for nationally by citizens, according to the country surveys, making for greater credibility and integrity of EMBs and reducing the influence of the executive or other arms of government. In 17 of the 40 countries, at least 75% of the expert respondents agree or strongly agree with this position (figure 7.3).

*Autonomy for electoral management boards*
The autonomy of EMBs resonated in almost all the country reports. The clear reform message from the Expert Opinion Survey is that EMBs should enjoy relative autonomy in political, administrative and financial spheres: in 39 of the 40 countries, more than half the expert respondents agree or strongly agree that EMBs should enjoy relative autonomy in political, administrative and financial independence (figure 7.4).

*Election adjudication and dispute resolution*
The importance of transparent, impartial and expeditious adjudication of election disputes is now well accepted as crucial to defusing pre- and post-election violence in Africa, and to enhancing the legitimacy of electoral outcomes and political succession (see chapter 5). For that reason, some countries have introduced electoral reforms.

The general objective of electoral adjudication is to protect and promote diversity, provide remedies for electoral irregularities (national and local elections, party nominations) and protect the electoral mandate from being stolen. It is also to ensure the accountability of EMBs and to prevent them from being judges in their own cases. Thus constitutional and other legal provisions such as electoral laws spell out the institutions and processes for adjudication. Equally important are the legal framework for conducting the elections and general confidence in the judiciary's independence.

Confidence in dispute management though is not high: only in eight countries did more than half the expert respondents consider election disputes to be well managed to the satisfaction of all political parties, pointing to the need for policy reform (see figure 5.4).

The country reports suggest that such reform needs to create independent and credible institutions to handle election disputes; institutionalize dispute adjudication for elections; ensure sets time limits for disposing of election disputes and petitions; issue information regularly to the political parties and citizens on how the dispute is being resolved; explore alternative conflict resolution mechanisms; and carry out regular review and auditing of the processes of election dispute management, including their efficacy.

> *The jobs of electoral commissioners should be openly advertised and competed for nationally by citizens*

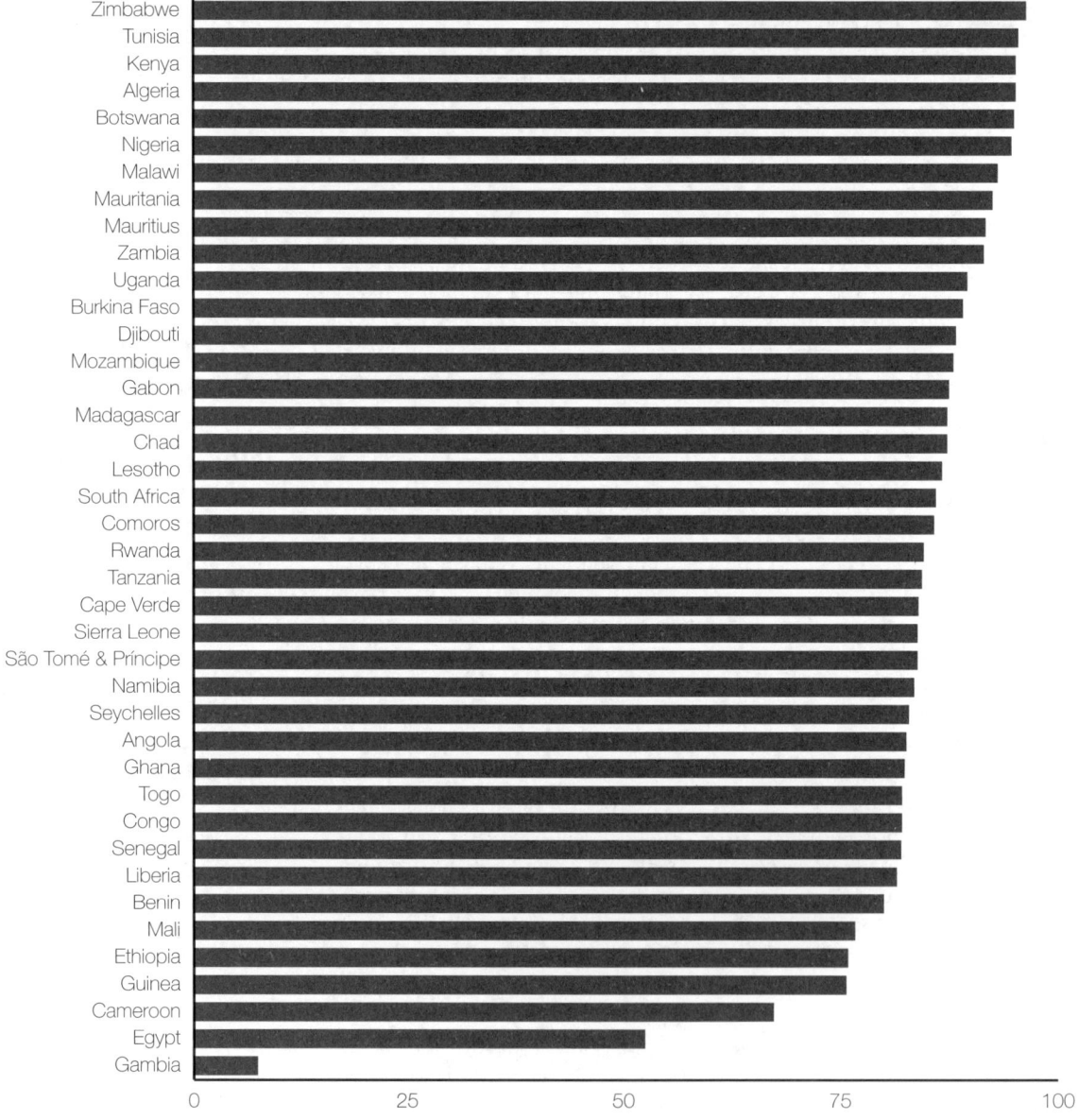

**Figure 7.2 Appointing and removing electoral commissioners should be handled by an independent non-partisan body—agree or strongly agree**

Share of experts surveyed agreeing with the statement, by country (%)

*Source:* AGR III Expert Opinion Survey 2012.

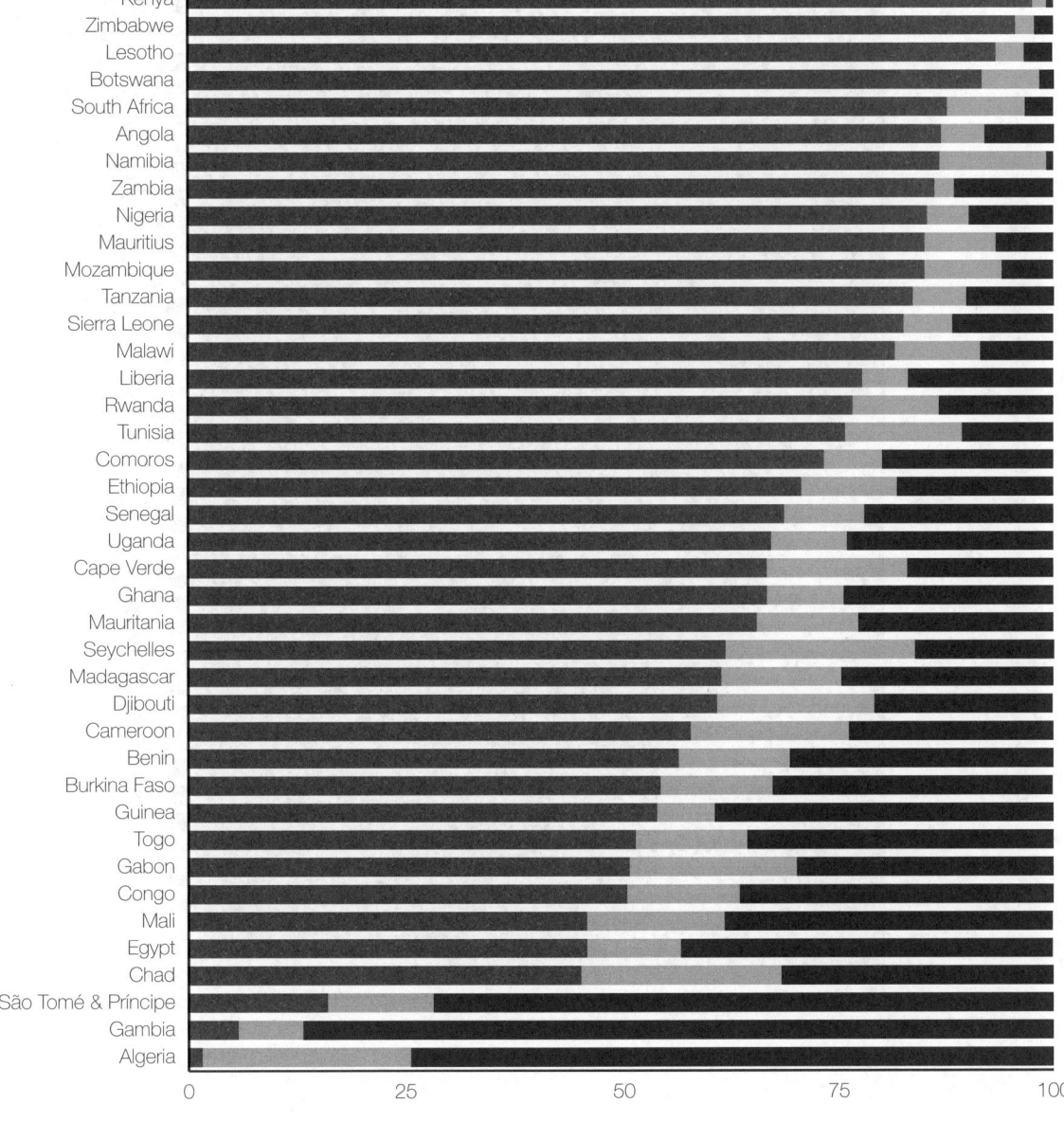

**Figure 7.3 Positions of electoral commissioners should be advertised for national competition**

Share of experts surveyed, by country (%)

- Agree or strongly agree
- Neither agree nor disagree
- Strongly disagree or disagree

Kenya
Zimbabwe
Lesotho
Botswana
South Africa
Angola
Namibia
Zambia
Nigeria
Mauritius
Mozambique
Tanzania
Sierra Leone
Malawi
Liberia
Rwanda
Tunisia
Comoros
Ethiopia
Senegal
Uganda
Cape Verde
Ghana
Mauritania
Seychelles
Madagascar
Djibouti
Cameroon
Benin
Burkina Faso
Guinea
Togo
Gabon
Congo
Mali
Egypt
Chad
São Tomé & Príncipe
Gambia
Algeria

0   25   50   75   100

*Source:* AGR III Expert Opinion Survey 2012.

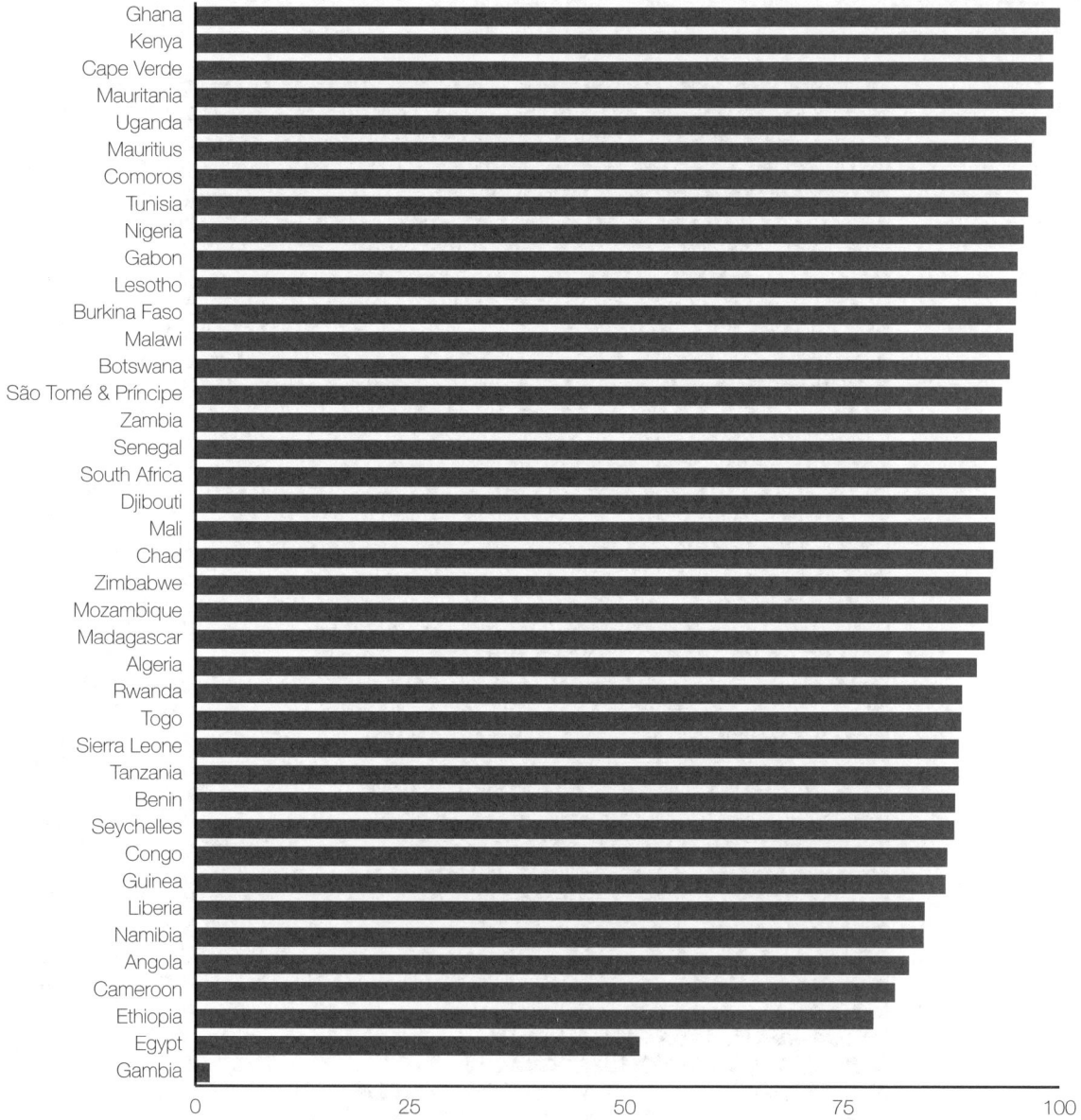

**Figure 7.4 Electoral management boards should have relative autonomy in political, administrative and financial independence—agree or strongly agree**

Share of experts surveyed agreeing with the statement, by country (%)

*Source:* AGR III Expert Opinion Survey 2012.

## Security of elections and the role of security agencies

The "security" of electoral governance may be seen along broad and narrow perspectives. The broad perspective focuses on securing the electoral process from distortions, violations and manipulations, in ways that will generate and sustain confidence in the legitimacy of democratic elections and democratic political succession. Critical is the notion of free and fair or credible democratic elections (see box 4.7). Securing the electoral process in this way has been the preoccupation of electoral reform in Africa since the 1990s. It requires planning, training, inter-agency coordination and interaction between electoral commissions and stakeholders in state and society. This aspect of securing the integrity of the electoral process is as important as the specific and election-related deployment and use of security agencies, to keep the peace and move men and equipment to difficult terrains just before, during and after election day.

The narrow sense of security refers to using security agencies, such as the police, for specific electoral functions and duties in the electoral cycle, beyond their normal law-and-order role. In this view, there is necessarily the need to determine what kinds of security agencies and security actors to deploy and use. When there is agreement on deploying security agencies for electoral duties, there may be disagreement over where the operational authority over them should lie. The operational authority lies in some countries with the electoral commission; in other countries, it lies with another neutral body. In both cases, what informs the arrangement is the need to insulate the EMBs from partisan party political use by incumbent political authorities.

In a number of countries, the debate is about who should be the controlling and disbursing authority of the financial arrangements for deploying security agencies, and who should bear the cost. Another problem concerns the control and coordination of the operational activities of the security agencies deployed for duty in the electoral process, and the nature of the training they must undergo for their election-related duty.

The challenge for African EMBs remains the daunting capacity-building one of how to engage in inter-agency coordination with security agencies, ministries, departments and other agencies of the state without alienating the EMBs' operational autonomy and their ultimate responsibility for ensuring credible elections. The problem then is how to ensure that the security and other agencies deployed for elections are under the control of the EMBs, in respect of the election-related assignments of the security agencies. This is further complicated by the problem of the extended span of control of the EMBs, in view of the necessarily decentralized nature of managing the electoral process in many countries, and the discretionary power on the ground wielded by local officials and temporary staff of EMBs.

Some African countries have reformed their party system to de-emphasize dysfunctional ethno-political and related violence in competitive party and electoral politics, by proscribing ethnic-based political parties (box 7.3).

These and similar provisions provided the legal basis for the attempt to engineer the emergence of political parties with a national outlook through structural or organizational requirements and regulations, spelt out in electoral and other laws, which political associations seeking recognition and registration as political parties should satisfy. The EMBs in some countries, for example, have the mandate to ensure political party compliance with the constitutional requirements of broad national outlook.

However, the character of political parties in terms of their functional spread and national outlook is a major contentious policy issue. Some argue that since political parties are free associations of like-minded people with same ideological orientation and conviction, parties do not necessarily have to be national and trans-ethnic in orientation; parties could be sectarian, local or community based, so long as they do not threaten national interests. But others argue that for parties to be agencies of diversity management, they need to be national in orientation and transcend sectarian identities. Whatever their composition, though, parties need to be instruments of social cohesion, national integration and political stability.

In the AGR III survey, in 19 countries at least half the expert respondents consider their security agencies to be fair and non-partisan in their roles in the electoral process, less than half in the other 21 (see figure 5.3). This point emphasizes the need to reform how security forces engage in the electoral process.

### Political party reforms

Political party reforms have been central to electoral reforms in Africa, if only because competitive party and electoral politics is one of the defining characteristics of liberal democracy. The challenges of reforms for political parties include how to prevent parties from being sectarian along ethno-regional, racial or religious lines; to be inclusive of different social classes and categories; and to practise internal democracy.

### Internal party democracy

Political parties in many African countries have a wide deficit in internal democracy: only in 12 of the 40 countries did more than half the respondents agree or strongly agree that political parties practise internal democracy (figure 7.5).

Lack of such democracy fuels internal party feuds and conflicts, undermines any credible process of leadership selection and compromises the quality of leaders presented as candidates for national elections.

## Constitutional and political reform issues

When the constitutional and political context of electoral governance does not provide for effective diversity management, the electoral architecture on its own cannot bridge social diversities in cohesion. Some of the more important issues requiring reform are now discussed.

### Constitutional safeguards to protect marginalized groups

Marginalized groups include minorities, women, youth and people with disabilities. Affirmative action is proposed in many of the country reports for those groups, beyond constitutional provisions, which themselves should be more explicit on recognizing diversity and protecting minority rights.

In practical politics, in 32 of the 40 countries more than half the experts agree or strongly agree that a quota system should be adopted for appointing women to legislative and executive positions (figure 7.6). The clear preference among expert respondents is for women to be mainstreamed in governance processes. This reinforces the position of regional institutions like the African Union and some regional economic communities like the Southern African Development Community for quota systems for women in public institutions.

### Effective constitutional checks and balances in governance

When there are effective checks on the use of power, the propensity is for group and minority interests to be well protected in the political system. More than half the experts in 33 of the 40 countries indicate that there are significant or full checks and balances among the three branches of government (figure 7.7).

But more needs to done. Many legislatures are quite weak (see chapter 2), with executive dominance still the norm in many countries. There is a need to reinforce the capacity and better fund the legislature, while ensuring transparency and accountability in its affairs.

### A competent, corruption-free and independent judiciary

A competent, corruption-free and independent judiciary is central to democratic governance, respect for the rule of law and ensuring that diversity is not compromised. Confidence in the judiciary may make all the difference in electoral governance as political actors who feel cheated can have recourse to the judiciary for electoral justice. In Nigeria, for example, the judiciary has been crucial in keeping the democratic project on course through landmark electoral judgments that

> *A competent, corruption-free and independent judiciary is central to democratic governance*

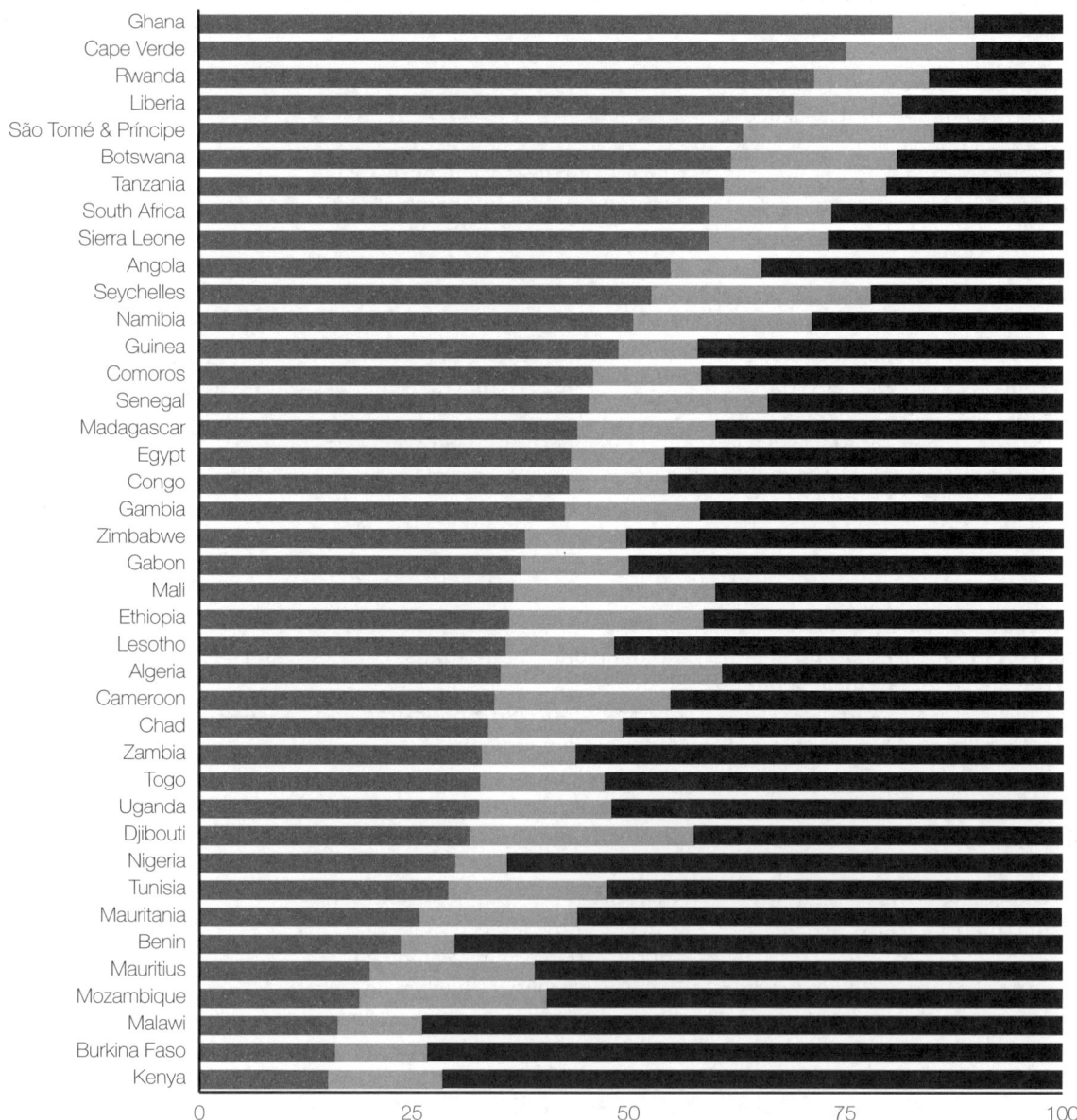

**Figure 7.5 Political parties practise internal democracy in electing party officials and party candidates for national elections**

Share of experts surveyed, by country (%)

- Agree or strongly agree
- Neither agree nor disagree
- Strongly disagree or disagree

*Source:* AGR III Expert Opinion Survey 2012.

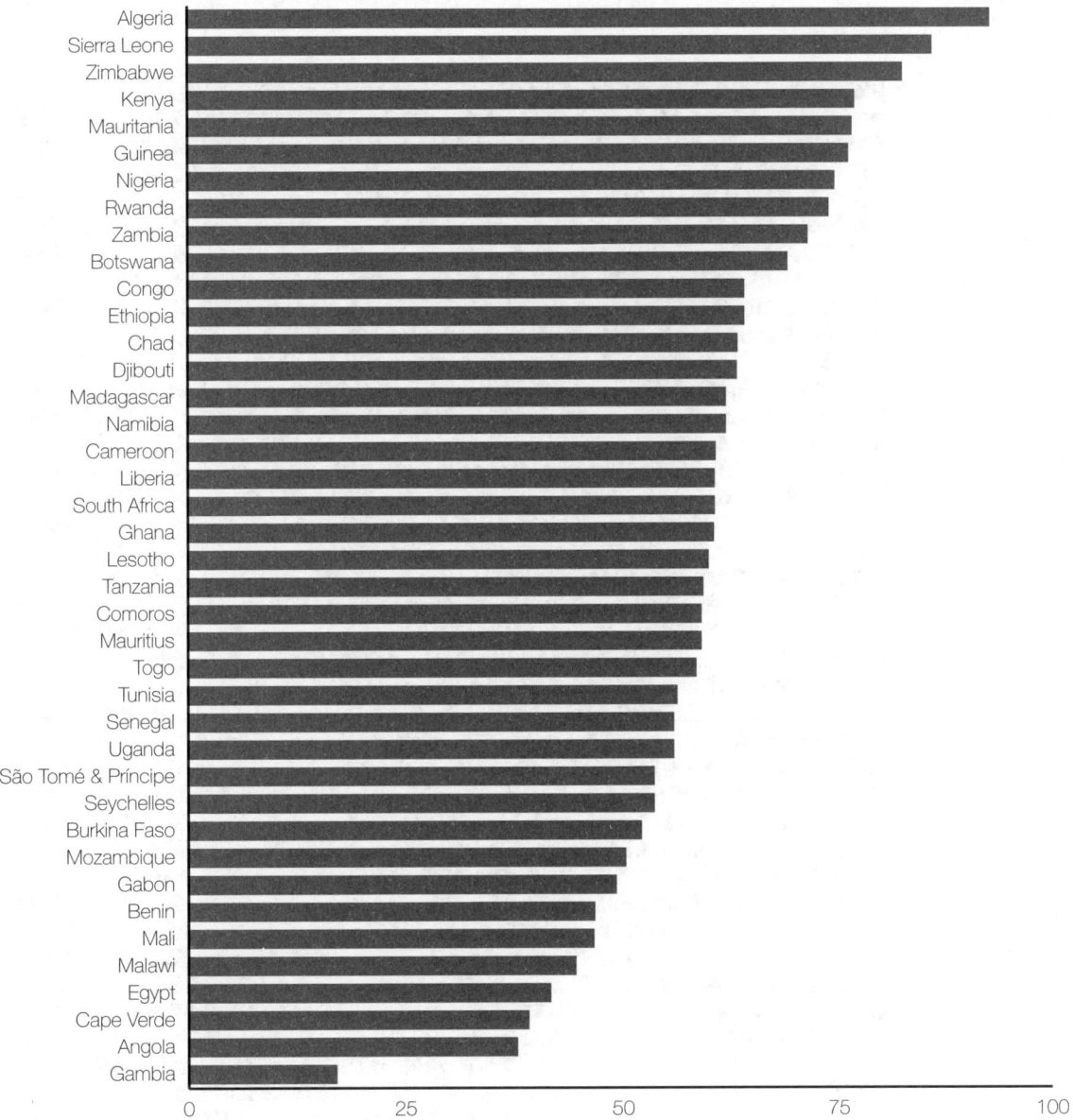

**Figure 7.6 A quota system should be adopted for appointing women to executive positions and parliament—agree or strongly agree**

Share of experts surveyed agreeing with the statement, by country (%)

*Source:* AGR III Expert Opinion Survey 2012.

# Figure 7.7 Significant or full constitutional checks and balances among the different branches of government exist in most countries

Share of experts surveyed, by country (%)

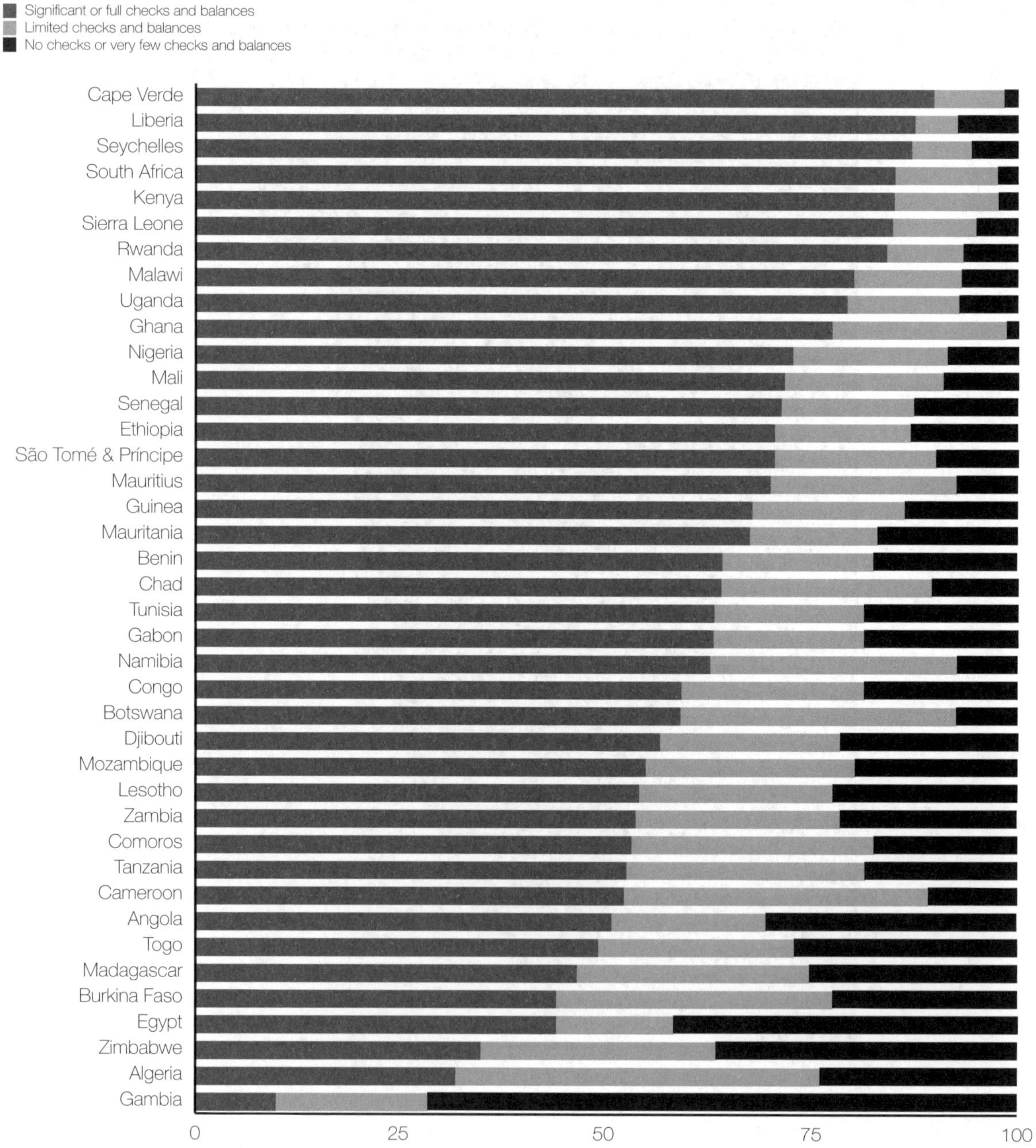

- Significant or full checks and balances
- Limited checks and balances
- No checks or very few checks and balances

Cape Verde
Liberia
Seychelles
South Africa
Kenya
Sierra Leone
Rwanda
Malawi
Uganda
Ghana
Nigeria
Mali
Senegal
Ethiopia
São Tomé & Príncipe
Mauritius
Guinea
Mauritania
Benin
Chad
Tunisia
Gabon
Namibia
Congo
Botswana
Djibouti
Mozambique
Lesotho
Zambia
Comoros
Tanzania
Cameroon
Angola
Togo
Madagascar
Burkina Faso
Egypt
Zimbabwe
Algeria
Gambia

0    25    50    75    100

*Source:* AGR III Expert Opinion Survey 2012.

gave justice to aggrieved electoral parties. In several states in Nigeria, electoral verdicts have been overturned by the judiciary and election tribunals, averting the possibility of violence (Adejumobi 2010; Agbaje and Adejumobi 2006).

However, while checks and balances are increasing, corruption in the judiciary remains daunting (figure 7.8). Many respondents regard the judiciary as corrupt: only in seven countries did at least half the experts consider their judiciary to be largely free from corruption.

The goal is that judiciaries should be purged of corruption. Policy reform measures may include appointment and removal of judicial officers based on clear procedure and, possibly, entrusted to an independent body (such as a judicial service commission); adequate remuneration and protection for judicial officers in their work; regular training for judicial officers to ensure state-of-the-art knowledge in dispensing justice; regular audits of the conduct of the judiciary, which should involve parliament, civil society and professional groups; and adequate sanctions for erring judicial officials tried through legal process.

### National unity government in post-election crisis

African countries have made important strides in promoting inclusive governance through redesigning institutions and governance systems, including decentralization, diversity in the constitution of governments and the executive, and reform of the electoral system (see chapters 1, 2 and 5). A frequent challenge after elections, however, is forming a national unity government that includes all or the main parties, against a backdrop of violence, as in Kenya and Zimbabwe.

The policy message from the country surveys is that this option should be adopted as a temporary measure in a post-election crisis, in order to ease the crisis and avoid destruction of lives and property. In 32 of the 40 countries, more than half the respondents endorsed the formation of a national government as a viable option (figure 7.9). However, this option should be only a temporary measure, and not assume permanence in competitive electoral politics. Reform of the electoral system towards mixed forms of proportional representation may provide an inclusive mechanism for ensuring a more national method of representation.

### Government delivery of services

A major expected dividend of democracy is the delivery of public services. When government services are inefficient, inaccessible and based on patronage, the result is usually low commitment and support to the democratic project— what some refer to as democracy fatigue—and possibly tension and conflict in society. The government's service delivery capacity is thus a key conflict-mediating mechanism. Individuals and groups that can access affordable public goods without relying on ethnic or other sectarian connections are likely to reinforce national unity and identity (UNECA 2009).

*African countries have made important strides in promoting inclusive governance*

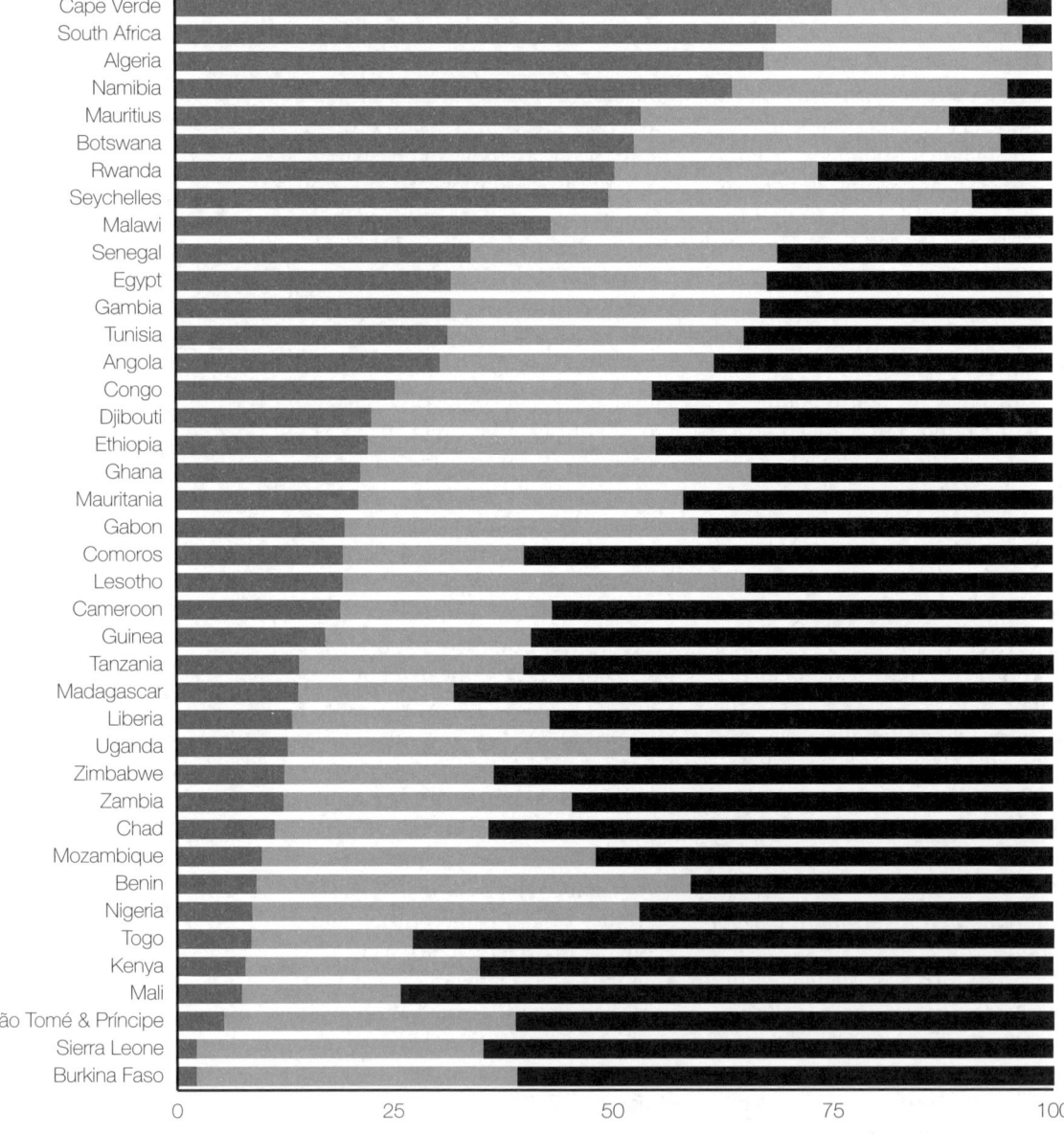

**Figure 7.8 Judicial corruption remains daunting**

Share of experts surveyed, by country (%)

- Largely free from corruption or above corruption
- Fairly free from corruption
- Completely or fairly corrupt

Cape Verde
South Africa
Algeria
Namibia
Mauritius
Botswana
Rwanda
Seychelles
Malawi
Senegal
Egypt
Gambia
Tunisia
Angola
Congo
Djibouti
Ethiopia
Ghana
Mauritania
Gabon
Comoros
Lesotho
Cameroon
Guinea
Tanzania
Madagascar
Liberia
Uganda
Zimbabwe
Zambia
Chad
Mozambique
Benin
Nigeria
Togo
Kenya
Mali
São Tomé & Príncipe
Sierra Leone
Burkina Faso

0    25    50    75    100

*Source:* AGR III Expert Opinion Survey 2012.

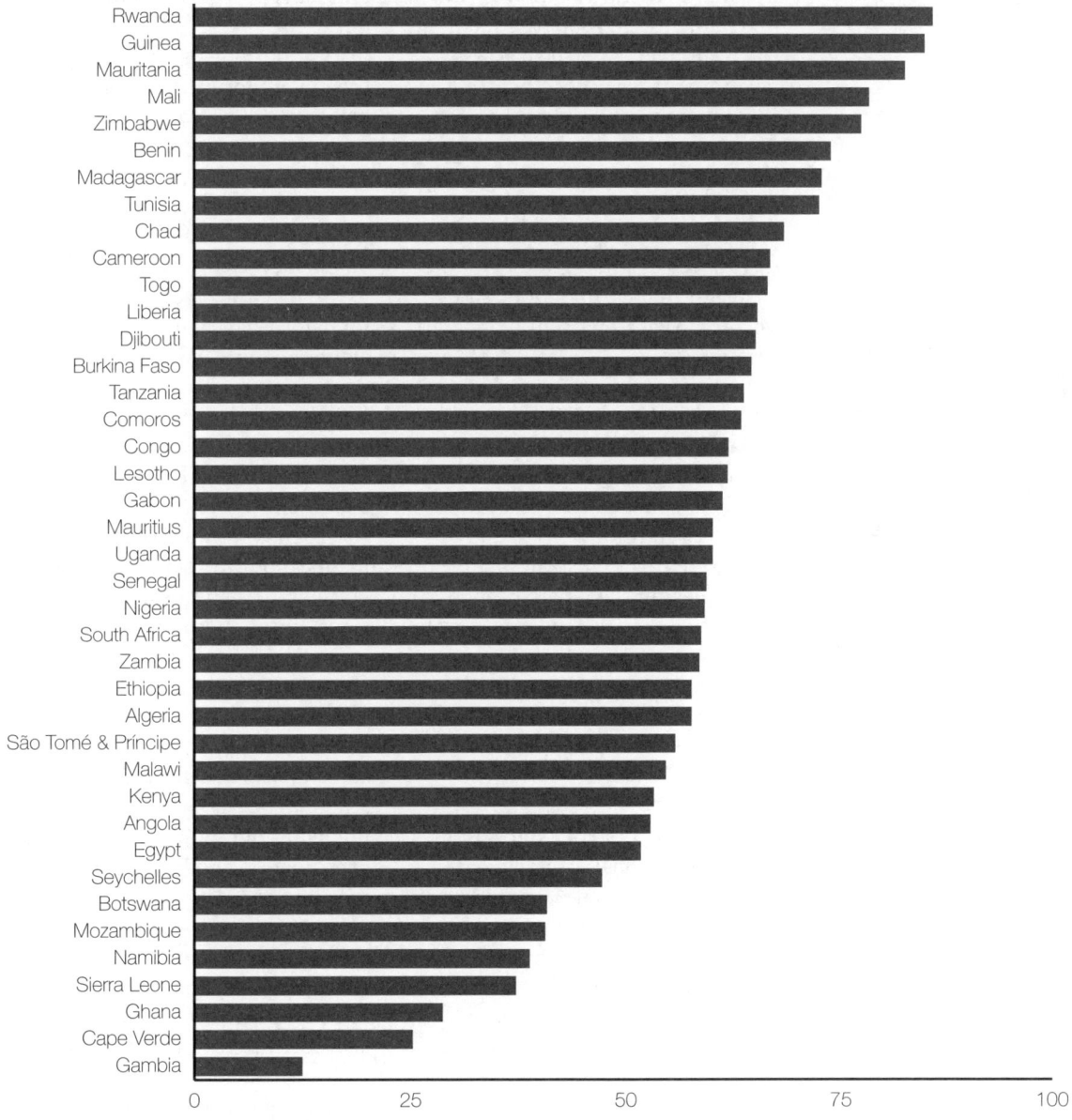

**Figure 7.9 Formation of coalition or national unity government is a viable option—agree or strongly agree**

Share of experts surveyed agreeing with the statement, by country (%)

*Source:* AGR III Expert Opinion Survey 2012.

Unfortunately, access to such services is a major challenge in many African countries, fuelling public disaffection and social conflicts in some of them. In only 7 of the 40 countries did more than half the respondents perceive access to government services to be readily or mostly accessible to the citizenry; in the remaining countries, the popular perception from the experts is that access to public services is either limited or difficult (figure 7.10). This is not a good snapshot in eliciting public support for Africa's nascent democratic systems.

*Governmental conflict-management capacity beyond elections*
Some countries have established conflict-management structures, including in rural areas, while others have failed to institutionalize them, leaving them patchy and ineffective. So, although inter-state conflicts have sharply declined in Africa in the last two decades, intra-state conflicts remain a disturbing feature of the political landscape.

These conflicts stem from various roots: indigenous/settler citizenship conflict; resource-based scarcity, including water, grazing and other pastoral rights; or relative economic deprivation. Whatever the source, African countries have to devise mechanisms that ensure that domestic conflicts are well mediated and do not assume national proportions, especially as experts in only 11 countries believe that the government has these mechanisms in place (figure 7.11).

> *African countries have to devise mechanisms that ensure that domestic conflicts are well mediated*

## Conclusions and recommendations

The backdrop of pressures for deeper electoral, constitutional and political reforms in Africa is painted not only by political parties and state institutions but also by society more broadly. Reforms must come from below as well as above.

Survey findings underline the need for such reforms, especially in countries that have to fully consolidate democracy. Reforms are required to improve the credibility of electoral governance, including ensuring autonomy for EMBs.

EMBs must be insulated from party political pressure by incumbent authorities. They should also build capacity to engage with security agencies, ministries, departments and other state agencies, without alienating their operational autonomy and their ultimate responsibility for ensuring credible elections.

EMBs also need to work with other stakeholders in state and society to secure the electoral process, including planning, training, inter-agency coordination and interaction. This is as important as the specific and election-related use of security forces around election time.

Resolving election disputes fast and fairly is crucial to stemming election-related violence and to enhancing confidence in electoral outcomes and political succession, so that the electoral mandate is seen as having been awarded freely and transparently.

# Figure 7.10 Access to public services remains a major challenge

Share of experts surveyed, by country (%)

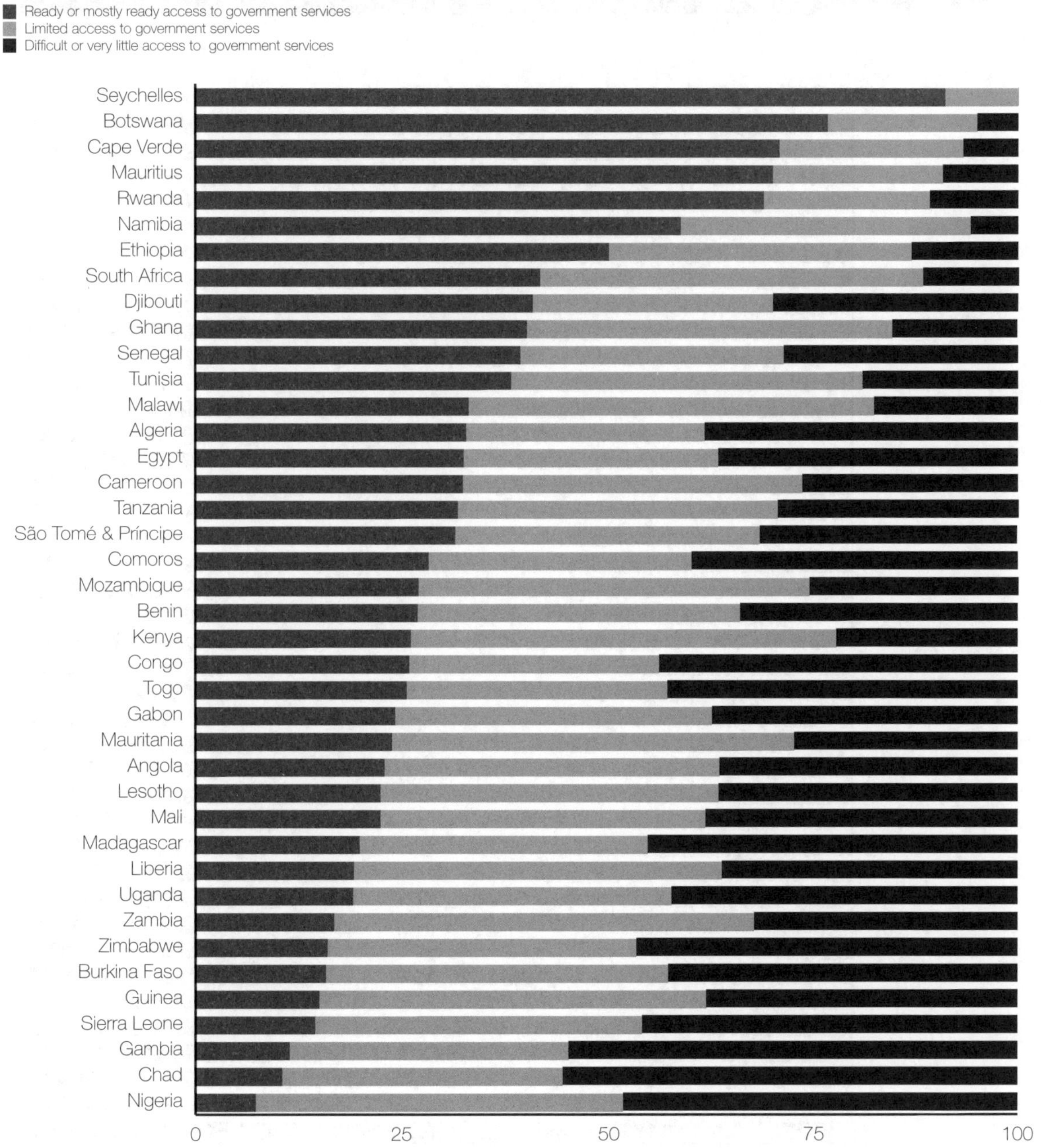

- Ready or mostly ready access to government services
- Limited access to government services
- Difficult or very little access to government services

Seychelles
Botswana
Cape Verde
Mauritius
Rwanda
Namibia
Ethiopia
South Africa
Djibouti
Ghana
Senegal
Tunisia
Malawi
Algeria
Egypt
Cameroon
Tanzania
São Tomé & Príncipe
Comoros
Mozambique
Benin
Kenya
Congo
Togo
Gabon
Mauritania
Angola
Lesotho
Mali
Madagascar
Liberia
Uganda
Zambia
Zimbabwe
Burkina Faso
Guinea
Sierra Leone
Gambia
Chad
Nigeria

0    25    50    75    100

*Source:* AGR III Expert Opinion Survey 2012.

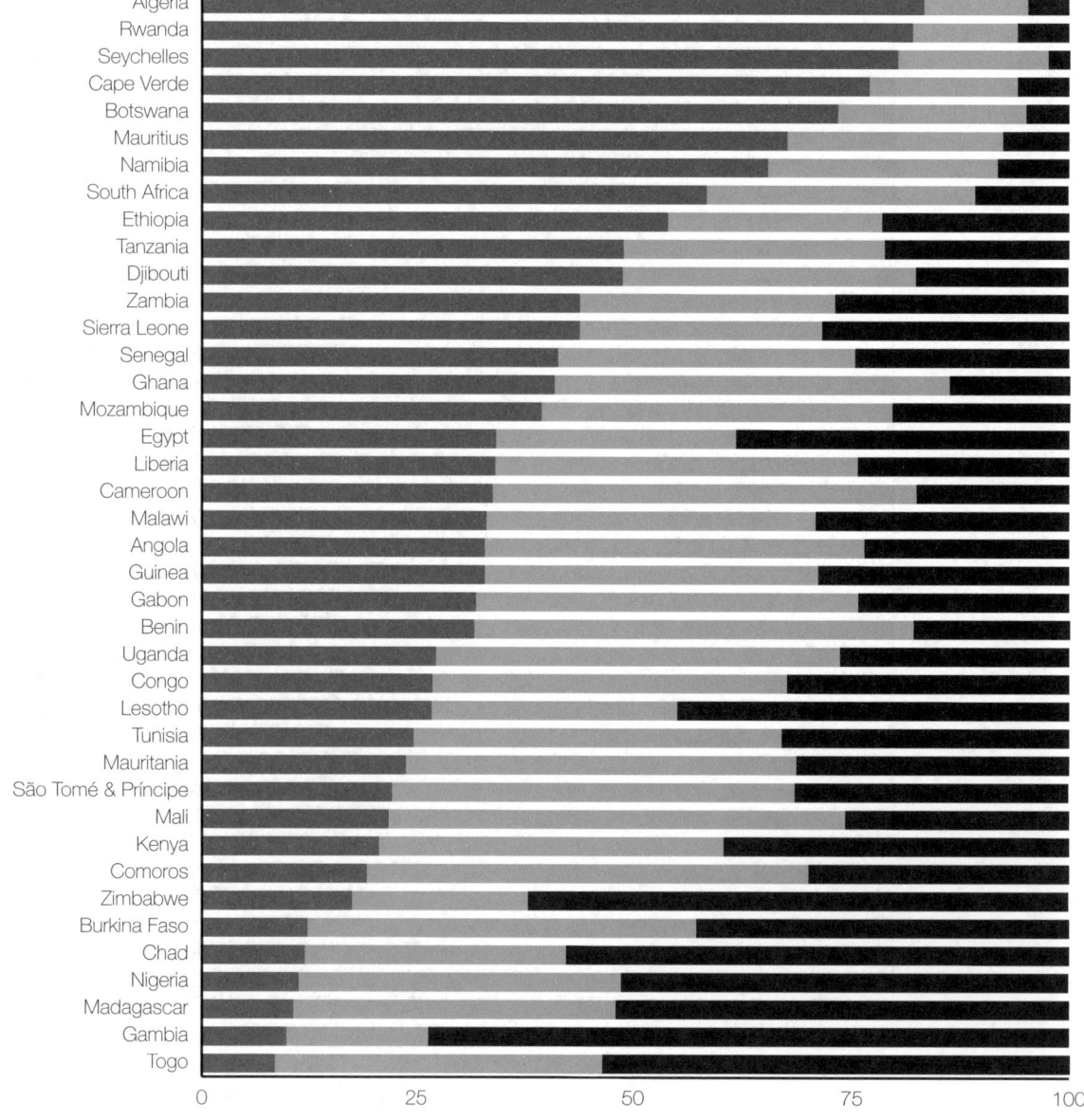

## Figure 7.11 States have weak capacity for managing intra-state conflicts in most countries

Share of experts surveyed, by country (%)

- Usually or always effective
- Occasionally effective
- Completely ineffective or rarely effective

*Source:* AGR III Expert Opinion Survey 2012.

Thus a mechanism or forum in which various groups in society, parties and state institutions consult regularly on issues of electoral and constitutional reforms would be valuable. It would also consider how to manage diversity issues.

Political parties need more internal democracy, both to promote a democratic culture and to help select good leaders. Trans-ethnic and national parties may better promote diversity management in multi-ethnic African societies, suggesting this is the approach to follow, but policy reforms will have to be contextual, based on the conditions and experiences of the countries involved.

African countries will have to devise incentives and sanctions to make their political parties democratic internally, which may include state financial support that is tied to parties' internal democracy, and moves by the EMB (or other agency) to ensure that political parties conform to the electoral law on internal democracy. Finally, African governments will have to scale up efforts at improving the delivery of affordable, high-quality public services.

## References

Adejumobi, Said. 2010. "Democracy and Governance in Nigeria: Between Consolidation and Reversal." In *Governance and Politics in Post-Military Nigeria: Changes and Challenges*, ed. Said Adejumobi. New York: Palgrave Macmillan.

Agbaje, Adigun, and Said Adejumobi. 2006. "Do Votes Count? The Travails of Electoral Politics in Nigeria." *Africa Development* 31 (3): 25–44.

UNECA (United Nations Economic Commission for Africa). 2009. *African Governance Report II*. Addis Ababa.

# 8

**Policy Recommendations**

The dominant theme of this report is how to organize elections in a credible, fair and transparent fashion amid an environment of wide diversity—whether in ethnicity, religion, region, class, gender or age. As democracy has deepened in Africa, elections have occupied a central place. Elections have become more regular but also more closely contested, making them tinder boxes that must be sensitively organized—and occasionally doused.

The report therefore argues for strengthening and democratizing electoral governance. Credibility, fairness and transparency are imperative in running an electoral process, even more so when conditions are diverse. Every stage in the process should have—and be seen to have—procedural certainty, and hence a level playing field for contending parties and candidates, to ensure the substantive uncertainty of an election's outcome.

This final section presents a synthesis of policy recommendations made by expert panels, focus group discussions, country reports and analysis in the preceding chapters. Findings from these sources are more consistent than divergent.

A major theme running through the report is not only the recognition of diversity as a possible source of conflict between and during elections— but the need to address it. The potential of elections to accommodate diversity depends on the measures designed to pre-empt or resolve diversity-related conflicts. Most countries have not fully resolved either the structural roots of these conflicts or the conjunctural triggers, although good practices are emerging.

The recommendations, in five parts, are candid, highlighting the need for further political and constitutional reform to secure yet greater gains in electoral governance. Resolving political, social and economic diversity through elections will be long drawn out, but putting the item prominently on African countries' political agendas is a prerequisite for the continent to continue its democratic transformation.

## The political system

*Constitutional reforms and diversity*
Most constitutional reforms in Africa were undertaken to accompany the democratic transition, but some were directed towards electoral change and diversity management. Across a large number of African countries, expert panellists did not believe that the constitution of their country promotes diversity and inclusive governance or adequately protect minority interests. Constitutional protection of diversity is uneven among countries, and enforcement also varies.

Constitutions should have provisions for protecting diversity and for assuring a national mechanism to monitor how those provisions are carried out. (The country reports for Ghana, Kenya and Namibia expound on this at some length.)

For diversity to be well protected through the constitution, the voices of the people and their aspirations must resonate in the constitution. The best way is to adopt a bottom-up and people-driven approach in constitutional engineering. As Kenya's experience with its 2010 Constitution suggests, this is a good pathway to promoting constitutionalism.

### Management of ethnic diversity

Constitutional provisions that merely forbid discrimination against minorities have largely failed to resolve ethnic exclusion. One policy response would be to establish a Commission for Diversity Management to champion groups' concerns and to oversee implementation of the diversity-inclusion agenda, especially in public institutions (as practised in Nigeria and now put in place in Kenya under the recent constitution). "Ethnic auditing" should be conducted regularly at both national and provincial or state levels to identify and penalize those who engage in practices that enforce ethnic exclusion in hiring as well as in distribution of public resources.

### Lingua franca and diversity

Language is a powerful instrument of social identity and diversity convergence. A common language facilitates inter-communal and interpersonal communication in a country and can crystallize a national culture that supersedes parochial affinities of race, ethnicity, regionalism, religion and class—recognizing multiculturalism. In Tanzania, national cohesion has been facilitated through the common national language of Kiswahili. This report does not urge countries to impose a national language, but through national dialogue and consensus explore the possibility of a common national language or languages (as in South Africa) being adopted.

### Indigenous people, settlers, migrants and citizenship

The political and economic rights of non-indigenous peoples in a given country need to be addressed urgently in an open forum to achieve national consensus. A legal framework should be constructed, to ensure that their relations with indigenous people at election time do not degenerate into conflict and violence. Citizenship should be redefined to emphasize birth, residency, tax obligations, and civic and national values rather than ancestry and ethnicity.

Strategies are also required for ensuring that citizens understand the benefits of diversity and the rights of migrants as well as their positive contributions to the country. Citizens need to be encouraged to learn about cultures and languages of others. There should be complementary programmes to nurture social cohesion in wider society.

### Institutions of horizontal accountability

Institutions of horizontal accountability need to be established or strengthened in promoting respect for peoples' rights and democratic management of diversity. These institutions include the office of the auditor general, ombudsman, anticorruption body, human rights institutions and the judiciary. The goal is to ensure that citizens' rights are

> **Institutions of horizontal accountability need to be established or strengthened in promoting respect for peoples' rights**

protected, public accountability is ensured, the rule of law is maintained and the democratic system is unhindered.

## Government of national unity and election outcomes

Electoral malpractice and disputes led to crisis in some countries (including Kenya and Zimbabwe) and to negotiations that subsequently resulted in a coalition government as an emergency or temporary measure to stop election conflict from escalating into violence.

The Expert Opinion Survey points to a strong view in most countries that a government of national unity is desirable in a post-election conflict, but this should be temporary and not a means of rewarding those who rig elections or commit other electoral fraud. (Indeed, fraud should be criminalized, where it is not already, and heavily sanctioned, to deter would-be riggers.) A government of national unity may also be necessary after a war but, as with post-election conflicts, should be well crafted based on local circumstances to avoid rewarding warlords with power.

## Affirmative action for women and other marginalized groups

Expert panellists in most countries show a strong consensus that affirmative action, including quotas for women, is necessary in electoral and political processes. This consensus recognized that women are still marginalized in most countries, but they are not the only ones: it has become customary to advocate affirmative action for youth and people with disabilities as well.

Recommendations from the country reports range from affirmative action in legislative and local elections to the placement of candidates from marginalized groups on party lists in proportional representation systems. Governments, electoral management boards (EMBs), parties and civil society organizations (CSOs) should adopt quotas for gender equality and women's empowerment including party quotas, candidate quotas and reserved seats.

Parties should adopt affirmative action measures by ensuring gender equality during party primaries and nomination of election candidates. More generally, special measures should be considered to raise the level of representation of women, youth, minorities and people with disabilities in bodies such as parliament and electoral institutions. There is a reasonable case for affirmative action that would empower these marginalized groups with resources to run for office and serve in electoral institutions. Polling stations, as well as centres for voter registration and issuance of identity cards, should have special facilities in order to encourage participation of people with disabilities and the elderly.

Marginalized communities such as the Basarwa (in Southern Africa) and Batwa (in the Democratic Republic of the Congo, Rwanda, Uganda and other countries) are poorly represented in parliament and state institutions. Governments should

> *Governments, electoral management boards, parties and civil society organizations should adopt quotas for gender equality*

undertake affirmative action to assist these excluded communities to run for office, and need to review citizenship-empowerment strategies to cultivate indigenous entrepreneurship and sustainable economic development. In a related vein, if a country is to succeed in managing diversities such as marginalized youth, it must pursue inclusive economic policies that embrace all social groups.

## Electoral institutions, processes and finance

### Reform of electoral management boards

EMBs are crucial to the electoral system, but the picture is not good, as evidenced by the country reports. Their institutional and financial autonomy is imperative, and should be enshrined in the national constitution. Most country reports recommended that the appointment of EMB members should not be the prerogative of a president but should be either a process that follows a mechanism of open advertisement or a vetted process in which CSOs and political parties are involved.

Other African Governance Report (AGR) III country reports recommended that the processes of appointing and removing EMB members should be handled by an independent non-partisan body. And the majority of surveyed panellists agreed. EMBs should be diversity-sensitive in their staffing, and include women and minorities with requisite skills and experience.

Furthermore, EMBs should be endowed with the necessary powers and authority to create mechanisms to promote cooperation among political parties, CSOs and candidates with the objective of building trust and consensus among those participating in the electoral process, and preventing or defusing electoral disputes.

### Political party reform and diversity
The country reports show great concern that most parties—central players in the electoral process—are formed to mobilize electoral support on a sectarian identity basis which can often be a polarizing factor in national politics. Expert panellists in most countries tend to agree with this proposition.

Most country reports indicate that parties generally lack internal democracy. Some parties have even split due to contestants' unwillingness to accept results of party primaries. There is therefore a need for genuine internal party democracy. And like other organizations, such as CSOs, parties should be required to register, and have appropriate governance mechanisms.

Parties should embrace diversity in their membership and outgrow their original ethnic and regional bases. They should also have a monitoring mechanism to ensure representation of various ethnic and social groups (including women, youth and people with disabilities) among their key organs and leadership positions.

### Reform of the electoral law
Electoral law provides the basis of the electoral process and electoral competition. If it is flawed, the

> **Political parties should embrace diversity in their membership and outgrow their original ethnic and regional bases**

electoral process will most likely be corrupt. Electoral legislation must not only guarantee that the requisite institutions, rules and processes of electoral engagements are clearly spelt out, but must also recognize and accommodate diversity in all its manifestations. Many country reports call for reform of the electoral law to make it more responsive to contemporary needs and demands, and to be more sensitive to diversity.

There are two major policy concerns across countries. First, the electoral law should be periodically reviewed and updated to keep up with changing political dynamics in the country. Second, the revision or reform of the electoral law must be an inclusive process that involves not only parliament and political parties, but also other stakeholders.

### Electoral system and diversity

The quality of an election hinges on the type of electoral system in a country. The capacity to manage diversity depends on the plurality and inclusiveness of the system, which falls into two broad categories. Proportional representation (or a hybrid) could balance legislative membership among ethno-regional parties and other minority groups, and, particularly in post-conflict countries, could counter the winner-takes-all, disenfranchising outcome that first past the post tends to encourage. Countries dissatisfied with the latter system may wish to review it and consider proportional representation or a variant of the two systems, consulting as widely as possible in an attempt to reach consensus.

### Voter registration

Voter registration encounters huge challenges in most countries, from manipulation, through inflation, undercounting of potential voters and inclusion of dead voters, to obstacles in registering certain groups—those in remote areas or slums, pastoral populations and internally displaced peoples. Its credibility, transparency and efficiency need to be vastly improved, which should include a post-election review by the EMB to yield disaggregated data on groups such as women and youth. These data will help in electoral planning.

Countries need to meet the challenge and responsibility of registering voters among their diaspora communities, especially as the diaspora vote is growing in importance. At home, identity and voters' cards should be harmonized to broaden the voters' register and ensure continual registration.

And relevant new technologies to speed up and vet registration should be embraced. The biometric voter registration has vastly improved the accuracy of the voter registration system in countries such as Sierra Leone and electronic registration through the Internet and mobile phones has made advances in Rwanda. African countries should adopt modern technology for registering voters, but it must be cost effective, affordable, adaptable to the local environment and locally serviceable.

### Voter education

More widespread voter education in Africa is indispensable.

> ❛ **Relevant new technologies to speed up and vet voter registration should be embraced**

Recommendations in the country reports are quite specific, and include:

- Voter education should be an instrument for addressing diversity in politics. Important as information about the technical aspects of voting may be, voter education programmes need to include the issue of diversity, as well as political and social tolerance. Not only should strenuous efforts be made to extend this education to marginalized groups, but the themes of unity in diversity, responsible citizenship and peaceful conduct of politics should be infused into such programmes.

- Continuous targeted civic education, especially at young people, should be undertaken to help eliminate electoral violence. As a matter of urgency, governance and leadership education should be carried out alongside civic education in schools and universities.

- Voter education should be made more widespread and materials more accessible, especially for marginalized groups. EMBs should publish user-friendly electoral lists and related texts on elections.

- CSOs—particularly youth, women's and professional groups—should work with the EMB to raise awareness of the election process in towns and villages using channels as diverse as radio, print, electronic and other

media. More women, young people and people with disabilities should be trained and deployed as voter education facilitators.

*Election observation and monitoring*
Election observation and monitoring —international and domestic— contributes to democratic change by exposing electoral malpractices, while new technology has made it possible to communicate posted results and reveal discrepancies immediately, helping to deter brazen rigging.

The capacity of countries to monitor local elections should be encouraged and reinforced, as in Sierra Leone in the 2007 national elections when domestic groups formed a network—National Election Watch —to monitor them across the country. Increased capacity of domestic election monitoring promotes greater national ownership of the electoral process and encourages political accountability through citizens' influence on the process.

*Political finance*
If democracy is to take firm root in Africa, governments should make election funding a national priority. Citizens and CSOs, too, play a crucial role in ensuring that their government treats elections as basic public goods.

Very few countries' political parties have equal access to electoral resources—the ruling parties are usually heavily advantaged. Other issues relate to campaign funding, donor and private funding, and regulation of political finance.

> **'** *Voter education should be made more widespread and materials more accessible, especially for marginalized groups*

The AGR III country reports offer several recommendations.

- Introduce and enforce strict regulations on campaign finance for parties and candidates and fully disclose private campaign funding. To receive funding, parties must disclose their sources of income and expenditure, cooperate with relevant integrity agencies, adhere to requirements set by law and observe codes of conduct.

- Grant political parties (ruling and opposition) equal access to electoral resources (media, state funding and public property). This should be codified in law and strictly enforced. Parties that disadvantage others in accessing state-owned electoral resources using incumbency powers should receive stiff sanctions.

- Safeguard against corruption in election funding. Election money-laundering poses a particular danger as does buying political influence through corrupt funding. The use of state resources for patronage should be outlawed.

- Consider setting up a national election fund, possibly with external donor support, to address the gap created by inadequate election funding. Countries may allocate money to this fund continuously through their national budgetary cycle, in election year or otherwise. This fund can therefore be relied on for elections.

African countries should endeavour to fully fund their own elections, and so reduce (and ultimately eliminate) their dependence on the West, both to establish national ownership and to reflect a new determination to erase the stereotype of a continent in perpetual crisis, dependent on others.

## Managing electoral conflicts and disputes

*Violence*
Some of the countries where violence is a major feature of political campaigns, according to the expert panellists, include Benin, Chad, Ethiopia, Madagascar, Mozambique, Nigeria, the Congo, Sierra Leone, Togo, Zambia and Zimbabwe. Violence during elections has reached serious levels in recent years in Côte d'Ivoire, the Democratic Republic of the Congo, Kenya, Nigeria and Zimbabwe, for example. The country reports show a consensus that this scourge of the electoral process should be eradicated. And when the credibility of the EMB is in doubt and the electoral process compromised, parties' disaffection often increases, also sometimes leading to violence.

The following policy measures are recommended:

- Tools for preventing electoral violence must be woven into each stage of the electoral cycle.

- All political parties must give a written commitment to a peaceful and non-violent electoral process through a binding code

> ❛ *Citizens and civil society organizations play a crucial role in ensuring that their government treats elections as basic public goods*

of conduct. Parties violating this commitment should be sanctioned by the EMB or other statutory body.

- Inter-party dialogue should be encouraged where parties can air their concerns and fears. This platform should be institutionalized and made more regular. The EMB should also be part of such dialogue.

- Party militia groups or violent youth wings of political parties should be outlawed. Parties who maintain them should be sanctioned.

- Political parties' regulatory authority needs to be supported in order to monitor abuse of public resources during campaigning by incumbents; to prevent and penalize verbal violence among parties and civic groups; and at the constituency level, to build capacity for parties and broaden ownership, monitoring and enforcement of party codes of conduct.

- The EMB must display transparency, non-partisanship and professionalism in managing elections.

- Countries may also consider drawing on existing modes of conflict management in the electoral process to pre-empt violence, such as party liaison committees in South Africa and the conflict-resolution model of the Electoral Institute for Sustainable Democracy in Africa.

*' The election atmosphere should be voter friendly in all situations*

### Role of state security agencies

The police, military forces, intelligence services and related bodies display partisanship in the electoral process in most African countries according to the Expert Opinion Survey, and often brutalize opposition political parties and supporters. Activities of civil servants, local government officials and traditional rulers have also provoked controversy over bias, compromising the credibility of elections and increasing the chances of conflict.

The following policy measures are recommended in the AGR III country reports:

- Security forces should be professional and neutral towards parties during elections.

- Clearer rules need to be introduced and enforced to ensure civilian control of security forces and insulate them from party politics. Checks and balances are required to subject security agencies to democratic rules even as they provide the necessary security during elections. Security agencies should be given human rights education and election-related training to improve their understanding of their role in the electoral process.

- The high visibility of soldiers, police and other security personnel at polling stations makes for an environment ill conducive to free and fair elections.

- The election atmosphere should be voter friendly in all

situations. Repressive environments during elections should be discouraged.

- Civil servants, public officials, local government officials and traditional rulers should be outlawed from using their official positions to intimidate voters or otherwise use their power in the electoral process (though they naturally keep their voting rights). They must keep to the ethics and electoral law in discharging their duties.

### Transparent and efficient adjudication of election disputes

Most countries have dispute adjudication mechanisms, although capacity and credibility vary. When these mechanisms are weak, partisan or corrupt, the propensity for violence is usually high.

The following policy measures are recommended:

- As failure to resolve conflicts promptly may result in incessant petitions catalysing conflict, properly institutionalized and credible dispute settlement mechanisms are required.

- The electoral law should be very clear and concise on adjudicating disputes and on the institutions responsible. It should allow for results to be challenged in the courts.

- The independence of such courts handling electoral matters has to be guaranteed.

- Special electoral courts may be needed in regions and districts, but their selection and composition must be secured by consensus among all political parties.

- As many current mechanisms are very time consuming, a set and short time-frame should be introduced and enforced for resolving election disputes.

- EMBs should keep electorates updated on progress in such disputes, including cases that have gone to court.

- Good practices in alternative dispute resolution should be widely publicized.

### Regional mediation in election disputes and poll outcomes

Countries are showing increasing recourse to regional and international mediation to resolve election disputes, including Côte d'Ivoire, Kenya and Zimbabwe, as well as Madagascar.

The powers of sanction by such organizations as the African Union (AU), the Economic Community of West African States (ECOWAS), the Southern African Development Community (SADC) and others have been used to deny legitimacy to those regimes that come to power through coups, and to intervene in election disputes. This role is significant and should be as proactive as possible. Countries should be encouraged to ratify protocols that relate to elections and democratic governance.

> *Properly institutionalized and credible dispute settlement mechanisms are required*

Regional organizations have a moral and political authority to encourage member states to ratify and implement necessary democracy charters and protocols as well as pursue strategies of peaceful settlement of election disputes. Their role in promoting democracy and good governance (beyond dispute management) should be supported by their member states and harmonized to maintain policy coherence Africa-wide.

### Conflict management and early warning systems

Elections should be transformed from conflict triggers into conflict managers. Conflict management structures and processes should be established to ensure that electoral disputes are handled amicably and dealt with early enough so that they do not escalate into violence.

Local initiatives should be boosted to reduce the necessity for external assistance or intervention. And national early warning systems should be set up to identify regions or areas prone to election-related conflict and head it off. The wealth of information available should inform decisions on such interventions.

### Electoral justice

Some countries have adopted provisions or mechanisms to deal with those who contravene electoral rules and engage in fraud, hate speech and violence. Country report recommendations include laws that cancel immunity for those involved in electoral violence and fraud, and that impose tough sanctions against

parties and candidates engaging in these activities.

Civil society should be empowered to build programmes around the courts' handling of election-based offences, and such programmes would seek to ensure that the police and courts are constrained from ignoring election offences. Information on election offences and trials should be collated and kept in the public domain.

## Regional and international organizations and promotion of electoral integrity

Electoral norms set by regional organizations like AU, ECOWAS and SADC have defined the framework and expectations for their members' electoral integrity. These bodies, as well as international organizations and development partners, can encourage states to adhere to basic norms of electoral integrity by applying peer pressure on states that do not respect them, but they need to stand up for such integrity before elections.

The AU should ensure rapid implementation of the 2007 African Charter on Democracy, Elections and Governance, which has already gone into force. The regional economic communities must do the same with their regional protocols and standards on democracy and good governance.

Regional organizations should create and clearly communicate their "red lines"—prohibitions of egregious

> **' Elections should be transformed from conflict triggers into conflict managers**

malpractices that, if violated, would trigger condemnation and sanctions.

## Policy dialogue, training and research

The country reports draw attention to a vacuum in capacity among key stakeholders—EMBs, political parties, state institutions and CSOs—to administer and influence the election process effectively. They recommend building capacity in EMBs, and introducing internal democratic values and practices in parties, as well as encouraging regular inter-party dialogue. Training and policy-oriented research would contribute to greater capacity, professionalism and institutional effectiveness.

Policy dialogue should be initiated where the key stakeholders do not already have it. It should also be used to consider and implement measures relating to cross-cutting diversity management issues. Policy dialogue should be initiated on how to implement election dispute management instruments more effectively.

Some of these instruments are weak and thus incapable of responding to the sophisticated election malpractices increasingly prevalent in African elections. Inter- and intra-party democratic deficits should be plugged, and credible forums and mechanisms for managing internal party disputes set up.

To deepen policy dialogue, platforms should be built for party-to-party dialogue and cooperation in responding to national issues on a non-partisan basis. There need to be programmes to develop the capacity of election administration staff in promoting policy dialogue between stakeholders and in managing conflicts. That conflict management training should draw on some of the best practices illustrated in this report (see chapter 5).

Finally, both policy dialogue and training would benefit immensely from research on key issues pertaining to elections and diversity. Comparative experiences of federalism and devolution show how some countries have sought to address socio-economic and political diversity. It would be useful to identify best practices and draw lessons from them, in which countries undertaking constitutional reform could reflect on these lessons and their possible relevance to them. Research should be conducted on:

- links between electoral systems and conflict, with a focus on whether particular electoral arrangements lead to or reduce conflicts (possibly including case studies);

- how to expand the African research base on elections and related conflicts, dispute management, and comparative experiences of African EMBs in promoting electoral integrity; and

- the role of regional organizations like the AU and regional economic communities in managing diversity in African governance and elections.

> *Policy dialogue should be initiated on how to implement election dispute management instruments more effectively*

Democratization in Africa, which began about two decades ago, has seen the collapse of authoritarian and one-party regimes and the ascendance of elections as a means of political change and an instrument for political legitimation.

In 1999, the United Nations Economic Commission for Africa (UNECA) started the "Assessing and Monitoring the Progress towards Good Governance in Africa" project, a background to the African Governance Report (AGR). The underlying premise of the project is that development in Africa has been slow and stunted because of poor governance on the continent. With improved governance, Africa's economic progress and development will be enhanced and sustainable. So UNECA embarked on the AGR project with the main objectives of promoting consensus on good governance and the capable state in Africa; providing a mechanism for monitoring good governance, while showcasing best practices for improving governance by African countries; and formulating policy recommendations to address capacity gaps and other governance-related challenges that face African countries.

The AGR, the most comprehensive report on governance in Africa, assesses and monitors the progress African countries are making on governance. It identifies capacity gaps in governance institutions. And it makes appropriate policy recommendations to improve governance on the continent.

The first edition of the AGR in 2005 covered 27 African countries, while the second edition in 2009 covered 35. This third edition covers 40.[1]

After the first two editions, there was a rigorous review of the entire project, with broad consultations with experts, stakeholders and partner institutions. A project review workshop was held in July 2009. Subsequently, two decisions were made:

- *To adopt a thematic approach in producing the report.* Besides the thematic approach to the biennial AGR report, there would be a general report produced every six years to monitor the general progress of African countries on improving governance.

- *To partner with the United Nations Development Programme (UNDP).* UNECA and UNDP have forged a new partnership to produce the AGR and the national country reports, which hitherto were produced solely by UNECA. UNECA continues to lead the project.

In choosing a theme for AGR III, UNECA and UNDP were guided by three considerations: the findings of AGR I and AGR II; the cross-cutting issues identified by the African Peer Review Mechanism; and general pressing African governance issues. And four major issues arose: elections and diversity management, corruption, gender and constitutionalism. After exhaustive deliberations and consultations, it was decided that AGR III should focus on "Elections and the Management of Diversity in Africa".

AGR III monitors governance performance in African countries by systematically collecting and analysing qualitative and quantitative data using selected key indicators. The selected indicators of AGR III were aimed at assessing how elections can be a tool for better management of diversity and at facilitating political inclusion while promoting the democratic values of transparency, freeness and fairness of elections in Africa.

In selecting key indicators and preparing for AGR III and its associated outputs, background papers were prepared, methodology refined and five workshops held. All were geared towards fine-tuning the framework, methodology and key indicators and training the UNDP focal points on the objectives, essence and strategic orientation of AGR III.

## Rationale and objectives

The overarching rationale for the AGR is the emerging consensus that for Africa to meet the international development goals in 2015 and reverse the continent's economic, social and political predicament, African states have to create an enabling environment of good governance. In addition, the project also provides a valuable analytical framework for realizing the various governance agendas adopted by the Heads of State Implementation Committee of the New Partnership for Africa's Development (NEPAD). Since the

AGR represents the most thorough and empirically substantial attempt to measure governance in Africa to date, it has become invaluable for enriching policy content and dialogue across the continent towards strengthening institutional governance.

Some main project objectives are:

- to monitor governance trends and the progress African countries are making towards promoting democracy and good governance on the continent;

- to provide a mechanism for monitoring efforts at creating and sustaining capable democratic states that support broad-based growth, sustainable development and poverty reduction;

- to better understand governance processes, mechanisms and policies and promote an analytically founded dialogue on governance;

- to maintain governance issues on the agenda of political leaders, policy makers and other key stakeholders for improving governance performance on the continent;

- to improve the capacity of national research institutions in conducting governance research and analyses in Africa; and

- to identify capacity gaps in governance institutions and present relevant policy recommendations and interventions to address them.

To ensure legitimacy for and ownership of the project within countries, national research institutions were selected to conduct the country studies. The collaborating institutions are required to establish national steering committees comprising government representatives, civil society, businesses and religious organizations. The committees were established through in-country consultations. Two workshops were convened—the methodology workshop to explain the research for the national country study to stakeholders and the validation workshop to present the findings after the research has been completed and the report prepared.

Apart from national ownership, the other core principles of the AGR process are:

- independence and objectivity;

- scientific rigour;

- inclusiveness and national consultation; and

- mainstreaming of peoples' views and voices.

## Methodology

### Research instruments

The AGR III methodology uses three research instruments: an Expert Opinion Survey, focus group discussions and desk-based research. The research instruments were designed to obtain information on elections and the management of diversity in Africa and monitor governance trends based on the political, economic and social affairs of each country.

*Expert Opinion Survey.* The Expert Opinion Survey has two parts. First, it deals with specific questions on elections and the management of diversity. Second, it asks 24 general questions derived from key components of governance from previous AGR studies. These indicators on governance monitor progress on good governance in African countries against the backdrop of AGR I and II.

Some of the indicators in the Expert Opinion Survey are presented in a "cafeteria" format with five options ordered that the condition most favourable to elections and management of diversity is the foremost option, and the worst is last.

The Expert Opinion Survey uses a national expert panel comprising 120–150 national experts in each project country. In each country, members of the expert panel were drawn to ensure representation with regard to age, gender, education, social status, political orientation, field of training and ethnic, regional and religious background, as well as representation from the private sector and civil society organizations.

The target panel members were also drawn from the academy, political parties, professional groups, independent civil society organizations, policy makers, media, bureaucrats, police service, election management bodies, judiciary, parliamentary and executive members, and enlightened citizen-voters such as retired professionals, church leaders active in community development and social issues and educated and experienced business leaders.

Once collected, the data from each expert panel study were further subjected to rigid quality control to ensure that they were consistent and reliable.

*Focus group discussions.* Focus group discussions were used by collaborating research institutions to ascertain how participants in each group feel about elections and the management of diversity. They were designed to stimulate free discussions, fresh ideas and new insights in the groups.

The number of discussion participants was limited to 8–12 people for each session, and they were selected from the same socio-economic group or with a similar background and experiences in relation to the issue under discussion.

UNECA identified five groups for the focus group discussions. The national research institutions organized the following five groups as targets for the focus group discussions:

- women groups;

- youth groups;

- political party members;

- community-based organizations in the field of governance; and

- the informal sector.

The focus group discussions were conducted in both rural and urban areas for each of the selected target groups. In all, between 10 and 12 discussions were conducted.

*Desk research.* Desk-based research was used to collect factual information and hard data to complement information gathered through the other two research tools.

By compiling data, the national research institutions extracted information from secondary sources like government documents and gazettes; electoral management bodies; available documentation from political parties and civil society organizations; publications at the local, national and regional levels; textbooks, journals, newspapers, magazines and periodicals; and other relevant sources.

### Calculating the indices

The indices are based on the data from the expert panel study only. AGR I and II contain 83 and 85 indicators, respectively, while AGR III contains only 24 indicators, which were clustered by UNECA. Some sub-indices are not mutually exclusive.

The overall index is calculated using all 24 indicators for each project country. There is no input from other countries in the overall index of any country. Each reflects the opinions of experts in the country. Each governance index is constructed using average scores, which are combined and rescaled to bring each to a common range of 0–100 using the following approach:

Let

$T_i$ = sum of the mean scores of the indicators in cluster $i$, $i = 0$, $1, 2, \ldots, C$, where $C$ is the total number of clusters in the study.

$K_i$ = the number of indicators in cluster $i$, $i = 1, 2, \ldots, C$

$G_i$ = Index of governance based on cluster $i$, $i = 0, 1, 2, \ldots, C$.

Then, $G_i$, $i = 0, 1, 2, \ldots, C$, the *index of governance* for the $i^{\text{th}}$ cluster, follows as:

$$G_i = \frac{T_i - K_i}{K_i\,(s - 1)} * 100 =$$

$$\frac{T_i - K_i}{4 * K_i} * 100, i = 0, 1, \ldots, C$$

where $K_0 = 24$, $T_0$ is the total of the average scores for all indicators in the study, and $s$, which is 5 in the Africa Governance Project, is the maximum score that is assignable in any of the 24 indicators, so that the corresponding "Overall Index of Governance" will also be given by:

$$G_0 = 100 * \frac{T_0 - 24}{96} = 100 * \sum_{i=1}^{c} w_i G_i,$$

$$w_i = \frac{K_i}{\sum_{i=1}^{c} K_i}$$

The weighted average formula is valid only if the $C$ clusters are strictly mutually exclusive and exhaustive. An index close to 100 is perceived to reflect good governance as perceived by the respective national opinion leaders of the country. Cross-country comparisons should be avoided since there are serious factors that negate the validity of such comparisons.

## Project implementation

### Selection of collaborating national research institutions

Only independent national research institutions were considered to conduct the study in each country. UNECA and UNDP country offices were responsible for recruiting those institutions. In all, they recruited 40 competent national research institutions in a highly competitive bidding process.

As per procurement rules and procedures, UNECA and UNDP solicited institutions to submit bids. Further to the submission of bids, a capacity assessment evaluation was undertaken to ensure if the institutions partaking in the highly competitive bidding would be best placed to undertake the AGR work. The collaborating research institutions were selected in accordance with United Nations procurement rules and regulations.

### Methodology workshops

The collaborating national research institutions in all countries held an official methodology workshop with government representatives, civil society, private sector, international partners and other relevant stakeholder groups to introduce the project, promote a suitable implementation environment and ensure the process of national ownership.

### Establishment of a steering committee

The collaborating institutions in all the 40 countries each established a National Steering Committee comprising people of high personality and impeccable credentials in the country to play an advisory role, to popularize the project and to support the project as necessary.

### Preparation of national country reports and country profiles

The collaborating national research institutions collected the data, obtained UNECA's quality control clearance, analysed it and produced a national country report in accordance with agreed guidelines. UNECA further provided technical oversight to ensure conformity with its detailed instructions and agreed upon work plans and report formats and reviewed the final results.

### Validation workshops

The collaborating national research institutions convened national stakeholder validation workshops to discuss the findings and draft report before the final report was submitted. In every country, it was an essential event for promoting national ownership, essential for the credibility and acceptability of the report.

### Collaborating research institutions

The national research institutions at the country level that implemented the in-country surveys, facilitated the focus group discussions, prepared the country reports and facilitated the national stakeholders' consultations in the 40 countries covered by AGR III are shown in the appendix table.

## Note

1. The 40 countries are Algeria, Angola, Benin, Botswana, Burkina Faso, Cameroon, Cape Verde, Chad, Comoros, the Congo, Djibouti, Egypt, Ethiopia, Gabon, Gambia, Ghana, Guinea, Kenya, Lesotho, Liberia, Madagascar, Malawi, Mali, Mauritania, Mauritius, Mozambique, Namibia, Nigeria, Rwanda, São Tomé and Príncipe, Senegal, Seychelles, Sierra Leone, South Africa, Tanzania, Togo, Tunisia, Uganda, Zambia and Zimbabwe.

## Appendix table: AGR III collaborating research institutions

| Country | Research institutions |
|---|---|
| Algeria | Centre National d'Études et d'Analyses pour la Population et le Développement |
| Angola | Agostino Neto University, Center of Excellence in Public Politics and Local Governance |
| Benin | Académie Alioune Blondin Beye pour la Paix |
| Botswana | Botswana Institute for Development Policy Analysis |
| Burkina Faso | Centre pour la Gouvernance Démocratique |
| Cameroon | Centre d'Études et de Recherche en Économie et Gestion |
| Cape Verde | Afrosondagem |
| Chad | Cabinet MAGI Communication, Presse et Services |
| Comoros | University of Comoros |
| Congo | Unité de Recherche en Analyse Sociétales |
| Djibouti | University of Djibouti |
| Egypt | Ibn Khaldun Center for Development Studies |
| Ethiopia | African Institute of Management, Development and Governance |
| Gabon | Directeur des Études de la Recherche Appliquée |
| Gambia | University of The Gambia, School of Business and Public Administration |
| Ghana | Ghana Center for Democratic Development |
| Guinea | Stat View International |
| Kenya | University of Nairobi, Institute of Development Studies |
| Lesotho | National University of Lesotho, Political Science Department |
| Liberia | Agency for Economic Development & Empowerment |
| Madagascar | Études, Conseils et Assistance à la Réalisation |
| Malawi | Director of the Centre for Social Research |
| Mali | Cabinet du CATEK Groupe |
| Mauritania | Council on Economic and Social Development |
| Mauritius | StraConsult |
| Mozambique | Centre for Democracy and Development Studies |
| Namibia | Institute for Public Policy Research |
| Nigeria | Center for Democracy and Development |
| Rwanda | National University of Rwanda, Center for Conflict Management |
| São Tomé and Príncipe | Sociedade de Consultoria e Gestão Lda (Consultant and Management Firm) |
| Senegal | University of Dakar |
| Sierra Leone | Alternative Consultancies |
| Seychelles | StraConsult |
| South Africa | Institute of Democracy in South Africa |
| Tanzania | University of Dar es Salaam |
| Togo | Université de Lomé, Faculté des sciences économiques et de gestion |
| Tunisia | Institut Arabe des Chefs d'Entreprises |
| Uganda | Centre for Basic Research |
| Zambia | Center for Policy Research and Analysis |
| Zimbabwe | Mass Public Opinion Institute |